SHATTERED

TO: Bruce
Enjoy the journey!

STEVE SEFTEL

Cover Design: Laura Duchene c/o Westmount Signs & Printing
www.westmountsigns.com

Layout: Marquis Interscript

Printed & bound in Canada by Marquis Book Printing

Published and distributed by
The Art of Hockey
Waterloo, Ontario, Canada
Tel: 226-218-3059
sjseftel@gmail.com

Legal Deposit: 3rd quarter, 2019
ISBN 978-1-9990581-4-2 (paperback);
ISBN 978-1-9990581-1-1 (e-book);
ISBN 978-1-9990581-2-8 (audio)

1. Seftel, Steve, 1968-, 2. Hockey Players-Canada-Biography 3. Hockey-Canada-History
1. Title

Library and Archives Canada Cataloging in Publication data available upon request.

Every effort has been made to search for & receive permission necessary to reproduce the photographs contained in this book.

The publisher welcomes notice of any omission or error.

Table of Contents

Foreword
By Doug MacLean

I first met Steve Seftel at the Washington Capitals' 1988 training camp. I was an assistant coach with the Capitals. Steve was a 20-year-old aspiring NHL hockey player, who was the Capitals' 1986 2nd round draft pick from the Kingston Canadians of the Ontario Hockey League. Jack Button, the Capitals', assistant GM, introduced me to Steve with the words, "Mac, this is a kid you will love. He's big, he plays a complete game both offensively and defensively, and has great skill." Steve had an excellent training camp and was assigned to the Capitals' AHL affiliate, the Baltimore Skipjacks. He started his professional career as a top-grade NHL prospect.

Early in 1990, I was named the head coach of the Baltimore Skipjacks. Steve and I quickly developed a positive player/coach relationship. The Skipjacks had veteran players like Chris Felix, Bob Mason, Doug Wickenheiser, Nick Kypreos, Mike Richard, Alfie Turcotte, and Steve. The team also had a roster of talented rookies such as Tim Taylor, Steve Maltais, and John Purves. The group had NHL written all over them. My relationship with Steve really blossomed as I quickly realized that he was a player you could trust in all on-ice situations and that he was a tremendous team player. He played on a very important line with two quality veterans, Doug Wickenheiser (former NHL #1 overall-pick by the Montréal Canadiens) and hard-nosed winger Robin Bawa. They were a dominant checking line and played an amazing role in our regular season and playoff success. I was convinced the Capitals had a tremendous young player in Steve and that he would go on to have a great NHL career.

The next season, 1991, I was coaching with the Detroit Red Wings. We played a game against the Washington Capitals, and Steve was there, playing his first regular-season NHL game. We talked during warmup and I felt like a proud father. He had made it!

SHATTERED ICE is a great read and follows Steve's childhood hockey days from Kitchener, Ontario all the way to the NHL. It chronicles the challenges young players face as they chase their dreams of playing in the National Hockey League. Great lessons about hockey and life are woven throughout his story.

SHATTERED ICE brought back great memories of playing, coaching, and the special people you meet along the hockey journey. I've coached and managed many players in my 22-year NHL career and I have to say, Steve Seftel was one of my favourites. A quality family man, talented hockey player and an even better person, I'm very proud to call him a friend. I hope you enjoy SHATTERED ICE as much as I did.

Sincerely, Doug MacLean

Introduction

A few words about a special uncle of mine. This book would not be what it is without the dedication of my Uncle Gerard Girodat who committed himself to cutting every article on the Kingston Canadians from the Kingston Whig-Standard day after day while I played junior hockey in the OHL. The fastidious detail and personal special notes he wrote were secured in binders for my later enjoyment. No longer with us, I still have a part of him with me today.

Thanks to Heather Kirk for her tireless efforts working with me to square up every detail of my writing and for encouraging me to start the project, although it took a few years before I was ready to begin, and for challenging me to dig deeper with the story and the writing. I'm grateful for your perseverance and understanding and knowing there was a story I wanted to tell. I will never forget your patience and support during this amazing experience.

A big thank-you to my parents, Bob and Joan Seftel. I'm grateful for your support throughout my life and for providing me with the opportunity to skate and run in the arena. I'm appreciative of the long hours you spent there with me, in the cold of the winter and the heat of the summer. It takes a personal commitment to be the parents of kids in minor sports and I am forever in your debt for making that commitment.

To Calvin and Nick: You have both made me proud. You have grown into mature, respectful, young men who have both picked unique paths. Your mom and I tried hard to protect, shape and prepare you, and while sport has always been my passion and it's true I showered you both with athletics, I always wanted the choices in the end to be yours. How else could we have Bills and Patriot fans in the same house? We've shared hockey games, football, lacrosse, baseball, and so much more. At times, my story may have seemed like a mystery and providing the details of my journey for you inspired me to write this. The written words in the book may make you smile, cry, laugh, or motivate you. More important than my story though, I want you both to know that you are loved and always will be by me and your mom. I love you! I never want to leave those three words unsaid.

I am one of the lucky people in the world who was able to marry their best friend. There are too many words required to explain my feelings for Lisa. Perhaps that will be the makings of another book. She is the rock of our family of four. Putting the boys and me before herself time and time again, Calvin, Nick and I have leaned heavily on her strong shoulders. A kind, passionate mother and wife, she has a positive energy that people find immediately infectious, and her positive outlook has the ability to sway the most negative of souls. She has stood by my side through all of my personal struggles, trials and tribulations, sharing a lot of joy and pain, and picking me up at my lowest, darkest moments. Thank-you for being you. I love you! You're my best friend!

Queensmount Arena

I don't remember a time without hockey; perhaps I was born with my hockey stick in my hands. I don't recall. However, I do remember being in my mom's kitchen shooting plastic pucks at her stove. The small hallway is my rink, and the yellow seventies-style stove, my net. In her kitchen, I wear a loose-fitting CCM helmet with no mask, a plain red jersey with no logo, long underwear, two different coloured socks – one orange and one black. I pretend to skate up and down the narrow hall as I aim pucks at the tiny stove door, throwing myself against the wall to imitate body checks given and body checks taken. In these innocent games, I never lose, always score the winning goal, and they're done when I say so, or when my parents say it's time for bed. "How did I do Mom?" I ask. "Really good," she says. "Really good!"

Passion and dreams grow at this impressionable, budding age. For me, the dream is inspired by a shiny blue-satin Buffalo Sabres' jacket purchased by my Grandma Betty on a trip to Buffalo, and my eager enrollment in the Sammy Sabre fan club.

I receive my wallet-size membership card in the mail, along with the Sammy Sabre stickers, which I secure to my plastic lunch box. Sabres' games are on television Tuesday nights, and I rush to the T.V. to watch as much as I can until bedtime. I love watching the French Connection skate up and down the ice. Fan favourites, the Québec-born trio are the Sabre's number one line: Gilbert Perreault, René Robert, and Rick Martin. However, my favourite player is #18, Danny Gare, because he scored fifty goals last season.

When I play road hockey down the street in the neighbour's driveway, I'm Danny Gare, I tell everyone. Game on! I bank the tennis ball off the side of the house, run to the net, and shoot into the top corner over the goalie's glove. "He shoots! He scores! Another goal for Gare," I proudly shout to anyone who's listening.

At school recess, I can't wait to play with my friends. Goal posts are made out of snow about five-feet apart at each end of the pitch. It looks like soccer played with a green tennis ball, but we call this game foot hockey. My goals are still scored by Gare, while others shout Sittler or Lafleur after scoring their goals.

Hockey journeys start on this small scale. A child's world, my world, seems large at this age. However, looking back, it's ever so small. Brandon Avenue in Kitchener, Ontario is my street. My parents' house, a yellow brick, storey-and-a-half with a long paved driveway. On Saturday mornings before hockey, I watch *Bugs Bunny* and the *Looney Tunes*; there isn't much choice on TV.

In the mid-seventies, my crosstown rivals seem far way. My home rink is Queensmount Arena; an odd-shaped structure built for our growing neighbourhood. The lobby is the gathering place for players, coaches, parents, and siblings. It is also the location for parents to engage in banter. I hear parents asking, "How was your drive in? Who are we playing today? The coffee here is terrible!

Have you tried the new Tim Hortons down the street?" Not much has changed in Canadian minor-hockey circles. Walk into any rink on a Saturday morning today, and you will hear the same chatter taking place.

The canteen, located in the lobby, is a favoured gathering spot for me. Wait times for service are short, and it provides the lone place to find food and drinks. It's a source of coffee for tired parents needing a boost, and fast-food for siblings who have been rushed to the rink in the wee hours of the morning. Here, I smell delicious comfort foods: hot dogs cooking on the rotisserie and popcorn popping, with both the smell and sound drawing me over to the counter. Chocolate bars, licorice, hot chocolate and pop, of course, are in abundance; sugary drinks are a staple of the cramped canteen to be sure.

The trophy case sparkles across from the canteen. Trophies, awards, and photos are pristinely secured on shelves, never to be touched, only viewed through glass, protected behind lock and key. Local sporting heroes, and legends one and all look out onto the young hopeful. I stare at the faces, and read the names on the awards. Champions, most-valuable players, and top scorers, from years past and present, all assembled as a tribute, an inspiration, a remembrance. Perhaps one day my team, my name, or my picture, will get the honour of the trophy case.

Queensmount has a skate sharpening room. Here, for a small fee, skates can be sharpened, the blades ground to allow for precision cuts on the ice. Most days, my skates are sharpened by the same fellow who floods the ice. "Can you sharpen my skates sir?" I ask. "I sure can," he replies. "It won't take me long," he adds.

I watch as the rink attendant turns on the noisy exhaust fan, and fastens the dull blade to his block. I listen to the distinct sound as he grinds the blade from front to back. I watch closely as hot sparks fly off the steel with each precise pass. After a few passes, he disconnects the skate, raises the blade above his eye, and stares into the light, looking closely for those sharp edges that will propel me across the ice. A nod of his head, and he lowers my skate onto his workbench, and slides a stone along each side of the blade. That grey stone, called a honing stone, is about four-inches long and a half-inch thick. The newly sharpened skate is set aside, and my other skate goes through the same stringent routine. Once complete, he passes the skates back to me like they are brand new and says, "Careful, those blades are sharp!" "Okay, thank-you," I reply, and quickly place my skate guards on to protect the razor-sharp steel. This expertise doesn't come for free; he asks for a dollar; a small price to help me skate faster. It's worth it.

The arena lobby houses large bulletin boards that display standings from local leagues, men's leagues, beer leagues. I scan the stats, and on a lucky day I see a familiar name. Posters are secured to the large information boards: play lacrosse, the fastest game on two feet, says one yellow sheet. I thought hockey was the fastest game on two feet? Maybe my dad will let me play lacrosse one day. It looks like fun!

The storage room is the minor-hockey equipment vault. If by chance the busy attendant forgets to close the door, I get a quick look inside the cavernous room. Like a small sporting goods store, this equipment is free with the appropriate approvals. Access is by appointment only to this treasure trove that contains endless rows of jerseys, socks, and goalie equipment. For players daring enough to try the position there is the loan of the brown goalie pads, brown blockers, and trappers.

I see the lost and found. The rink attendant is in charge of the loosely guarded lost and found, which is a stop on the arena to-do list for me. Single mittens, toques, skate guards, scarves, hockey socks, and battered equipment left behind, or discarded, all find their place here. In certain instances, it contains a gem left behind and ultimately recovered by the rightful owner. I hear people in the rink say, "Did you check the lost and found?" The hockey community is always looking out for one another.

The dressing room is the sanctuary for the players; a private spot for me, my team, and my coaches. Parents are permitted in the dressing room until about ten-years-old, at which time most coaches insist they stay out. Even when parents are permitted, they're required to leave before any last-minute instructions are given. The dressing room is my safe place where I'm under the shelter of coaches and trainers, accompanied by teammates, who are like my brothers.

My first hockey team is the Barons and we wear plain green jerseys with white trim. This is novice house league. I'm 7-years-old, and so happy to be playing hockey! We play one game each week against kids from my neighbourhood, in the end winning the league and city championship. My dad is taking me to McDonald's after today's championship game to celebrate. This victory must be big if I'm getting a juicy Big Mac out of it.

At 8-years-old I wonder if I have the skills to represent my home rink on a novice select team. Tryouts take place at each city arena. This is my first opportunity to experience tryouts, to have the chance to prove myself. Each section of the city will pick a team to represent their corner of the community. Rinks from various wards – arenas named Don McLaren, Grand River, Wilson, and my own Queensmount – representing north, south, east and west Kitchener, will square off for city bragging rights. My team is the Queensmount Kavaliers, and I wear the jacket with pride. At the end of a successful season, we win the city championship.

Like a drug, winning is addictive, and for me leads to feelings of pure joy and happiness. I love the feeling winning gives me. I want to win so badly; I can taste it. My coaches say, "My team must be hungrier than our opponents." I want to win; all the time. The feelings I get from winning are incredible and motivate me.

By 9-years-old AAA (triple A) hockey, an opportunity to represent my city playing the game I love, is on my mind. Parents line up in arenas across the country with their children to register for these tryouts. AAA provides players with more practice, games, tournaments, and training. In my minor-hockey days – 1975 to 1985 – all Kitchener AAA team names start with the letter K with one exception – the major midget Greenshirts. There are the minor atom Krackers, major atom Krauts, minor peewee Keewees, major peewee Kruisers, minor bantam Knights, major bantam Kings, and minor midget Kavaliers. Maybe one day I will play for the Greenshirts.

My Kitchener minor atom AAA team is called the Krackers. It sounds like a funny name for sure, but I love it nonetheless. My new coach is Larry Lyman who moved to Kitchener from Burlington; an arch rival of Kitchener. We have fun, and early season laughs, as we tell Mr. Lyman he will have to burn his Burlington minor-hockey jacket. This seems like the obvious destiny for his old colours.

Remarkably, throughout my entire career, I remember to adhere to messages and lessons from Coach Lyman. Some coaches have an ability to leave a permanent imprint on a player, and he left his on me. He says two things that I will never forget. One, he says, "The puck moves faster than any person on the planet." At that point he shoots a puck down the ice. He then says to our team of bright, wide-eyed nine-year-olds, "I challenge any of you boys to skate as fast as that puck." His lesson is: pass the puck. Passing is a fundamental and essential skill for hockey players of any age. Two, Coach Lyman says being successful in hockey, and life, comes down to four words that he affectionately calls the 4Ds: desire, dedication, determination, and discipline. I will remember these words, and write them down. He says these four simple words will help me become a better hockey player, and help our team win. I want to be a better hockey player, and I like winning a lot! C'mon, we're going on a hockey journey, a Canadian hockey journey, my journey.

Rink Rats

We're a Catholic family, so Sunday mornings mean church. My family attends mass at St. John's. Most stores close on this day of rest and tasks like shopping are left to the other six days of the week. Hockey though doesn't take Sundays off. Since another religion in Canada is hockey, going to the arena instead of, or in addition to mass, is seen as okay or even necessary by many.

Dad plays pick-up hockey at Queensmount Sunday mornings. He played minor hockey as a kid, just like many who come out to the one-hour weekly games. The two assembled teams consist of an assortment of skill levels. The familiar players include my dad's buddies, Jim, Ray, Lloyd, Pinky, and the Newf. I've never heard his real name, but guess logically that he's from Newfoundland.

Watching my Uncle Dennis move, I know he is a smooth skater and, a well-polished hockey player. Dad says he once had a tryout with the Guelph junior team, which impresses starry-eyed me. Hanging out in the dressing room, I like listening to the lively chatter, the sharp barbs flying around the room as the men hold their weekly hockey roast. This motley crew barking at one another is sure to carry over onto the ice.

For me, Sunday morning hockey is a chance to play hooky from church, and to put on my skates instead. I don't get to play the game but still, I get to skate. The tractor goes out to flood prior to Dad's ice time and the rink attendant lets me skate. I stay on the opposite side to avoid the noisy tractor, and remain out as long as I can. Soon the ice is resurfaced and the equipped players slowly start to appear through the lobby doors. Pucks fly as they start their short warm-up. Shots are fired hard at the glass, mixed with shots at the two goalies. It's not so safe now!

I leave the ice through the bench door, totally satisfied with my ten-minutes of skating. Pushing my way through the swinging doors to the warm lobby I find a seat on the wooden benches. The lobby is quiet. The rink attendant returns to his office after flooding, smiles at me as he passes by, and I smile back.

The pick-up game starts, my skates come off, and the search for pucks begins. Pucks are like tiny jewels, and any six-ounce, one-inch thick, three-inch wide, vulcanized rubber disc found rinkside falls under the finders – keepers laws. A good day may see a five puck take and slow day fetches me nothing. All pucks collected are added to the home stash to be used in the driveway, or on the outdoor rinks.

My first outdoor hockey experiences, as for so many kids, take place at the neighbourhood rink. Westmount Public School is visible from the large front window of my house. Through some sort of hockey miracle, a sheet of ice magically appears every winter in the schoolyard. Of course, the magic is created by friendly neighbours flooding the rink, allowing the ice to thicken, and harden to the desired consistency. These neighbours work long hours and late nights so we kids can play like our heroes and act out our dreams.

Once the ice is ready, the hockey-loving neighbourhood kids start to gather at the rink to skate and play shinny hockey. Shinny, that so Canadian outdoor, informal, unscripted version of the real game I love so much. Games are played with minimal or no rules. All we need is players, a puck, and two nets.

In the event a game is underway, and the snow starts to accumulate we yell, "Time!" Young hockey players quickly learn the routine: time-out, stop what you're doing, and go grab a shovel. Shovels are sticking out of the snowbanks for exactly this purpose. The players, me included, secure our hockey sticks in the snow, and form a line of shovels that can clean off the fresh cover in minutes. Once complete, we yell, "Game on!"

Games are played daily and if no one else shows up, I shoot pucks at an open net. If I'm alone, I pretend to score the winning goal in Game Seven of the Stanley Cup. I do my own play-by-play while I shoot and score.

When I can, I walk up the street in my boots and put my skates on at the rink. On these rinks, there are no rules, no referees, and no scoreboards; it's just kids skating and playing hockey. As I approach the ice surface, the sound of passing pucks and skates reverberates through the large field at the school. These soft sounds are soothing to my soul: the tapping of sticks on the ice; skate blades turning and stopping; voices calling out for the puck.

Today, walking toward the ice with my skates on through the snow, my feet are heavy and slow. Once I make it to the side boards though I hop onto the ice and feel like I'm achieving liftoff as my skates propel me. Forward, backward, inside turns, outside turns, skate, pass, shoot! No instruction is needed or given; I just wing it. I play until it is too dark to see, and even then, try to stretch it out.

The side boards are short, allowing for low bank passes, and helping keep pucks in play. The end boards are higher; the added height to accommodate wrist shots and slapshots. A shot over the wooden boards sees the shooter have to make the unenviable trek into the snowy field, following the trail of the rolling puck to hopefully recover the black disc. If it is not found today, it will be easily discovered next spring after the snow melts. Again, finders

– keepers' laws will apply. There are two nets, one at each end, made of steel posts with wire mesh to make the cages durable against long, cold Canadian winters.

It is game on, and I find myself stuck playing goal. The play continues at the other end and I'm bored from the lack of shots on my net. I turn around and stare at the steel cage I'm protecting. It's bitterly cold and I focus on my breath which I can see slowly escaping my mouth. Each exhale cuts through the crossbar with ease. My eyes become fixated on the icy bar. Inching forward, I place my lips on the cold steel. I pause a moment, and try to pull away, but I can't. My lips are glued to the frozen pipe. Fear takes over and, in that instant, I pull away fast. I'm free, and as the adrenaline wears off, I taste warm blood running down my burning lips. Ahhh! Running home in my skates, I learn a valuable lesson about outdoor cold-weather hockey, or at least, about warm skin on cold metal.

Like many kids, I anxiously look forward to Christmas for time away from school, and a chance to skate on the outdoor rinks playing Canada's national winter sport. Victoria Park contains a good-sized lake that freezes in winter and is used for skating and better yet, shinny games. My dad takes my brother Brad and I and turns us loose on the large, frozen surface. I can skate for what seems like miles on this enormous ice. Flipping the puck in the air, I take three quick strides and chase it. However, the real excitement is the game, and we need competition.

Today, older boys play us in a game of three-on-three. I skate hard after the puck when we lose possession. I dig my blades in to skate faster to get it back. It's an even game, and we need a goal. I pick up the puck, drive hard to the net, and attempt to dodge the oncoming larger kid. His stick meets mine at the puck, causing it to flip up in the air, and with a thud, hit me in the little space between my mouth and nose. I drop my stick and grab my face as red blood streams down. Suddenly my lip feels bigger, and I yell for my dad. This game is over! A short five-minute drive to Dr. Miller's office and I'm cleaned up. He suggests we go home and enjoy the Christmas holidays quietly, perhaps without shinny hockey. That may be good advice, at least for the remainder of today. Shinny can wait until tomorrow.

We move to a larger house in a new neighbourhood. The Laurentian Hills area is busting with new homes and new schools. Sunday mass for the new Blessed Sacrament Church takes place in the school gymnasium at Monsignor Haller until a church can be built.

A fresh blanket of snow is the perfect time for the hockey-mad gang I've found to play another version of the sport: road hockey. Roseneath Crescent is the location where kids gather for spirited fast-paced road hockey games. The white snow cascading down permits winter boots to become skates. Sliding over snow and ice in boots is as quick as awkwardly trying to run through it. The Canadian fluffy stuff makes moves slick for goalies too: two-pad slides in snow pants, butterfly to the knees. The powdery snow is much more forgiving on our legs than the normally rough black asphalt.

A couple of Kitchener Rangers' players are billeted in a home on the quiet crescent. If it's our lucky day, they will come out and take shots with us. "Paul Coffey from the Rangers lives there," my buddy says to me. "Really?" I reply with excitement. "Yah, he played with us before," he says boastfully. "I hope he plays today," I call out as I stickhandle with a frozen tennis ball.

Trillium Public School is the location of the outdoor rink and it's just a short walk from my family's new home. The weekends are busy there. On weeknights, the ice is less crowded. To assist in feeding my hockey addiction, I put my old skates on at the front door of my house, walking on my tiptoes carefully down each step on the front porch until I reach the snow and ice-covered sidewalks. Once on the slippery sidewalks, I push with my blades. When I reach a dry patch, I step until the icy path continues on again, propelling myself until my skates meet up with the schoolyard field.

The field is full of white stuff, and separates me from the rink. My skates become makeshift snowshoes as I step through the snow-covered grass, making sure my pants are over my skates to prevent large amounts from being lodged in the leather skate boots.

The ice surface is now in range; only a few more steps. One last obstacle: fresh snowbanks that are taller than the last time I was here. I sprint up the front, cautiously descend down the back, and hop onto the rink. My steel blades are now cutting through the ice the way they were intended to.

Game on! The players determine the rules: first team to ten wins; no slapshots. Sticks are thrown into the middle in order to pick teams, and one volunteer throws a stick at a time to each side. Finding a willing skater to play goal is a challenge. If there is no volunteer, the fairest thing to do is random switches on the fly. The faceoff starts the game at centre and draws two players to the middle. We tap sticks three times, tap, tap, tap, and the puck is swatted away. The sounds of pucks hitting sticks echoes in the schoolyard backed by the sweet sound of blades cutting through the ice, and spraying snow when we stop sharply. He scores!

We play hard and compete for bragging rights. Without even noticing, my skill level is rising and I'm trying new tricks on the ice. Without the structure of a formal practice, I demonstrate my keen, individual creativity. The game continues until players start to depart. Kids leave because their toes are frozen, and have homework to finish. There are only a couple of us left playing two-on-two, and then one-on-one. The game ends and those of us not yet ready to leave shoot pucks at the boards. Finally, the rink goes silent. A volunteer will show up long after we have left and flood the large surface with fresh water. Tomorrow's game will be played on a new sheet of fast, crisp ice.

Eat, sleep, hockey! Not necessarily in that order. Play away from the arena helps develop my love for the sport. Unregulated, unsupervised, unstructured play nurtures my passion for the game and fills my endless appetite for hockey. Time spent with friends, outside, having fun, and playing my favourite sport, yes please!

Kitchener Bauer Krauts

The name Bauer is synonymous with hockey and especially skates. In 1927, one of the local Bauer families established the Bauer Skate Company in Kitchener. The Bauer name is also known in hockey circles because of the exceptional talents of icons Father David Bauer, and his brother Bobby.

Milt Schmidt, Woody Dumart, and Bobby Bauer played hockey for the Kitchener Greenshirts. These boys would go on to dominate the NHL, brilliantly skating together for the Boston Bruins. Centre Schmidt, left-winger Dumart, and right-winger Bauer were eventually given the nickname the Kraut Line. This line was so accomplished that in the 1939-1940 season, the talented trio was 1–2–3 in the NHL scoring race, and while the line was intact, the Boston

Bruins won, and hoisted, the Stanley Cup in the 1938–1939 and 1940–1941 NHL seasons. All three legends are inducted into the Hockey Hall of Fame: Schmidt in 1961, Dumart in 1992, and Bauer in 1996. The famous Kraut Line helped put the growing community of Kitchener on the world hockey map.

In 1959, mild-mannered coach Murray Fried started the first atom rep hockey team in Kitchener. Known as the Bauer Krauts, they gained a reputation across minor-hockey circles for icing competitive teams and displaying sportsmanship. Fried coached the team for twenty-one years, and after passing on the coaching duties, managed for nine more. All told, his respectful influence encompassed 2,020 games and 79 tournament victories, along with many Ontario Minor Hockey Association championships.

September arrives, and it is time for hockey tryouts again. The annual Canadian minor-hockey ritual is underway. I don't think much about it at the time but, across the country, from Vancouver to St. John's, kids like me are attending tryouts.

Kitchener is a hockey hotbed, and it's quite obvious to me that tryouts this fall are different. This is the Kraut year – that's what is heard as parents of 10-year-old hockey players in town chat with each other – this upcoming hockey season is different. Young ears, including mine, listen at home, in the car, and in the lobby of the arena. Parents throw the name Krauts around like the Greenshirts, Dutchmen, and Rangers, making the name synonymous with minor-hockey royalty in Kitchener.

Another indication that this is a special hockey season is the team name: Bauer Krauts. The atom AAA club is sponsored by local skate manufacturer, Bauer. Parents and players are keenly aware that each player who makes this team will receive a free pair of skates, free hockey sticks, and endless rolls of green and gold tape for the upcoming season, courtesy of the team sponsor. Further to this perk of free skates and sticks is the annual trip, planned by the team, and that routinely requires a flight to a far-away hockey locale.

Reporting to the rink with my hockey bag on my shoulder, I find players are lining up alongside their parents to pay their tryout fee.

After paying, I'm given a white sticker with a number for the back of my helmet. This number allows evaluating coaches to identify me and other kids on the ice.

Dads stand in the corner at Don McLaren Arena when tryouts start. This vantage point provides an unobstructed view of the entire ice surface from which they stoically watch every shot, pass and stride. Moms sit up in the stands and engage in quiet conversation. Siblings play mini-sticks in the corner of the rink, oblivious to the action on the other side of the boards.

For the players, myself included, this evaluation is the early stages of defining ourselves as hockey players. A pecking order begins to take shape. I want to be the best player! I'm acutely aware of these thoughts, and I feel fearless. I've grown taller, stronger, and have a size and skill advantage over many players. A competitive drive is developing inside me, an ambitious spirit growing internally. I want to be here, I want to succeed, and this is what I want to do.

This is my second winter of AAA hockey, and another lesson has to be learned. Even at this young age I have to be prepared to lose good friends who are either cut from the team, quit the sport, pursue other interests, and so on. Having said that, my cousin Ronny and I have a close relationship. I was born in May of 1968 and Ronny in October of that same year. We've spent a lot of time together, playing hockey, playing lacrosse, sleepovers, biking, and trading hockey cards. This fall he is cut by Coach Fried. I never ask him how he feels; ten-year-old boys don't do those things. He will now play for the AA Komets. This is the first time I learn the hard lessons of the separation that hockey can cause. Fortunately for Ron and me, we will have many more summers together playing lacrosse for the Kitchener Braves.

The Bauer Krauts are selected. Coach Fried makes several changes to a team that won the minor atom AAA OMHA championship last season. Left-winger Clark Day is added; defencemen Rob Warren, who moved into town from our crosstown rivals in Waterloo joins; and the Schlegel twins (Brad and Jamie) are added – they played minor atom AA for the Klippers last winter.

I'm excited to start this new hockey season; free skates, free sticks, and trips. I feel rewarded for my passion, dedication, and talent. It's amazing! What 10-year-old boy wouldn't want to play for this team?

The first important event for the Krauts is the annual K-W Oktoberfest Tournament. Every October since 1969, Kitchener-Waterloo hosts the biggest Bavarian festival outside of Munich, Germany, and the atom hockey tournament is a staple of the local tradition. The high-profile tournament gets underway, and the newspaper, the Kitchener-Waterloo Record, shows up for photos and watches us open the event with a win. Post-game, the photographer snaps a photo as we proudly smile wearing our festive Oktoberfest hats and accompanying pins.

An early highlight for me is a meet and greet event put on by our sponsors from Bauer with Toronto Maple Leaf stars Darryl Sittler and Lanny McDonald that includes an autograph session with the two players. People are pushing toward the front of the line to get a glimpse of the star NHLers. I slither my slender body through the expanding mob, and find myself standing directly in front of Leaf captain Darryl Sittler. I secure autographs from him and Lanny McDonald. They sign pictures of themselves sporting all of their hockey gear (no Maple Leaf jersey mind you) and holding their new Bauer skates, obviously to support the sponsor. Leaf jersey or not, it doesn't matter, I just got Lanny McDonald and Darryl Sittler's autographs. Real NHL players!

The Maple Leafs are on television twice a week, on Wednesday and Saturday. I can't miss *Hockey Night in Canada*. Sittler and McDonald are now my favourite players; sorry French Connection. On Saturday night I ask Brad to watch the Leafs with me. Bill Hewitt calls the play-by-play, and I listen closely. I tell Brad to stay sitting when the first period ends because the five-minute animated program known as *Peter Puck* is on tonight. *Peter Puck* provides young and old hockey fans an easy-going, lighter look at the game and its rules.

Every hockey season, the Bauer Krauts embark on an exciting trip, and this year is no different. In fact, there are two trips to help celebrate the team's 20th anniversary. The first is a trip to the nation's capital, Ottawa, for a Christmas tournament. The second trip, in March, will be to New York City and Boston.

First up, Ottawa. The Krauts do not drive to Ottawa, the Krauts fly to Ottawa, and I experience my first ever flight on a plane. This is also my first time billeting with another family. Billeting is when families from the host city take in players during tournaments. They feed you, drive you to games, and look out for you during your stay. Even away from home, the hockey community takes care of one another. Parents and coaches tell us to behave and use our manners; after all we're guests in the homes of these hockey families. We're reminded to say please and thank-you; you represent your city, team, and family. The message is always the same: don't embarrass us! These words reverberate in my ears; the instruction is loud and clear.

At the end of January 1978, we have our regular 5 p.m. practice at the Kitchener Memorial Auditorium. The Kitchener Rangers major junior 'A' hockey team have long played home games on Friday nights at the Aud, as it is called. The Rangers have provided the NHL with many stars including Walt Tkaczuk, Larry Robinson, Bill Barber, Dwight Foster, and Paul Reinhart. For me, the Rangers seem like the next best thing to the NHL and its players.

On this day, after practice, Coach Fried enters the dressing room. "I have a special guest here," he says. From behind enters a slim blond-haired teen. "This is Wayne Gretzky," he says. "Wayne is going to come around and sign an autograph for each of you." Wayne Gretzky is playing for the Sault Ste. Marie Greyhounds and the Hounds are here to play the Rangers tonight.

Gretzky will play one season of major junior hockey before turning professional and taking his golden scoring touch to the Indianapolis Racers of the World Hockey Association. Incidentally, Wayne Gretzky, in his only season with the Greyhounds, scored a remarkable 70 goals and added 112 assists for 182 points in 64 games played. Oh, and did I mention he was only 16-years-old?

Dad secures my Gretzky autograph in a scrapbook he made for me. The autograph still sits in the same spot on the first page, alongside an article from the K-W Record that states, "Kitchener Atoms: You can't beat 'em." The road to hockey dreams is a little clearer all of a sudden.

The huge trip for the Bauer Krauts comes at the end of the season and sees us fly to New York City and billet with a team from Oyster Bay, N.Y. We land at LaGuardia International Airport where we're met by a welcoming committee from the host team. They're friendly people with a funny accent. They don't say "hockey" like me, they say, "hackey". They don't say "car", they say, "caa". They tell me I say "eh" a lot but I don't notice it.

We visit the enormous Empire State Building and the Statue of Liberty, where we're filmed for the intro of the *Good Morning America* T.V. show. *Good Morning America* is a news program that runs from 7-9 a.m. Monday through Friday on the ABC television network. The show opens with random people, or a person, proclaiming the famous tagline. The Krauts are spotted exploring the 305-foot Statue of Liberty, and the GMA production people invite Coach Fried to tape the catch phrase for the opening of the program. We line up in an orderly fashion, and the director says, "Action." Coach Fried exclaims, "We're the Bauer Krauts from Kitchener, Ontario, Canada," and then in unison we call out the familiar phrase, "Good Morning America!" To the 10-year-old brain we are now TV stars; next stop Hollywood!

Departing the Big Apple, the team buses to Boston for a couple of exhibition games with an atom team from Reading, Massachusetts and a stay with more billet families. I double up with Robbie Brown on this stop, staying together with the same billets. He plays lacrosse with me as well, and I like his confident company. A highly-skilled player, he will leave after this season, and return to Kitchener in 1984 for the Memorial Cup as a member of the Kamloops Jr. Oilers at only 15-years-old.

Before we leave for the airport, our billet family decides to show us the historic Boston Garden, which is the home of the Boston Bruins, and the location where the famous Kraut Line once played.

Entering the Garden, we start to meander around, following our billets' lead. We're down at ice level near the Zamboni area, literally in the belly of the rink when a pair of athletic men approach. Could these two be hockey players? Yes, they are. It is Rick Middleton and Dwight Foster. Rick Middleton played 1,005 NHL games and Dwight Foster played 541 NHL games. After brief introductions, my billets give Robbie and I paper for autographs. I hand over mine slowly but I'm busting inside. These guys play in the NHL. That's my dream! The two Bruins return the signed papers and I stare at their faces. I'll put these autographs beside Sittler, McDonald, and Gretzky. What a way to end the trip!

For me, the experience of playing for the Kitchener Bauer Krauts is memorable to be sure. Even though the players are 10-year-olds, it helps shape an expectation of the work ethic, attitude, and team-work that will be required to play elite-level hockey. This is the beginning of my first real sense of purpose as a hockey player. Being a hockey player is now my focus, my goal, my mission!

Advanced Hockey Clinic

Summer for me is lacrosse. I love lacrosse! The speed, the physicality, the summer season, and perhaps the added bonus that school is out for most of the schedule all combine for a great experience. Lacrosse shapes my rapidly developing hockey IQ: a two-on-one in lacrosse is the same as a two-on-one in hockey. Added to that, I play with a mean streak that carries over to winter hockey. The fast-paced sport forces me to play in tight spaces, use hand-eye coordination, give hits, be hit, run, and run, and run more. Without question, the fastest game on two feet enhances my hockey skills and conditioning.

In addition to playing Canada's national summer sport, and to maintain a competitive edge, refining my hockey skills in the

off-season is a summertime ritual. In other words, I attend hockey
school, taking the opportunity to improve my craft, and remove
the hockey rust before tryouts.

A resident named Fred Nichols operates the Advanced Hockey
Clinic for players who want a more intense, hockey-driven experience and the opportunity to refine important skills with professional instructors. This hockey school takes place over one week
and includes two weekends. The sessions on Saturday and Sunday
are two-a-days, that is two ice times and two dryland training
workouts.

Young hockey players, including me, arrive at Don McLaren carrying our equipment bags on our shoulders, and proceed to the
dressing rooms. Dryland training is done in the summer heat,
while wearing our lower hockey gear. We file out the back door
onto the grassy field in behind the rink, some days dodging the
tractor as the attendant dumps the snow from the flood of the ice.
The straw-like field is dry and shows slender paths worn into the
grass by sneaker-wearing hockey players. Dryland begins with a
run along the side of the arena, up the tree line along Glasgow St.,
across the parking lot, up a steep hill, and down the other side. It's
a badge of pride to wear if you lead the pack of hungry players
during the run. I struggle to stay ahead of the slower kids in the
rear, push myself in order to stay away from the back, and to avoid
the chirping that will follow. I hate jogging, especially in hockey
equipment.

Local minor-hockey volunteer, Peter Douglas, who is trainer of
the midget AAA Greenshirts, is the pack leader of our dryland
training. The Greenshirts have a proud hockey tradition and have
sent numerous aspiring players to the Ontario Hockey League.
Much to my amazement, the fit and trim Mr. Douglas runs with us
and leads the way. We all understand that with him, hard work is
not an option. He speaks with an English accent and sternly if the
youthful pack get distracted. Just don't piss him off. If the pack
works hard, we'll be okay. However, if we're goofing off, laughing,
or being smart-mouths, the entire pack will suffer with an extra
workload of laps, push-ups, sit-ups or worse.

A few curious parents observe while we finish the workout, and now it's time for the on-ice portion of the day. I can do what I love. Playing hockey, on the ice, is where I want to be! This is why I'm here. I want to play hockey, not to run and do push-ups, says my saucy 12-year-old self.

The Advanced Hockey Clinic already has something in the name that suggests this hockey school is only for players who are serious about the sport, and Mr. Nichols hires a few ex-pros like Kitchener-native Myron Stankiewicz. The sharpshooting winger, who played for the Philadelphia Flyers and St. Louis Blues, had six seasons of twenty goals or more with the Hershey Bears of the American Hockey League.

Jimmy Loree, a stocky firefighter with a raspy voice, leads the on-ice activities. Mr. Loree is a no-nonsense instructor. In his gruff tone, he tells the young pack to listen to the pros like Mr. Stankiewicz and to learn. If a player dare be late to the ice, that kid will skate alone, while the rest of us watch. Just don't piss off Mr. Loree.

When Mr. Loree calls the pack in after warm-up, he turns it over to the instructors. They demand hard work, respect and the packs' attention. Knacks and tricks for skating, shooting, stickhandling, passing, and checking; I can't get enough, and I'm eager to learn. I strive to be a student of the game. My appetite to improve the essential skills of hockey turns me into a sponge and I soak up the knowledge Mr. Stankiewicz and the other experienced instructors have to share.

At this hockey school, we're taught how to body check. I thrive on the physical nature of hockey and lacrosse. Using a boxing heavy bag suspended from the rafters, the instructors swing the sturdy bag back and forth. I must wait for the right moment to strike the bag with the full force of my body. If my timing is off, I arrive too early or too late and miss the large swinging bag. With practice, I time it right and stop the heavy bag dead in its tracks with a giant thud. The instructors like my big collisions and are frustrated with the boys who can't get it right. I feed off the positive reinforcement and work hard to execute correctly. "Can I hit the bag again," I ask eagerly. Without being aware of it, the heavy bag is helping me develop balance on my skates while being hit by a moving object; a necessary skill needed in hockey. "It's hard to score when you're sitting on your butt," the instructors shout to the pack members.

Coaches tell me I need to get stronger. Perhaps I will start lifting weights in a couple of years I suspect, but not now; I'm not mentally ready for it. I mess around in the basement with free weights but nothing too intense. No one has ever said I need to get stronger to play lacrosse. When I play lacrosse, I work my ass off and everyone is okay with that. I'm just as physical, just as determined, just as emotional. Hmm. It must be the game; the sport. Yes, it is the game, it's hockey, and hockey in Canada!

The Advanced Hockey Clinic ends for another season. Summer is almost over. I walk up the street to call on one of my road hockey buddies, Marc Potvin. The future power forward will one day play 121 NHL games. On this summer day, I see he has lined up a bunch of sticks on his porch. The short wooden twigs look like batons. "What are these for?" I ask. He is standing on his long porch in a t-shirt, shorts, and in his sneakers. "For jogging," he says. "What do you mean?" I ask curiously. He responds quickly like he's on a mission, "I run a lap of the street with one stick, when I return, I put it down, and grab another. I'm not done until I run with each stick around the street." I'm impressed but don't want him to know. "Okay, maybe we can take shots tomorrow," I suggest. This commitment by my buddy Marc is the type of hard work needed to become a better, stronger hockey player. Maybe this pack member needs to do more too.

Bumps, Breaks & Bruises

I believe NHL players are the best athletes in the world. Playing hockey requires aerobic power, anaerobic power, speed, flexibility, strength, skill and more; too much to mention. All of this is required while standing on two thin pieces of steel attached to leather boots on your feet. Added to that hockey players must be brave; warriors, not unlike Montréal Canadiens' legend Rocket Richard with his memorable bloodied face shaking hands with Bruins' goalie Jim Henry after a 1952 playoff game; or Maple Leaf defenceman Bobby Baun, shockingly scoring on a broken leg in the 1964 Stanley Cup final versus the Detroit Red Wings; and Flyers' captain Bobby Clarke's famous, toothless smile while hoisting the coveted Cup. All of these were warriors of their time.

A physical sport indeed, injuries are part of the game. In my hockey life I suffer, in no particular order, a fractured thumb; fractured hand; fractured ankle; fractured wrist; fractured finger; concussion; multiple "green fences" which is a variety of visual images appearing in assorted colours (seeing stars); multiple stitches; a root canal and other dental damage; torn left anterior cruciate ligament; bucket handle meniscus tear; am knocked unconscious in a fight; torn right anterior cruciate ligament; torn medial meniscus; hip pointer; and separated shoulder. There was a bizarre incident in which a chunk of an opponent's wooden hockey stick became embedded in my chest after a cross-check, requiring surgical removal when it became infected and was oozing pus; and other bumps, breaks and bruises. In time, my teammates and I will encourage each other to pay the price and sacrifice our bodies; whatever it takes to pursue the dream and complete the mission!

The Advanced Hockey Clinic is in my rearview mirror and the boys and I are playing foot hockey before a peewee game. Seeking out a quiet corner in the arena, we play this sport with a tennis ball. One of my teammates, Steve Donnelle, takes a shot, and it rebounds off my body. I reach out to grab the loose ball, but at the same moment, he loads his leg up for the rebound kick. His winter boot meets my hand at the ball, and I scream, "Ahhh!" Grimacing in pain, I walk back to the dressing room holding my aching, trembling hand.

I still have a real hockey game to play tonight, and I endure my first experience of playing through pain. In this instance, I play injured out of guilt. We've been explicitly told not to horse around before games and my violation will not be received well by the coaches or my parents.

Game on! Perhaps if I ignore the pain it will go away. Nope! My hand throbs with each beat of my heart. It beats faster, and the throbbing increases. The minutes tick away slowly, the buzzer sounds, and the game ends. Carefully I remove my equipment, and walk out to the lobby with my head down to face my dad. Looking up, I explain my dilemma, and can see the head-scratching look on his face. Boys will be boys, eh Dad?

This game is at home, Don McLaren. K-W General Hospital (which is now known as Grand River) is located across the street. Dad and I walk down Green St. to the big hospital for X-rays, and the results – a fractured hand.

Despite the freakish injury, I'm on top of the world; my dad is taking us to our first NHL game at Maple Leaf Gardens. The famous building on Carlton St. is the home rink of the Toronto Maple Leafs. My first live NHL game, this is huge! The added bonus is that the Buds are playing up-and-coming, Wayne Gretzky and the Edmonton Oilers. The phenomenal talent from Brantford, Ontario makes me get out of my seat when he touches the puck and skates.

Driving to Toronto, we park near the Gardens, and walk a short distance to the arena that Conn Smythe built. The Gardens look and smell like hockey. Photographs of Maple Leaf legends hang on the walls, along with past Stanley Cup champions – players like Syl Apps, Charlie Conacher, Tim Horton, Johnny Bower, and Frank Mahovlich. George Armstrong was the last Maple Leaf captain to hoist the Stanley Cup in 1967, the year before I was born. Maybe they'll win the Cup this year. I sure hope so!

Walking the concourse, the smell of popcorn and hot dogs fills the air, blending with the sounds of people chatting, creating a buzz, as fans prepare in their own way for the game that is starting soon. I want to watch warm-up so we better find our seats. In order to get there Dad says we must ride the escalator, therefore, this must be the big-time; the NHL. Our seats are across from the Oilers' bench, on the blue line, and just over half-way up. I watch warm-up intensely, and focus on #99, Gretzky. The ticker on the wall posts his stats and key information about tonight's game which I absorb like a sponge. I love stats, streaks, and numbers related to hockey.

Warm-up is in the books; I impatiently wait for the ice to be resurfaced. The Leafs and Oilers reappear and we stand and listen to the national anthem, and then the puck drops. The game goes by quickly. The score isn't important; it is the experience that matters most to me, the memory, the players, #99, the Gardens, the thrill of the NHL, the dream of the NHL!

I'm 13-years-old, and today is Thanksgiving. I have a game in Hamilton, and my parents are staying in the city while I travel to play the Huskies since they've committed to hosting family for the festive dinner. I get a ride down to the Steel City. Hockey parents are more than willing to help each other out when it comes to driving to games and practices.

Game on! I'm skating hard, and playing my regular defence position. The puck is on my stick continuously. A loose one squirts out through the neutral zone towards our blue line. Moving forward to the black disc, I can see a Hamilton player dart towards me. We're going to meet at the puck simultaneously so I reach out and poke it forward. I stretch and my opponent steps into me with a body check. Contact is made with my extended stick, and then my exposed arm. Forced back violently like an accordion, a piercing pain shoots through the nerves in my wrist. I immediately skate to the bench and sit down. The trainer takes one look at me and we leave for the dressing room.

In the empty dressing room, I sit down as concerned hockey dads join the trainer and me. They announce that I look really white; my face is pale and ghostly looking. They say I must go to the hospital immediately. Happy-go-lucky goaltender Paul Henriques' dad works in Hamilton, and is familiar with the city. He volunteers to drive me to McMaster General Hospital.

Arriving at Mac, I'm put in a wheelchair, and taken for X-rays. I feel alone in this large, unfamiliar medical centre. Returning from the radiology department, the nurse says, "We need to call your parents." I provide my phone number and sit and listen. "Can I speak to Mr. or Mrs. Seftel please?" says the friendly nurse, and there is a brief pause. "Hello, Mrs. Seftel," another pause. "We have your son Steven here." Another pause, followed by, "Yes, he has a fractured wrist." Whisked away again, a plaster cast is fitted to my arm for the next eight weeks.

The weeks pass, and I start to skate with the team but no stick-handling is allowed. Approaching six weeks I begin shooting pucks because I'm feeling better. Skating and shooting is my way of asserting that I am in fact ready to play. The cast is removed. It's been difficult watching the team play without me, and I'm anxious to get back into action on the ice.

Returning to the lineup, the coaches decide to make a change: I will no longer be playing defence, but will finish the hockey season as a left-winger. I've played both defence and forward up to now so I'm fine with their decision. Whatever I have to do, for my pack, my hockey dream, and my journey.

Kissing Disease

A gangly, five-foot-eleven, 155-pound, adolescent 15-year-old, I'm anticipating the minor midget tryouts with the AAA Kavaliers. Dad calls me upstairs. "I just had a phone call from the midget coach, George Knisley and he wants you to attend Greenshirts' tryouts," he says. A rush of energy engulfs me as I process that the respected coach and leader of the Shirts wants me to play for him. If I can make the team, I'll be playing up a birth year with the 16-year-olds. This is a bold move by Coach Knisley because he didn't only invite me, he invited nine of my teammates, and the news sends ripples through the local minor-hockey world.

Playing plenty of lacrosse and hockey develop my tenacity and competitiveness. Be first to the puck and go for it, enter the dirty areas, like the front of the net and the corners are among my mantras. I will need these valuable skills to make the Greenshirts.

An exhibition game for the boys is in Oshawa. The puck is dumped into the Oshawa zone. Moving my feet quickly, I read and react. Beating the opposing defenceman to the corner, I seize the loose puck. A quick head fake and I dodge the defender, and skate to the net. Sliding a cross-crease pass to my linemate waiting on the back post, he buries the puck past the sprawling goalie. Yes! Raising my stick, I cruise over to celebrate. Skating back to the bench with a bounce in my step, I begin to believe. When tryouts are complete, myself and eight other underage boys make the 17-player Greenshirts' roster. Here we go!

Having kids playing sports puts a strain on my parents. Driving to games and practices while working and taking care of family needs creates challenges. In this case, mid-week 5 p.m. practices at Don McLaren are a problem for my hardworking mom and dad. When we can, we ask teammates to assist with driving, but in this instance, we're forced to be creative.

My grandmother lives within walking distance of the rink. Dad and I drive my equipment over to Grandma Betty's house the night before practice. After school, I take the #4 Glasgow St. bus to Mabe's Lunch, located across from the Uniroyal tire factory. Grandma works at Mabe's and I show up from school like any other ravenous teenage boy.

Mabe's Lunch is a small eatery with one counter and silvery swivel chairs to sit on. The cash register sits on the end of the counter with colourful candy tucked behind glass below. A large pop cooler with an accompanying bottle-cap opener, and a narrow storage room complete the setup. Pushing the door open, I'm greeted with my grandmother's friendly smile. She's always eager to cook for me. "Would you like a hamburger," she asks. "Yes, and a chocolate milk please," I answer happily.

The regulars line up on the stools: firemen, policemen, tire builders and neighbours. Lively chatter fills the joint and she proudly introduces me to the patrons I've not yet met. After devouring my hamburger, I walk a few minutes to her house on

Gruhn St. to watch T.V. or, less likely, finish homework. Watching the clock closely, I hike the ten-minute trip up the street with my hockey bag on my shoulder. Practice complete, my parents arrive to pick me up. My family does whatever it takes to get me to and from hockey.

Christmas 1983 is approaching and I'm primed for a big hockey week; the Greenshirts are attending the prestigious Ottawa International Hockey Tournament. The boys are looking forward to the opportunity in front of us. The tourney will have loads of OHL scouts in attendance. It's exciting knowing that real scouts will be watching us.

We're visiting relatives this holiday season. It is after all, the most wonderful time of the year; at least that's what the song says. After a hefty dinner, I'm shaking and shivering under a wool crocheted afghan, and a fever hits hard. I'm burning up. It's not the most wonderful time of the year for me at the present moment.

Mom takes me to see Dr. Miller. 'Only the flu,' I hope. 'You know, maybe forty-eight hours, then Christmas, and off to Ottawa.' Dr. Miller asks me to sit on the examination table. Performing a routine exam, he slowly nods as he feels the painful, swollen glands in my neck, and says he suspects he knows the problem.

"Well Steve," he says in his Scottish accent, which I like hearing, but not today. "I believe you have mononucleosis." Mononucleosis! Ahhh, no! "What about hockey?" I desperately inquire. "No hockey or strenuous activity, get plenty of rest, and drink lots of fluids," he says.

Infectious mononucleosis, or mono, is called the kissing disease. The virus that causes mono is transmitted through saliva, and though it can be acquired through kissing, you can also be exposed through a cough, a sneeze, sharing a glass, or food utensils with an infected person with the contagious virus. Teenagers are often diagnosed with mono but, in fact, you can contract it at any age and I have. Kaboom!

A mental wreck after the news, I don't show it outwardly. I have the infamous kissing disease! I have a girlfriend. I'm unsure if my parents like her, or maybe they don't like me having a serious girlfriend at 15-years-old with OHL dreams dancing in my head. Easy come, easy go? Hell no, this sucks!

The captain of the Greenshirts, Brian Pedlar, surprises me with a knock on the door, and a giant fruit basket from the team just before they depart for Ottawa. It feels good knowing that the guys are thinking about me, but I really want to be travelling with them. Mononucleosis zaps all of my energy reserves and for the next few weeks it is difficult just walking up the stairs from the basement rec room to my bedroom. Despite missing the tourney, it does pass as Dr. Miller predicted and the hockey season rolls on.

The Greenshirts' coaching staff selected this group with the goal of playing in the Air Canada Cup. After a league championship and series win over Niagara Falls, the boys are facing off against the Peterborough Petes in the OMHA (Ontario Minor Hockey Association) final. The powerhouse Petes are highly ranked in the province, and the talented team includes future NHLers Herb Raglan, Kerry Huffman, Dallas Eakins, and Glen Seabrooke. The Peterborough Examiner gives us little to no chance of winning this final series. However, the article provides us with solid bulletin board material to motivate the team in the room. The upstart Greenshirts win the best-of-five series and will represent the OMHA at the Air Canada Cup Regional Championships in Nepean, Ontario. This means more opportunities for the team and more scouts in the stands.

At the end of a competitive week in Nepean, the Greenshirts do not advance and the tournament is won by a dominating North Bay hockey club, led by future NHLer Darren Turcotte who will play 635 NHL games.

The 1984 OHL draft is up next, and the Kitchener Greenshirts have four players selected on draft day. My teammates who will be moving on include winger John Keller, selected in the 6th round by the hometown Kitchener Rangers; defenceman Randy Curran, in the 9th round by the Ottawa 67's; winger Peter Lisy, in the 13th round by the North Bay Centennials; and defenceman Brian Pedlar, in the 16th round by the Peterborough Petes. Although eligible, none of our nine underage midgets, including myself, are selected. Perhaps our time will come next spring.

I finish the season with 61 games played, 36 goals and 25 assists for 61 points; a point per game pace. Having seen my teammates drafted only stokes the fires burning inside me. I know and believe I can do this. This dream is becoming reality, and I need a plan to keep my journey on track.

Raw Eggs

In the warming summer, the upbeat song *Jump* by Van Halen is the #1 single on Billboard's Hot 100. The boys and I debate over who is a better guitarist, Eddie Van Halen or Angus Young of AC/DC. At the movies, we wait in long lines to watch Arnold Schwarzenegger in the *Terminator* and Eddie Murphy in *Beverly Hills Cop*.

A senior now at St. Jerome's Catholic High School and, with the previous hockey season a not too distant memory, I make a few important decisions that will impact my hockey life. The choices focus on my dream to make hockey a career. Keeping that goal in mind, I make three conscious declarations to myself.

One – I will no longer play lacrosse. It is with a heavy heart that I decide to stop playing a sport I love to focus primarily on hockey.

Lacrosse is a great game, but I will make this sacrifice for my hockey dream.

Two – There will be no steady girlfriends in my life for the next twelve months. This particular decision seems right after the infamous mononucleosis-gate from last season. The kissing disease turns me off girls and I'm making another sacrifice for hockey.

Three – I will commit to getting stronger. Coaches the past two years said I needed to improve my upper body strength.

For the upcoming season, the Greenshirts' coaching staff is back and intact with the addition of assistant coach Bob Turow, or Rocket, as we call him. We call him Rocket because when scrimmaging before practice starts, he joins in and tries to dangle through us, thus, earning himself the nickname Rocket after the Montréal Canadiens' great goal-scorer Maurice 'Rocket' Richard. Bob is a young man and former Greenshirt. He turned to coaching after his playing days and he relates well to the boys that he's only a few years older than.

The staff is once again hoping for a berth in the Canadian Midget Hockey Championships, the Air Canada Cup. The upcoming hockey season will be special for another reason: the Greenshirts will be travelling to Czechoslovakia for 17-days in November.

The AAA team's conditioning camp takes place throughout the hot summer days with on and off-ice training. The busy training regimen helps fill the void left by the absence of my friends playing lacrosse. The girls I do not miss; at least not this summer. The strengthening goal I set for myself is in high gear.

Purchasing a membership at the busy YMCA. I bike there in twenty minutes from home. A few of the guys invest in memberships as well. After weightlifting, we play racquetball, run the indoor track, swim in the pool, or play basketball. Training feels good, both physically and mentally. I start to see and feel the results and this drives me. I've also discovered bodybuilding magazines that belonged to my Uncle Tony. Flipping through the pages, I study the articles on nutrition and discover information on how to build muscle and improve strength. It is in these magazines that I find ads for protein powder.

Protein supplements are designed to increase muscle mass when combined with regular exercise. In my pursuit of gaining physical strength and weight, the next logical step is to buy protein powder, which I do. Quite frankly it tastes horrible, but that's okay. I need to fill out my slender frame.

To further my protein consumption, and inspired by the motion picture *Rocky*, I realize that raw eggs can be ingested like a drink. It appears to have helped Rocky Balboa become a champ. I mix the slippery raw eggs with milk in a glass and drink the slimy liquid as a fast, simple method to consume protein and calories. Family members are disgusted by my new habit, but I'm hoping that the concoction will bear fruit or added pounds. I learn what I can from books or magazines; there is no Google or Alexa for quick reference. The raw egg drink theory now appears to be fake news. As it turns out, muscle is built by doing resistance training, getting proper sleep, and nutrition. Basically, it is hard work. Remember the 4Ds: dedication, desire, determination, and discipline.

I'm not playing lacrosse but I officiate to fill the void. I'm managing to stay girlfriend free, and physically I'm stronger. Staying true to my plan, the extra effort is paying off. I'm growing and maturing. Entering the new hockey season, I'm now six-foot-one, 172-pounds. This puts me two inches taller and twenty pounds heavier than last season as tryouts begin.

Tryouts are complete and there are considerable expectations for a team that is icing nine returning players from last year's Greenshirts. The sweaty group of skaters is sitting in the dressing room after an exhibition game in Oshawa when the coaching staff appears. Coach Knisley announces they've made a decision on captains. "We've chosen Steve Seftel as captain, Jeff Noble and Rod Thacker as assistant captains," he says to the boys. Hearing Coach Knisley tell the team that I will be the captain is incredible. I'm proud and honoured to have their confidence and trust as the leader of this hockey team. For me, the news validates the three decisions I made at the start of summer.

In order to allow for two-and-a-half-weeks in Europe, we will need to play a condensed schedule early in the season. I'm eagerly anticipating the upcoming trip. 'What will it be like to fly across the ocean? Will the people in Czechoslovakia be friendly?' We're still deep in the throes of the Cold War and I don't really know what to expect.

In 1980 this coaching staff, minus Rocket, had taken the Greenshirts to Czechoslovakia and beat the Czech national midget team, and our pack is well aware of that fact. What will it be like playing hockey behind the Iron Curtain? Ladies and gentlemen, boys and girls, please fasten your seatbelts.

Czechoslovakia

Czechoslovakia is a Communist country; it had been since 1948. Perhaps some of what we believe to be true about Communist countries comes from the fact that we are only twelve years removed from the profound emotions of the '72 Summit Series.

The Summit Series was 8-games of extraordinary hockey played between the Soviet Union and Canada in September 1972. It was the first competition between the Soviet national team and a Canadian team made up of professional players from the National Hockey League and was devised with the intent of creating a true best-on-best hockey series, resulting in international chest-pounding bragging rights for world hockey supremacy.

An article in the sports section of the K-W Record on November 1st, 1984 presents the headline: "Powerful Greenshirts set for Czech Trip." Expectations are certainly high for the team and me. Departing from Toronto on Thursday, November 8th, it will be a long journey with stops in Montréal, Helsinki and finally, Prague. Here we go!

After crossing the Atlantic Ocean and arriving in Prague via Helsinki on Saturday, the boys are tired and physically drained from our travels. At the airport, we're met by our friendly, always smiling tour guide, Jon. I'm taken aback by the conspicuous military presence on hand as we depart on our bus and drive to the Prague International Hotel.

The coaches assign roommates and hand out keys. My large double room sleeps four and I'm happy to have company in this foreign land. Noble, Thacker and Jamie Schlegel are my roomies. There's comfort knowing I'll be sharing living space with this trio.

The next item of business is to find the elevator in this sizable hotel. The elevators are old, made of wood, and have manual doors. Inside, it is small, and has room for one player, and a hockey bag. Stepping into the elevator reluctantly, I press the button for my floor. The elevator doors close, and it begins to move. First floor, second floor, crack, boom, bang, and the elevator abruptly stops. As if warm liquid is poured over my head, I begin to sweat profusely and internally vibrate. Intense feelings swarm my body like a cloud of smoke, and I feel trapped. Seconds feel like minutes and minutes like hours; this is panic!

There is pounding on the walls. I hear a voice. 'I know that voice, it's Gary Watson.' He calls out to me, "Hey Sef, how you doing in there?" Instantly, his familiar voice is gone. Frantic, I shout, "Help!" I hear noises, and strange voices calling out. The voices aren't speaking English. I faintly hear words I recognize. Like the charging cavalry coming to the rescue, the boys show up. Together with hotel staffers, they manage to free me from the elevator. A sense of relief comes over me as the doors open and I hustle out. I can always count on my pack to have my back, on and off the ice. After this episode, I'll take the stairs for the remainder of my stay. Avoidance of the elevator you ask? Yes!

After the elevator trauma, and settled in our large hotel room, I try to get normalcy to my schedule. Hockey is a continuous flow of routine that helps create conditions for team and individual success. The coaches give us a strict curfew and lights out time; no ifs, ands or buts.

Anxiety takes hold of my internal thoughts and I can't sleep. My roomies fall asleep, and I'm the only pack member awake. The Iron Curtain feels like it is closing in on me without the security of idle chatter, the type of banter that calms my anxious, overactive mind. While I lay in bed, a flurry of images enter my thoughts...Perhaps armed guards patrol the streets at night. I heard people have been shot and killed trying to escape these Communist countries.

Without noticing, I drift off to sleep. Bang! Stirred up by a loud crack, I scramble to my feet and race across the room. Stumbling across the floor in the dark, the boys call out to me. Their voices awaken me and I regain my bearings. 'It's only a dream and I'm sleep walking.' The boys continue to chirp and laugh. I quietly return to my bed, and we all lay wide awake. What a day!

We receive our early wake-up call the next morning, and breakfast is ready in the big hotel's dining room. Teenage boys and specifically, teenage hockey players, need food. Breakfast here is far different than what we're used to; that is to say, the choices are minimal. The scrambled eggs are okay, but the buns are hard and difficult to chew. At lunchtime, schnitzel is popular and the most familiar item on the menu for me.

Monday it's time to get the gear on for the first time in Czechoslovakia for an exhibition game against Prague's Sparta midget team. It's explained to us, this will be the equivalent of playing the Toronto Red Wings, a top team in the current Greater Toronto Hockey League. Playing in a mostly empty 15,000 seat arena, we are stiff, and rusty. Pacing the team, I pot-a-pair of goals in the 4-0 shut-out win.

Post-game, we explore the outer edges of the hotel looking for food and drinks to purchase. There's shopping in the adjacent stores, but they're stark, and the shelves bare. Choices are at a minimum. We walk down the street like a pack of wolves. There's strength in numbers as the pack moves together along the sidewalk. Finding a plain convenience store, we enter, exchanging sideways looks with the shop owner as he assesses the pack of young Canadians. We are unsure if he speaks English and I assume he doesn't.

"Hey look, Coke," yells a voice from the group. Coca-Cola, a familiar brand in this unfamiliar country, makes us all feel a little closer to home as we carry bottle after bottle to the counter. "Five korunas," says the clerk. Rushing out the front door with our new-found treasure, we retreat to the hotel to tell the rest of the waiting pack of Greenshirts. We return, eager to purchase more Coke, but this time the clerk asks us for eight korunas. Tomorrow it will be ten and we offer little resistance to the rising prices. This wise clerk understands supply and demand.

For most of us, we've never played for more than a hundred friends and family at Don McLaren. Today we're playing an exhibition game against the Prague Selects in front of 4,000 screaming, elementary school children. One vocal group of kids are enthusiastically waving Canadian flags for us.

Skating onto the ice for the short five-minute warm-up, the kids scream as both teams circle in their respective zones. The boys line up with half the skaters in each corner and start with the traditional swing drill to warm the goalies; one player at a time moving out to the blue line for a pass and shot on goal.

The referee blows his whistle, and there are handshakes and an exchange of pins before puck drop. Game on! With fast-paced action at both ends of the ice, the young school children cheer and holler, the clock ticks down to zero, and we shutout our Czech opponents 6-0.

After removing our gear and showering, we leave the building and encounter the waiting school kids and teachers. Prior to leaving home, we were given pins for trading on our trip: Canadian flag pins, Oktoberfest pins and others. The enthusiastic kids swarm us, waving their arms in the air. Even though we cannot understand each other, everyone knows how to barter and trade using hand signals and facial gestures. Holding up one finger to a young fan, I display my pin: a Canadian flag. His wide eyes light up as he passes me his hockey organization's pin. The team is thrust into a trading frenzy as the kids continue to shout, the mob pushing forward waving their treasures. Suddenly, the locals are offering multiple pins for one pin from Canadian soil, and unknowingly it turns into a contest to fetch the largest swap. One boy offers me his entire collection of pins, which are conveniently housed in a wrinkled, brown folding case for just one of my pins. In the midst of the trading chaos, I quickly pull the trigger on the lopsided deal.

In a short period of time, the crowd disperses and I proudly present my haul to my mates. There is genuine excitement on the bus as we compare our new treasures. Upon reflection, I can't help but feel I've taken advantage of the situation. Guilty feelings come over me, and I stare at the boy's entire collection. I hope he's equally pleased with his swap but I'll never know. That pin collection and brown folding case still sit with my hockey memorabilia and I think of that boy whenever I look at it.

Moving on to Sumperk for a tournament, playing an aggressive Canadian-style of hockey, we overpower the Sumperk, Mlada Boleslav, and Hradec Kralove teams. Our short-term goal is to win this five-team tournament. A game against the pre-tournament favourite Slovak Nationals appears by most to be the matchup that will determine the tourney champion. The Slovaks score first less than a minute in, to take a 1-0 lead. Grinding it out, forcing turnovers, skating stride for stride with the wheeling fast-breaking Slovaks, the boys outlast them, winning 5-1. Crowned champions, the boisterous pack of Greenshirts proudly hoist the tournament trophy at the on-ice closing ceremonies.

The trip will end with the much-anticipated games with the Czech national midget team coached by the country's former national team goalie, Jiri Holecek. Game One in Sumperk, we play in front of a jammed, raucous crowd of 3,000 local hockey fans and our outnumbered, cheering parent group. The Czechs skate with blazing speed and win a tight game 5-3 to the delight of the noisy fans. Our manager Jack George knew the team could play better. "We ran around a lot and didn't play disciplined hockey," he told the Kitchener-Waterloo Record. Time to regroup!

For Game Two, we travel to the city of Olomouc. Fearing, but not believing we're overmatched, the pressure is on us for a win. Laser-focus permeates the room pre-game while each of us thinks about the mammoth task that is only minutes away. Playing in front of a smaller crowd of 1,500 fans, we have to control our emotions and play smart. It's time for good old-fashioned, Canadian bump-and-grind hockey.

The fired-up Greenshirts come out smoking hot in Game Two, matching the Czechs' speed, but they open the scoring and take a 1-0 lead in the intense, tight-checking first period. Playing fast, and physical, we finish the period up by a 2-1 score. Making more than one trip to the penalty box in the second and third periods, Jon, our interpreter, gives me the hand sign for calm down son. I'm getting frustrated and have to keep my composure. I'm not helping the team sitting in the penalty box.

The group believes in our hungry pack, our passion for hockey, our country, and in the end, we win 5-2 led by twins, Brad and Jamie Schlegel who combine for three goals. Hopping the boards at the buzzer, proud parents pass us Canadian flags to carry and wave. Post-game relief and elation bubble up in the relieved dressing room. None of us wanted to go home without beating the Czechs. Mission accomplished!

The entire group is welcomed at the Canadian embassy in Prague. Canadian flavours are a welcome refreshment for the players, coaches, and parents. We're enjoying the Canadian turf at the embassy when Jack pulls me aside. He asks if I can give a short speech to thank our hosts for their hospitality. I look at Jack and let the request sink in for a moment. I wanted to be captain of this team and along with that role comes responsibility and expectations. I need to do this for the pack and the parents. I agree, begin to pace, wandering around anxiously from room to room as I prepare a speech in my head. Okay, start it off with, 'on behalf of our players, coaches, and parents,' that sounds good.

I'm nervous as I wait for Jack to call my name. Within minutes I'm asked to the front of the room. Walking up, looking out at the assembled group, I clear my throat. Annunciate, speak loud and clear, I tell myself with my inside voice. "On behalf of the Kitchener Greenshirt players, coaches and parents..."

As captain of the team, I'm honoured to thank our hosts on behalf of the group. This is a memorable moment for me! I'm proud to be Canadian and feel lucky to live in Canada. In my mind, at this satisfying point in my journey, I know I live in the greatest country in the whole world! It's time to go home.

Déjà Vu

Returning to Canada, the boys and I need time to decompress from an emotionally draining trip. Routine is not so easy after seventeen days in Europe. I find myself suffering from jet lag and trying hard to get back into the fixed school schedule. As a team it's time to refocus on the hockey season and our long-term goal of playing in the Air Canada Cup.

Immediately after Christmas we're back on the road, travelling to our capital city for the annual Ottawa International Hockey Tournament. This event will provide an opportunity for scouts to see a large swath of players in one location. The OHL draft is less than six months away and even though the team is the number one priority, individual goals and dreams creep into our conversations.

In the hallways and in quiet locations of the arenas, scouts start to ask coaches questions about their draft-eligible players.

Parents and players can't help but notice the scouts in the rinks. Some are finely dressed men, some wear team jackets, carrying paperwork and rolled-up programs for note-taking. Some sit together, others sit alone. They watch the games intently, occasionally glancing down at their information sheets. As their pens and pencils start to move across the pages, players and parents start to think about the future.

After completing a successful round-robin, the Ottawa tourney ends with a spirited 4-2 semi-final loss to Detroit Compuware. The skilled Compuware midgets are led by future-NHL defenceman Adam Burt.

Rolling into the month of January, we prepare to start playoffs and resume the journey to the Air Canada Cup which, in 1985, will be hosted by the City of Regina, Saskatchewan.

OMHA playoffs include a league championship win over Burlington and another series win over Sarnia. Next up is an OMHA championship rematch against the Peterborough Petes. The winner of this series will advance to the provincial regional tournament for a chance to represent Ontario in Regina at the Canadian midget hockey championships.

It's déjà vu for the Greenshirts! We're getting ready to play Peterborough in the OMHA final for the second consecutive season. It will be the Petes' maroon and white jerseys versus our green and gold once again. The difference this time around: amongst hockey pundits, Kitchener is seen as the favourite.

A hard-fought battle ends for us in crushing fashion in the Lift Lock City and the Petes exact their revenge, winning the best-of-five series, ending any Air Canada Cup dreams we have. The Greenshirts are given a serious dose of their own medicine after the previous year's unexpected victory.

Back in the small visitor's dressing room, the finality of the hockey season sets in; it's over. Losing leaves a cut on my competitive spirit, and truthfully it makes me physically hurt inside. I want to scream but the room is eerily quiet. It feels like the end of the world. I keep my emotions locked inside, while some players cry, and others bury their faces in their hands. Our coaches praise our effort and commitment, and this starts the healing process and growth that comes from losing. The hurt felt today heals with time. I learn from it, and feel stronger mentally. The sun will rise tomorrow.

With the hockey season over, my focus becomes the upcoming draft. Coaches say team success will lead to individual success. On a personal level, I'm happy with my season. In 69 games played, I scored 58 goals and added 52 assists for a total of 110 points.

The month of March starts to evaporate; draft day is getting closer. My parents sit me down for a family discussion. "We want to discuss a request we received," my dad says. Sitting on pins and needles at the kitchen table, I look up as he continues. "A gentleman called us and he wants to represent you. He would like to be your player agent," says my dad as he slowly hands me a letter. The top left corner has the agency name, Branada; the three letter 'As' are red stars, the other four letters in royal blue. It looks sharp, and underneath it says Branada Sports Group. Excited by the news, my insides shake. It all seems so surreal. "He wants to be your player agent," they say again. I'm flattered! "His name is Rick Curran," my dad says.

Rick is a hockey player agent and vice-president of Branada Sports Group. Partnering with Bill Watters to help shape Branada Sports, he assisted in building it into one of hockey's premier agencies.

"He wants to meet you this week," my dad says, and the arrangements for a one-on-one meeting are set. Mr. Curran picks me up at home and we drive to Mother's Pizza on Highland Road. I'm in awe of this man. He represents numerous high-profile clients in the NHL. Rick is well spoken, sharply dressed and I'm overwhelmed by his genuine interest in my hockey career. We have a great conversation that goes by quickly. It all sounds great to me, and with that, he is now my agent.

In early April I receive a letter from the OHL, signed by league Commissioner David Branch; a letter many other players also receive. I see my name and address, followed by: "Dear Steve, on behalf of the Ontario Hockey League, it gives me great pleasure to write you at this time." The envelope contains an "Information Questionnaire" that I'm to complete and return by April 15th. The letter states, 'be honest and factual.' Why wouldn't I be honest and factual? Maybe this is when players somehow grow an inch or two and gain twenty pounds only to show up at camp as smaller versions of themselves.

Driving over to meet my humourous teammate Steve Herniman, I step inside his house and he hands me a copy of an article from the April 2nd edition of the Windsor Star. "Hey look at this," he says as he passes me the print. "This copy is for you," he adds. Taking the paper, I begin to read: "Across Ontario, the top players include defencemen Marc Laniel of the Toronto Red Wings, Brian Chapman of Belleville, Bryan Fogarty of Aurora, Steve Herniman, Rod Thacker, each of Kitchener, and Steve Bisson of Ottawa, along with forwards John Anderson of the Toronto Marlies, Steve Seftel of Kitchener, Lonnie Loach of St. Mary's and Jody Hull of Cambridge." I act calm and cool, while I finish scanning the info. However, inside I'm busting! This is a time with no Internet, no Facebook, no Twitter, and no social media. Information has to come by word of mouth, newspapers or radio. I'm trembling as the contents sink in; my name listed as one of the top players in Ontario.

The month of May continues to tick down. More calls and letters are coming to the house from junior clubs, including letters from the Peterborough Petes and North Bay Centennials; phone calls from the Kitchener Rangers, Ottawa 67's, Oshawa Generals and Guelph Platers; and a home visit from the London Knights. My world is frantic as I anticipate the big day. The draft is slated for June 2nd at the North York Centennial Arena. Shortly, my hockey career and entire life are about to change.

Coming Alive in '85

May of 1985 the OHL draft is fast approaching. Anticipation for draft day is building. I feel like I've been waiting for this moment for a long time. Having said that, I've never considered the U.S. college route which would require me to finish high school; two years away. Honestly, to me, that seems like delayed gratification.

There is a buzz amongst the minor-hockey community, friends, teachers and schoolmates as draft day approaches. I have the sense that the larger community is saying, "Hey, these are our boys, developed right here in our city." It reminds me of a famous proverb: 'It takes a village to raise a child,' or in this case, a Canadian hockey player.

The K-W Record publishes a draft preview, written by Record staffer Larry Anstett. I study the clip which reads: "The OHL draft list has four Kitchener Greenshirt midgets, one Kitchener Ranger 'B' and four other area players rated in the first four rounds. The Greenshirts are defenceman Rod Thacker, the 14th ranked player; left-winger Steve Seftel, 16th; defenceman Steve Herniman, 22nd; and forward Jeff Noble, 33rd."

In '85, the OHL consists of 15 teams. With only fifteen teams and being rated sixteenth overall, I surmise I could potentially be a first-round draft pick or at worst, second round. On draft day, potential draftees assemble to see how their future hockey lives are about to change, or not. Predictably, not all players present are drafted and as a result, the potential for a permanent and painful mark can be left on a young player's mind.

Attending the draft with my parents and our good friends, Chuck and Elv, we enter the building. It is an understatement to say I'm anxious. Inside, players and parents are mingling in the lobby and sitting in the stands. We partake in nervous chatter while waiting quietly for the proceedings to begin. After a handshake and brief discussion with Rick, I sit up in the stands with my Greenshirt teammates who are in attendance.

Hockey etiquette starts early for aspiring players, and is on full display today. The customary code for hockey players is passed on from year to year because, if you're going to be in this profession, you need to learn how to conduct yourself. I've watched Wayne Gretzky interact with the media and fans – he's classy. Canadian hockey etiquette involves dressing sharp. I've listened to Don Cherry on Coach's Corner heaping praise on the well-dressed players when they file off the bus and walk into the rink. To that end, I wear a suit and tie for this important day.

David Branch is a Canadian hockey architect, with a long involvement in junior hockey. He's served as Commissioner of the Ontario Hockey League since 1979, and as President of the Canadian Hockey League since 1996.

Commissioner Branch takes to the podium to start the proceedings. After a brief welcome, he invites the Kingston Canadians up to the microphone to make their first selection. Gazing around the arena, I can see the entire surface where the ice would be if it were hockey season. Instead, the large concrete floor is filled with busy tables where each team and their general manager, coaches and scouts sit, feverishly shuffling through papers and quietly speaking to one another.

'Are they talking about me? Maybe they're talking about Adam Graves.' He is the top-rated player in the draft according to the pundits. In the future, he will go on to play 1,152 NHL games, and be a two-time Stanley Cup champion. Not too shabby! 'Maybe they're talking about Brendan Shanahan.' He's also highly rated today, and will go on to play 1,524 NHL games, and be a three-time Stanley Cup champion. Also, not too shabby!

The Kingston Canadians finished last in the 1984-85 season and own the first-overall pick today. The Canadians' brass move towards the podium to make the all-important first selection. I have butter-flies in my gut and I squirm in my seat as I look at the faces of the Greenshirt boys. The club representative slowly steps up to the podium, and adjusts the microphone to the appropriate height. There is a pause and then silence in the building. Everyone is wait-ing for this call. A voice calmly speaks, "The Kingston Canadians select…from the Aurora Tigers…defenceman Bryan Fogarty." There is applause in the rink. Bryan Fogarty is a talented, smooth-skating defenceman. He's a future NHL first-round draft choice who will be selected 9th overall in 1987 by the Québec Nordiques.

The second-overall pick belongs to the Sudbury Wolves who use it to select centre Ken McRae from the Hawkesbury Hawks. The third-overall pick belongs to the Guelph Platers and they select left-winger Lonnie Loach from the St. Mary's Lincolns. First-round picks continue to fly off team draft boards.

The Cornwall Royals have the ninth-overall pick. The Royals' staff moves into position at the podium, "The Cornwall Royals select…from the Kitchener Greenshirts…Steve…"Oh man! This is it, I'm going to Cornwall, where is Cornwall exactly?'…"Herniman." …I hear loud and clear from the podium! What? Who's on first? What's on second and I don't know is on third. Who? First base!

I'm not going to Cornwall and my buddy Steve Herniman is. The huge defenceman is the first Greenshirt off the draft boards. He's six-foot-four and over 200-pounds, so we naturally call him Peewee, and he's going to Cornwall in the first round. We congratulate him as he descends to the floor. The first round ends with defenceman Steve Bisson selected by the Sault Ste. Marie Greyhounds. My name is not called. A total of fifteen players have been selected, including top-rated Adam Graves, selected 6th overall by the Windsor Spitfires and Brendan Shanahan, selected 13th overall by the London Knights. Future NHLers Adam Burt, Bryan Marchment, and Jody Hull are also picked in the first round by the North Bay Centennials, Belleville Bulls and Peterborough Petes respectively. First round was a target for me. Second round; this is my round. I know it!

The round starts and the Kingston Canadians select left-winger Scott Pearson from Cornwall, Ontario. The second round finishes with the selection of highly-touted goaltender Shawn Simpson by the Soo Greyhounds. Two more of my Greenshirt teammates have their hockey futures made clear. Rod Thacker is selected 22nd overall by the Hamilton Steelhawks and Brad Schlegel is selected 28th by the London Knights. They're both defencemen, as is stay-at-home d-man Herniman. A total of thirty players have now been selected. At the conclusion of round two my name is not called. This sucks! The collar on my shirt becomes a little tighter, and my breaths shorter. I feel warmer, and become fidgety in my seat. My first and second-round predictions for myself are wrong.

The proceedings are moving a little quicker now. To begin the third round, Commissioner Branch calls upon the Kingston Canadians again. They approach the podium, and I hear: "The Kingston Canadians select, from the Kitchener Greenshirts, Steve Seftel." Suddenly, the weight that has been pressing down on my shoulders vanishes into thin air, and is replaced instantly with an immense feeling of pride and pure joy.

Hockey etiquette says to be humble. I shake hands with the boys, and make my way down the steps to the floor. I'm intercepted by

Rick, who shakes my hand and congratulates me before I move towards the podium.

On stage, I'm greeted by general manager Ken Slater with a handshake. I was told to shake hands firmly and look directly into the eye of the person I'm meeting; in other words, be strong and confident. I'm escorted over to the Canadians' draft table to meet other members of the franchise's hockey-operations contingent.

The draft continues as I walk over to the concourse area. It is also customary to have returning veteran players on hand, almost like a welcoming committee. My first meeting is with Canadian's hard-nosed winger Scott Metcalfe. I know he's a dual-sport athlete like me – a lacrosse player from Brampton. I know this from my obsession of reading tournament programs throughout my youth.

Shaking hands, I'm trying hard to be cool. I break some awkward silence by blurting out, "So, do you have a car?" 'Ah geez, is that the best you can come up with?' I ask myself. Lame! Scott gives me a stare. We have a short chat about future car purchases and hockey. I'm intrigued to find out he is going to be attending the NHL draft in a matter of days. Needless to say, I'm impressed with that notion. The scrappy, skilled Metcalfe will be drafted by the Edmonton Oilers with their first pick, 20th overall at the 1985 NHL Entry Draft.

In the future, he will also play for Team Canada at the 1987 World Junior Hockey Championships which featured the infamous "Punch Up in Piestany," a bench-clearing brawl between Canada and the Soviet Union during the final game of the tournament in Piestany, Czechoslovakia. The incident resulted in the ejection of the two rivals. I remember watching the crazy events unfold. We were in shock as the brawl escalated and overwhelmed tournament staffers decided to turn off the lights in the chaotic arena. The nasty melee continued in the dark. Back in the CBC studios, host Brian Williams and red-faced co-host Don Cherry fired up a heated debate over the young Canadians' actions in the fierce brawl.

After jumping another hurdle on my journey, we depart from Toronto and drive to Chuck and Elv's house in Brantford for a celebratory dinner. The unknown is now known and Kingston is my future hockey destination. Driving down Highway 403, I think about my Greenshirt teammates. The Greenshirts left their mark on this draft – four players selected in the first thirty-one picks: Herniman (9th overall), Thacker (22nd), Schlegel (28th), and myself (31st). Three more were also picked today: Jeff Noble, 6th round by the Kitchener Rangers; Jim David, 12th round by the Rangers; and goalie Paul Henriques, 13th round by the North Bay Centennials.

Following the draft, the Canadians invite the draftees and their families to town for a weekend as an opportunity to see the city. The team provides us with accommodations at the Howard Johnson Hotel on the Lake Ontario waterfront. A tour of the city and a BBQ at GM Ken Slater's house are on the weekend's agenda, and I feel like the red carpet has been rolled out for me and my parents.

Coach Fred O'Donnell sends us home with a summer conditioning program, upping the ante for intensity and our commitment to hockey. I've never trained with an actual manual to guide me so this is new. Before leaving the city, each player is given a Kingston Canadians' baseball hat and, on the front, it says, 'Coming Alive in 85.'

We're impressed during our weekend visit, as Kingston is a summertime gem, situated on the eastern-end of Lake Ontario, and the beginning of the St. Lawrence River. Nicknamed the "Limestone City", Kingston is also rich in Canadian history as the birthplace of our first Prime Minister, Sir John A. Macdonald. It's also the hometown of The Tragically Hip and NHL stars Doug Gilmour and Kirk Muller who cut their hockey teeth in Kingston. We cannot forget that hockey-icon Don Cherry is also a proud Kingstonian! Next stop training camp!

Kingston Canadians

The Kingston Canadians' arrival in the OHA (Ontario Hockey Association) for the 1973–74 season was a result of the Montréal Junior Canadiens' switch to the QMJHL (Québec Major Junior Hockey League) in 1972. During the summer of '72, the QMJHL threatened a lawsuit against the OHA to force the Junior Canadiens to return to the Québec-based league. To solve the dilemma, the OHA granted the Junior Canadiens' franchise a one-year suspension of hockey operations while team ownership transferred the team and players into the QMJHL, renaming themselves the Montréal Bleu Blanc Rouge.

The OHA then reactivated the suspended franchise after completion of the one-year hiatus, under a new ownership group, with new players, naming the team the Kingston Canadians. An inspired crew of Kingston businesses and professional individuals negotiated the terms of the acquisition from the Montréal Arena Corporation. The Kingston Canadians are the genuine successor of the Montréal Junior Canadiens' legacy.

The newly established Kingston Canadians used the same colours and uniforms as the NHL's Montréal Canadiens, and the QMJHL's Montréal Junior Canadiens. However, the logo replaced the familiar and historic letter "H" on the famed Habs' jersey with the letter "K" for Kingston.

With my new opportunity only days away, the Canadians make a significant announcement prior to the start of the 1985 training camp. GM and director of hockey operations Ken Slater resigns his position with the club to become a full-time scout for the Vancouver Canucks.

For three seasons prior to the 1985-86 campaign, the Canadians finished in last place in the Leyden Division. After a three-year play-off drought, newly assigned GM and head coach Fred O'Donnell expects significant improvements from the team, icing 20-returning players.

O'Donnell is entering his first season as head coach and general manager of the team. The former Boston Bruin spent the past few seasons at Queen's University coaching the Golden Gaels men's hockey team. Coach O'Donnell is quoted in the Kingston Whig-Standard newspaper saying, "Our prime objective this year will be to make the playoffs. We missed the playoffs the last three years and it's no doubt affected everything from attendance to attitude." The Canadians have depth and talent entering the new season. Veteran defenceman Todd Clarke is acquired from the Ottawa 67's, as is veteran pivot Brian Verbeek, who is picked up in a trade with the Sudbury Wolves. The organization is hoping for big contributions from the returning forwards, including recent NHL draft picks Scott Metcalfe and Herb Raglan. On the defensive side, the team has six returning veterans including 19-year-old Flyers' prospect Jeff Chychrun, plus number-one-overall draft pick, Bryan Fogarty. The brilliant rookie has tremendous potential. The goaltending duties will go to local boy and Chicago Blackhawks' draft pick, Chris Clifford, entering his third season.

Kingston is about 350 kilometres east of Kitchener and seems like a distant city to my teenage mind. Seldom have I travelled to the eastern end of the province. I didn't realize it at that moment, but this is the last time I will be home with my parents and my brother for anything other than a couple of months here and there. I'm 17-years-old and starting the next chapter of my hockey journey. I've driven down Highway 401 many times but this time it is different. In my mind, when I arrive in Kingston, I'm staying.

The day arrives to leave home for training camp. My hockey bag is ready and checked. I always check it twice, and pack it in the same order each time. On many occasions I return to my bag and check it again. Some say that's one of those superstitions players have, or it might be an obsessive-compulsive behaviour. However, I'm nervous and antsy, I don't want to forget anything, and this is the best way to accomplish that. With my large suitcase packed, we load everything into my parents' Pontiac Phoenix. I fit my six-foot-one, 182-pound body into the back seat and we're off.

Arriving in the Limestone City, my dad pulls the car into the parking lot outside the arena. The home rink for the Kingston Canadians is the Memorial Centre. It's an older building with a pointed roof, a large grassy area out front, and a horse track in the back. The asphalt parking lot is medium-sized and there are stables for the horses beside it. Inside the decades-old rink, the ice surface is larger than most, a 200-by-90-foot, big sheet of ice, and in the east end of the arena hangs a picture of Queen Elizabeth II, as there is the case in many local rinks across Canada.

I walk slowly to the west end entrance to find the dressing room. Stumbling across the coach's office, I stop and stare at the blue door with the Kingston Canadians' logo painted on it. This is it; I'm here! The door is open a crack so I knock and walk in. On my left shoulder, I have my hockey bag and in my right hand, my big blue suitcase. Returning players will check in with billets before the team meeting or leave their luggage elsewhere. This is a veteran move!

I meet trainer and athletic therapist Peter Campbell. Peter makes me feel right at home. He's an easygoing, funny guy. I wander into the dressing room. The returning veterans are standing around, shaking hands, discussing their summers, and other stuff teenage boys talk about. I feel very conspicuous at this moment and want to ditch my luggage. Now I'm the new guy, the rookie, here to earn a spot, or maybe take one from an older player who'd already been on the team last year. In Kitchener, I was the big fish in the little pond when playing for the Greenshirts, but now, I'm the little fish in the big pond trying to make this club.

Coach O'Donnell spots me and asks if I can find my parents and join him in his office. We sit down across from Mr. O'Donnell at his desk, and he places a sheet of paper down for us to review. It is an agreement, or as I like to say, a contract. That sounds more official. The first line states: 'Agreement between the Kingston Canadians Hockey Club herein known as the club and Steve Seftel.' Sounds like lawyer stuff to me. The next line catches my eye. 'Provided that the player signs a major junior "A" card, the club agrees to provide the player the following.' So, you're telling me I still have to earn my spot on the team during camp. Okay, that seems fair and I plan on it, so no biggie. There are now four items to cover in this agreement.

In short: For each season completed with the organization, the club agrees to pay me $1,000 to be applied towards tuition and books at a credited Canadian post-secondary school. So, I could earn up to $4,000 here; fair enough.

Two, if I'm traded by the Kingston Canadians, my new team is obligated to all terms of this deal. Sounds legit, the new team shouldn't get off the hook.

Three, the player, that's me, must commence post-secondary schooling immediately following the completion of his major junior eligibility or the agreement is null and void. Okay, so I can't travel the world for two years after junior hockey. Fine.

Four, in the event the player signs an NHL professional contract, this agreement is null and void. Okay, so now you're telling me this is a small insurance policy because I plan to sign an NHL contract one day. I think insurance is good. Okay, where do I sign? My parents, Coach O'Donnell, the team president, and I all put pen to paper. Paperwork is done, I'm here to play hockey!

My parents stay long enough to make sure I'm settled in. They have a long drive back to Kitchener. We say our good-byes. I recently asked my mom how she felt as she left me that afternoon. "Your dad and I were proud of you and excited. We knew you were a mature young man and ready for this new part of your life," she said. "I wasn't expecting to have to come back and get you," she added.

Slowly more players arrive for the start of training camp. We have a team meeting to review itineraries, schedules, and expectations. I look around the room and see that it is loaded with skilled athletes who were the big fish in their hometowns. Everything is all business from Coach O'Donnell. Players are divided into four teams for training camp: Aces, Frontenacs, Red and Blue. Daily curfew is set for 11:15 p.m. and we're reminded to be on time for all on-ice and off-ice activities. He asks if there are any questions, and like a typical teenage boy, I say no and just stare straight ahead. Coach O'Donnell finishes the meeting, and slowly the boys disperse.

Next on the itinerary is billet assignments. Billets serve an important role in junior hockey. Billet families open up their homes to the players, and provide a stable family life while you're away. They treat you like one of their own, and believe me, it is not a moneymaking venture. Instead it is done for a modest weekly stipend and a pair of season tickets. Being a new player in town, I have no idea where I'm going to be billeting. In a short period of time, I will be greeted by a new family, who, just a couple of hours ago, were complete strangers to me. Unlike my weekend experiences with billets on short-term tournaments, I will now count upon this family to help and guide me through a much longer, and more turbulent time of my life.

Most of the team will live on the west side of the city and attend Bayridge Secondary School. Myself, Scott Pearson and Brian Verbeek will all reside on the east side of the city in a neighbourhood named Grenadier Village, and attend LaSalle Secondary

School. I figure Brian billets out here at the Moran's home because he's 19-years-old, and has a vehicle. We're rookies and have no access to an automobile, therefore we need Brian to get us to and from the rink.

Before we leave the arena, I'm told I will be living with the Stone family. Scott will be billeting with Ken Slater's family, and live on the same street as me. I take comfort in the fact that a fellow rookie will be living on my street, and think perhaps we will become good friends. In fact, we become best friends, supporting each other through our early trials and tribulations as rookies. In the future, he will be the best man at my wedding. In time, Scott Pearson will be drafted by the Toronto Maple Leafs in the first round, 6th over-all, in 1988, and play 292 NHL games.

I'm dropped off at my billet's house and introduced to Dennis and Ellen Stone. "Welcome Steve! It's nice to meet you," says Mrs. Stone. She's a warm, friendly, kindhearted woman with a great sense of humour. "Nice to meet you too," I reply respectfully. I enter the tight front foyer. Mr. Stone is a quiet, polite gentleman. They live in a modest two-storey, three-bedroom townhouse. They're nice people and that is reassuring. Mr. and Mrs. Stone show me around the house, introduce me to their two cats, and my new bedroom. Sitting down in the living room for a few minutes, we discuss tomorrow's early wake-up call and breakfast plans. I tell Mr. Stone I usually eat cereal and toast. Easy stuff. It's been a long day and I have an early morning tomorrow with camp start-ing. It's show time!

I go to my room, close the door and sit on the bed. As I think about what lays ahead, I begin to get warmer. Suddenly, there's a churning in my stomach, and an uneasy feeling comes over me. I look around at the walls and then just stare at my luggage. I think about my family hundreds of kilometres away, tryouts, scrim-mages, my bed at home, my bedroom, my backyard and other arbi-trary thoughts that infect my spiraling mind. My heart begins beating quicker, the room seems smaller, each breath shorter and then, without any notice, tears form in my eyes. Wait, wait, get a grip..., my mind suddenly starts thinking hockey and almost on cue, changes focus to why I'm here, and why I'm here starts tomorrow morning. As Tom Hanks said in the movie, *A League of Their Own*, "Are you crying? Are you crying? There's no crying in baseball. There's no crying in baseball!" If there's no crying in baseball, there is certainly no crying in hockey!

Training Camp

Kingston Canadians' training camp opens and I'm on the ice bright and early for the first intra-squad game. The competition for roster spots is about to commence. The Whig-Standard is here for photographs. They ask Coach O'Donnell for a picture. He collects a bunch of us, along with assistant coach Shawn Babcock, and we huddle around him for a quick photo op. I take my place down in front, on one knee, in the photo that will launch camp. Rookies are not given equipment from the team to start, therefore I sport my green Kitchener helmet and a white Aces jersey.

I have butterflies as the scrimmage begins but what I know is, all I need to do is get that first bump in and my nerves will sort themselves out. Early in the intra-squad, I pick up a loose puck, beat the oncoming defenceman, and find myself all alone on the goalie. When you're in that position, it's time to do what you do best, so I do. I go to the backhand deke, lift the puck up high and find the back of the net. I raise my hands and tap gloves with my linemates. I pick up another goal before the first scrimmage ends. A solid outing follows in the afternoon and I feel good about the way I'm playing. The early success I have on the ice washes away any uneasy feelings about moving away from home and keeps my mind on the task at hand which is making this hockey team.

After a good night's sleep, I return to the rink for the second day of camp, wanting to build on yesterday's scrimmages. Each day is a clean slate on the ice so you take nothing for granted. Today, more scrimmages are on the schedule, and my team is up for our next tilt.

Game on. The puck drops and away I go, following it into the offensive zone. Forechecking has always been one of my stronger assets. 'Be first to the puck.' That's the way I play hockey. Getting there first creates possession. I beat the d-man into the corner and grab the loose puck, then turn to make a play at the net. One of my linemates is streaking towards the back post and I'm preparing to pass. In an instant, the charging opposition defenceman uses his momentum to drive me into the west end boards. My heels hit the dasher first and send lightning bolts of pain shooting through my leg. Ahh! I attempt to skate away but I can't; my ankle is in serious pain. I lift my skate off the ice and glide on one leg. Hockey etiquette dictates that you don't make the trainer come onto the ice if you can get to the bench under your own power. I continue to glide over to the bench. The door opens and I sit on the end, wincing in pain. I slump over at the waist and inhale a deep breath. Peter comes down to see me, having just watched my pained reaction. We leave the bench together and he leads me down the runway into the training room. I sit on the table and stare straight ahead. After an assessment, he concludes that it's just a bad bruise and I need to take the remainder of the day off. No, c'mon man, things are going so well.

The third day of camp begins and I have to sit and watch in the empty Memorial Centre seats. The fourth day the team plays the annual Red versus White game in front of a sparse crowd. Unfortunately, my ankle is still sore and I'm not able to play. I'll have to be patient and take a wait-and-see approach. The team starts its 8-game exhibition schedule tomorrow afternoon in Peterborough.

The group loads the bus at the rink and it moves comfortably down Highway 401 for the two-hour trip. I've decided to drop the clip-on ties from midget hockey and now possess real ties that require proper technique to manipulate and wear correctly. However, I've never tied a tie.

The bus stops in the city located on the Trent-Severn Waterway, we exit one by one, and enter the barn in Peterborough. I quickly find a public bathroom for privacy to deal with my tie. I'm struggling with it and hoping nobody sees me while I figure it out. Experienced 19-year-old Brian Verbeek discovers me butchering my half-Windsor and gives me my first lesson on the proper technique required to complete a knot. I feel good about myself as his instructions work and I get it done. I tied my own tie. This is progress for a green rookie.

Game on! I watch the boys' first exhibition game from the cheap seats, resting my gimpy ankle. It's a combative hockey game with loads of aggression. Referee Bill Prisniak calls 147-minutes in penalties in the prickly fight-filled affair. The final buzzer sounds and we are thumped 9-3 by the hometown Petes.

Like other teams, the Canadians are the biggest game in town on home ice. A noisy crowd of 3,500 people are in attendance to watch our first home exhibition game versus the Belleville Bulls. The veterans say the Bulls are our arch rival; we don't like them and they don't like us; our fans don't like them and their fans don't like us. Crowds are always bigger for games against Belleville and this one is no exception.

Wandering around the Memorial Centre, I'm shocked by the size of the crowd since this is a pre-season game. The fans are ready and perhaps they know something about this rivalry that a rookie like me does not. The game starts and there are fisticuffs everywhere; a fight here, fight there, a line brawl. I've never seen anything like it, at least not live and in person. It's a big change from midget hockey where fighting is rare. Between the two teams are some of the toughest players in the Ontario Hockey League and there is no shortage of raging altercations to prove it. The game is filled with fast hockey and fast fists! The two squads combine for 299-minutes in penalties in just two periods of play. The game is suspended after the middle period because the steamy September temperature causes large amounts of fog to form on the ice and visibility is terrible for both teams and referees.

Man, we dislike the Belleville Bulls. Even my billet-mom, Ellen, engages with a rival Belleville fan today, as she tells me after the bitter contest. "Steve, one of the Belleville fans sitting near me was giving you guys a hard time tonight," she quips. He shouted, "Look at the Kingston Comedians!" "So I shouted back at him, Steve, I yelled, that's a lot of Bull!" I burst out laughing; she is witty! Even friendly Mrs. Stone gets excited when Belleville comes to town.

The exhibition games go by, one by one, and I continue to rehab my ankle as the regular season is starting shortly. I'm growing more impatient each passing day. I want to get back skating so I can play our first game. I attempt to skate at practice but my ankle is aching and just doesn't feel right; pushing off leads to sharp pain.

Hockey is not the only thing on my mind; I have to go to school. I'm entering grade 12 at LaSalle located in Kingston Township. I'd be lying if I said I wasn't excited to start. The reason you ask? I spent grades 9 through 11 at St. Jerome's in Kitchener, and it's an all-boys Catholic high school. The thought of attending school with girls, is intriguing to say the least and is a much anticipated change. There is a buzz in my new school and among the students, mostly girls is talk about three Kingston Canadians who will be attending this fall.

I make new buddies and at lunch we play volleyball. I love all sports and I'm very competitive – hockey, lacrosse, basketball, base-ball, volleyball, whatever. I want to win each time I'm competing – checkers, cards, road hockey, you name it. During this particular lunchtime volleyball get together, a strong serve comes sailing over the net directly at me. I plant my foot with the bad ankle onto the floor and put all my weight on it as I prepare to hammer the ball back over the net. Eee-ahh! Piercing pain shoots through my lower leg. The pain is excruciating, and I want to jump through the high ceiling. 'What the hell is going on?'

Saturday morning, the team has a rare early season day off. I've made plans to attend a Queen's University football game with a buddy, Gerard. He was on my summer hockey team back home and is attending the prestigious university. I make arrangements with him to be picked up for the match that will be played at Richardson Stadium later this afternoon.

Before the game, I decide to visit the emergency department at Kingston General Hospital just to be sure my ankle is okay, or at least improving. Mr. and Mrs. Stone drop me off and I go through the normal routine, check in, waiting room, X-rays. 'Better to be safe than sorry,' I figure.

It doesn't take too long before a nurse appears. "Steve," she says. "Yes," I reply. She's staring at me with a puzzled look on her face, eyeing me, up and down. She curiously observes my legs. "How did you get here?" she asks. "I walked in," I reply. Beside her is a wheelchair. "Sit in this chair please," she says abruptly. But, why? I think to myself as I take a seat.

A doctor appears from around the corner and he introduces himself. "Steve, you have a hairline fracture in your ankle," he says. 'What? That can't be right. I've been walking and skating on and off for three weeks.' I tell myself. "I'm going to have to cast your leg from the knee down," he says. This is not the news I was expecting! My brain is having trouble making sense of what is being said. I'm in disbelief, and confused as my fluttering heart sinks into my stomach.

With a fresh cast applied, just below the knee and engulfing my foot, I hobble to the exit and leave the hospital on my new crutches. Maybe I should go home to my billets' place? Ah, I'm just going to the game with Gerard! Screw it! I can't play hockey for weeks anyway so I might as well go to the football game. I call Gerard and ask him to pick me up. I walked into the hospital under my own power and now I'm leaving on crutches with a cast on my leg because I have a broken ankle. "Bullshit!"

Gerard arrives to pick up the new hamstrung version of me. We watch the Gael's game in front of a packed house. Being around screaming and yelling university students, armed with leather flasks and willing to share for a few hours, helps with the bitter feelings I have buried inside. 'What do I tell Coach O'Donnell?' 'What will I tell my parents?' 'When will I get to play for the Canadians?' 'Man, this sucks!'

Canadians vs Rangers

Our mission this season is to qualify for the playoffs and challenge for a championship. While sitting on the sidelines waiting for my broken ankle to heal, the regular season starts for the Kingston Canadians with a game versus the rival Belleville Bulls. The curtain-raising tilt disappoints an enthusiastic crowd of 2,202 and we lose by a nail-biting 5-4 count in our home opener. Watching from the stands is not the way I envisioned my junior career starting but with a cast on my leg and crutches securely in hand, there's no choice.

The team is off to a slow start, losing four games in-a-row out of the gate. Despite the losses, we know we're legit playoff contenders. After a lackluster start, there are smiling faces in the dressing room as we finally get in the win column in the fifth game of the campaign, thumping the Toronto Marlboros 7-2. It's a relief for Coach O'Donnell and marks his first win as an OHL bench boss. Postgame he tells the Whig-Standard, "It was a good win to get under our belts."

We're off to the races, and my daily schedule revolves around school and our two-hour practice from 4 to 6 p.m. at the Memorial Centre. School schedules allow for time at the end of the day to attend practice; hockey is now a full-time commitment. This new path in my journey shapes new routines. Off-days are rare and the team is on the ice each day. However, I will have to wait until I'm healthy enough to skate. Once back on skates, I become a creature of rigid habit. School, practice, eating, homework, sleep and repeat. Again, say it with me this time, school, practice, eating, homework, sleep and repeat. Deviation from this stringent schedule causes me to feel anxious and uneasy.

I want to be a well-rounded hockey player. Maintaining grades and attending class is important in my mind, and I have made it a personal goal to excel on and off the ice. Having said that, hockey will come first. If out-of-town games or road trips require time away from school then so be it, it will be done. No notes from parents or team personnel are required. With a short chat with the attendance folks – a game today, a road trip tomorrow, or an unscheduled event next week – is all I have to say to the polite ladies in the office and I'm given the school's permission to be absent.

Scott and I pick up a ride with Brian in his truck for practice daily. There is no need to call shotgun in my current condition. Scotty gives me the front passenger seat because I'm still sporting a cast and crutches and he takes the cramped bench seat in back. Thanks buddy! Veterans with cars typically drive the rookies to games, practices, and team events. To help cover gasoline costs, we pay Brian $5 of our weekly $30 cash allowance from the organization.

Brian, younger brother of New Jersey Devil winger Pat Verbeek, was raised on a busy farm in the rural, southwestern Ontario town of Wyoming. Daily drives to practice include playing the only cassette tape in the truck, meaning we listen to *Foreigner's Greatest Hits* most days. By the end of September, I know every song and hear the tracks when I lay in bed at night.

The team doctor says my ankle has healed enough that the cast will be removed. Having not played for six weeks means I need time to get back into game shape. With the cast off, I start practicing and training with the team. Oh, it feels good to be on the ice again! I'm ready to say good-bye to October and hello to November, because I'm more and more anxious to get into the lineup.

The first game for us this month is at home against the Soo, and the boys storm out of the gate with a first-period blitz, and take a commanding 5-0 lead. The Canadians pummel the visiting Sault Ste. Marie Greyhounds 11–2 in front of a crowd of just over 2,000 fans. Brian, with his deadly release, scores four goals tonight and now leads the league in that precious department. The win contributes to the squad being undefeated in the last eight games; something the team has only done once before in their 13-year history.

The unit weathered a potential early season storm and now have the fans taking notice, as the seats in the Memorial Centre are selling. The fans are hungry for a winning club and flock to games. There is a buzz in town for this hockey team. An article in the Whig-Standard says it all, "Happy days are here again – Canadians are winning, the seats are filled and Gretzky's kid brother is in town tonight." Gretzky's kid brother is Keith Gretzky who is playing for the visiting Windsor Spitfires. Yes, happy days are here again for the improved team, but I don't feel like they are for me. I'm struggling to fit in after being sidelined for multiple weeks. The team is on a roll, there is enthusiasm for us and I desperately want to feel closer to the on-ice success.

The good news: I'm off the injured list and on the active list. The bad news: it is very difficult to break into a lineup when a team is playing well, especially for an unproven rookie. I am happy though to be skating and practicing again; this is a step in the right direction. I'll have to be patient, and wait for an opportunity. In practice, I skate as the extra forward. The extra forward is clear to the team by the odd-coloured jersey they're required to wear. I work hard and sub in on line and team drills and I know I have work to do.

Examining the upcoming schedule, I circle a date on the calendar. Sunday, November 17th at 2 p.m., the team will visit the Kitchener Rangers at The Aud. Remember, I grew up watching the Rangers play, and vividly recall paying a couple bucks to sit on a yellow general-admission bench as a grade schooler. I recall the thrill of watching Brian Bellows, Scott Stevens, and Al MacInnis lead the Rangers to a title in 1982. In '84 I paid a whopping $15 to watch the Memorial Cup final between the Rangers and the Ottawa 67's. Ottawa won 7-2. That tournament also featured a future superstar from the Laval Voisins named Mario Lemieux. Incidentally, that season Mario Lemieux's regular-season statistics with Laval were 70 games played, 133 goals, 149 assists and 282 points. Yes, it's true!

Kitchener, of course, is also my hometown, which means family, and friends will be out to watch, hoping that I will be in the lineup. However, teams in the OHL only dress twenty players, even though they carry more on their roster to account for injuries, suspensions and other unforeseen issues. Those not dressed for a particular game are referred to as a healthy scratch. Those are words hockey players hate to hear, because they mean you are able to compete (play) but it is the coach's decision to have you sit out and watch from the press box. It's not fun for competitive athletes to endure!

Saturday's practice arrives and Coach O'Donnell informs me that I will be playing tomorrow and will be skating on the fourth line. Eagerly, I find a phone and call home to tell my parents. I can't wait for Sunday to arrive.

It will be down and back for the single road game. The city is just close enough that we do not need to stay in a hotel. Arriving at The Aud, the boys carry hockey bags on their shoulders through the belly of the barn on East Avenue. The dressing rooms are as I remember. Bags are dropped to the floor in the large visitor's space. I know these rooms from my minor-hockey days. The wooden chairs in the dressing rooms haven't changed much. It's spacious and houses tables in the centre with cups for drinks, tape and other game time necessities. Stripping my dress clothes off quickly, I change into my Bauer blues, stretch, tape the blades on my two red Titan twigs and check out the empty arena.

Time to get dressed in my gear. Minutes tick by slowly as I nervously wait for warm-up to arrive. Trying to be patient, waiting for this hockey game to start is challenging. "How much time?" a voice shouts out. "Three minutes," says another. It's almost here! In moments, our goalies will lead us out of the room, and down the tunnel to the ice surface. I'm ready!

"It's time," a voice calls out. This is it, let's go! Walking along the sturdy rubber mat, I follow the boys out and onto the ice through the penalty-box door. My skates are like miniature rockets as they propel me around the rink. Feeling like I'm eight-feet tall, peering up behind our bench, I can see my cheering section of family and friends. They're waving signs and shouting. What a feeling for me!

Game on! A scoring opportunity on my first shift catches me by surprise and stays out of the Kitchener net. The speed of the game is fast, and my opponents are physically strong. A third period fight between rugged-winger Scott Metcalfe and the Ranger's Paul Penelton gets the home fans out of their seats for a moment. We lose 8-3 but I'm not concerned. Today I'm just relieved to be playing real, meaningful hockey games again. My first game is under my belt, and it feels like a new beginning.

Changing in the room post-game, Tim Gordanier from the Whig-Standard approaches. Promptly, the Kingston reporter asks me about the missed scoring opportunity on my first shift. Surprised by his question, I search for the right words. "Ah, I thought I'd be just going up and down my wing," I reply to the friendly sports writer as he jots down my uninspiring answer.

Out in the concourse, meeting family and friends, I sport the traditional post-game look, wet hair, red cheeks, accompanied by a suit and tie. Soon the staff calls out, "Let's go boys! Bus is moving out." With that, the herd of players, parents, agents and friends meander towards the bus and say final good-byes. There will be many more opportunities for these short encounters down the road.

A dose of reality strikes upon returning to Kingston as for the next two weeks I'm a healthy scratch. I'm sitting and not playing.

Maybe Coach O'Donnell gave me the hometown benefit for the meeting with Kitchener.

Back into the lineup at home versus the Hamilton Steelhawks, I see minimal ice time, and end up being a placeholder or a grocery stick between the defenceman and the forwards. It's like this: defencemen are at one end of the bench and forwards are at the other end. When line changes occur, forwards slide to the middle. If your name is not called, you end up stuck between the changing defencemen and forwards. Voilà! I spend most of my night here, watching the game, and looking at the scoreboard above centre ice. The game ends, with a 3–2 overtime loss to the Steelhawks after Shayne Corson sets up John Purves for the game-winning goal.

Frustrated and pissed off, I shower and storm out of the rink thinking, why isn't Coach O'Donnell playing me more? Invasive thoughts accelerate my anger, and I make a decision to walk home. Marching briskly on Queen St. and closer to the downtown waterfront it's bloody cold. I've cooled off mentally and physically. Freezing, shivering, from the frigid winds off Lake Ontario, I determine a cab to take me the rest of the way home is a good idea.

The halfway point of the season is approaching quickly. At practice, I ask Coach O'Donnell what I need to do to earn more ice time. Coach says I have to improve my conditioning. I take his advice. At lunch, I jog up Highway 15 to improve my lung capacity. I see this as the extra effort needed to earn valuable ice time. Succeeding in sport is about commitment and dedication, asking myself how much I want it.

Sometimes you just need to wait for your chance, but what if you find yourself waiting behind a player like Cal Ripken? Cal Ripken set a major-league baseball record by playing 2,632 games in a row. You never know how long or short your wait will be, so you have to be prepared and ready.

Shadowboxing

Christmas of 1985 flies by and, as I ring in the New Year, my opportunity to get in the lineup presents itself. Scotty and Bryan Fogarty are attending the U-17 Program of Excellence Hockey Tournament representing Ontario. Scotty is a left-winger, like me. There is an opening and here's my chance...

January 2nd, 1986, the Canadians hit the road and drive two-hours to play in Cornwall against the hometown Royals. The city sits twenty-five minutes from the Québec border. The bus prepares to exit Highway 401 and the boys start to dress in the single aisle of the moving coach. On road trips like these, we wear tracksuits for comfort and one by one change awkwardly into our suits and ties to the rhythm of the swaying bus. Pulling into town, passing the massive paper mill, we arrive at the rink situated on the rugged banks of the St. Lawrence River. I'm pencilled in tonight on one of the top three lines. I need to make the most of this opportunity. It's go time!

Game on! Royals' sniper Ray Sheppard scores a pair of goals and the first period ends tied 2-2. Scoring three unanswered goals, we exit the second period with a 5-2 lead. Early in the third, towering, six-foot-six, 200-pound, right-winger, Daril Holmes scores his 20th goal of the season to expand our advantage. Now comfortably leading 6-2 at the six-minute mark of the third period, I crash the net, bang away at a rebound, and score my first OHL goal. It isn't pretty – given that I direct the puck in before getting knocked to my knees in the goal crease – but that doesn't matter. Elated, I reach out and grab the puck sitting behind the goal line with my hand. After celebrating with my linemates, I skate to the bench and toss the puck to Peter.

My heart is pounding. I can feel the adrenaline rocketing through my veins. Feeling like I'm on top of the world, I decide this is the night for my first fight! Fighting has always been a part of hockey. Strangely for me though, I've never been in a fight during a hockey game. Sure, I punched a few caged masks in midget with my glove on, but that's not fighting.

Let's backtrack for a moment. Fighting is rare in minor hockey. Players wear full cages and fighting will get you ejected from the game and suspended. It's not something I've ever done on the ice. I will always go into the corner first, will battle for every puck, take a hit to make a play, and do all the little things my coaches deem as tough, but I've never been involved in a toe-to-toe fight on skates.

Early in the summer of 1985, my Greenshirt teammates and I get together on a sunny afternoon at a friend's house for a teenage, hockey version of fight club. In anticipation of the expected fighting in junior hockey, the boys and I decide to participate in an activity known as buckets. We put on our hockey helmets and gloves, two combatants face each other, the group says go, and then the two in the middle fight, swinging away with their foam-filled gloves. The round ends when one contender quits or says, "Uncle". We partake in this experimental 'boys will be boys' activity on the front lawn.

I square off with my good buddy, rangy Steve Herniman and decide to go on the offensive and be the aggressor. When I do, I'm able to land a couple of hard punches to his head, and I end up with the upper hand in this bout. My next go is with tough, stocky Rob Warren. The eager onlookers say go and he delivers a huge smash to my caged face. I step back, dazed and seeing stars. An ache explodes in my skull, and I feel disoriented. I drop my hands, and say, "I'm out." That's the last time I ever played buckets.

During the pre-season, I watched numerous altercations that included fighting and brawling. The other rookies on the club had the exhibition games to sort out their fighting skills. I consider myself a team player and if it means fighting, then so be it. Preparing myself to play hockey games, I think often about what my first fight will be like.

To prepare for this fight that I imagine will come soon, I shadow-box when my billets are away. What is shadowboxing you ask? Shadowboxing is an exercise used in training for boxing, or in my case, fighting with skates on. For me, it is done by myself when nobody is watching. I just start throwing punches at nothing, essentially into thin air. This is how I prepare for my first fight. I walk up and down the front foyer of Mr. and Mrs. Stone's home and throw punches as fast as I can. I'd watched many hockey fights and picked up certain techniques from teammates who are good at it in our dressing room. I observe how my teammates approach a fight, but actually being in one creates a whole new set of challenges.

Tonight, in Cornwall, I will test my fighting skills. With my first goal under my belt, this will be the night I initiate my first fight. I just want it out of the way. The crazy thing is, I want it out of the way almost as much as I want my first goal out of the way.

With only a few minutes left in the third period, there is a scrum on the side boards as players on both teams battle for a loose puck. Mark Evans, a Royals' defenceman, skates in late with a hit. I give him a two-handed shove, he looks at me, and I drop my gloves. He does the same, and I start throwing lefts as fast as I can, having no idea what I'm hitting. The other players pair off, and the fight ends quickly as the linesmen intervene before any damage is done. Evans and I are sent to our dressing rooms by the referee as we each receive five-minute majors for fighting and there are less than five-minutes left in the lopsided game.

Back in the empty dressing room, I take off my wet equipment and walk to the shower. I'm pumped, and begin to shadowbox as I step under the showerhead. A goal and a fight! Continuing to punch at air, I soak my sweaty hair. The howling boys return to the room after the final buzzer sounds and I receive pats on the back and lots of, "Good job Sef." The Canadians double up the Royals 8-4 on this winter night, and I contributed with a goal and a fight. I officially feel like I'm part of this hockey club.

Rolling on through January and February, I score, add points, and fight more, including a toe-to-toe scrap at home against Ottawa with visiting Mom and Elv in the crowd. Another first, fighting in front of Mom and her friend! I'm feeling good about my play and gaining Coach O'Donnell's trust on the ice. Growing physically and mentally, I'm ready to play a greater role on this team.

Saturday night is Hockey Night in Canada, and on a cold, February Saturday evening, the Canadians arrive in Belleville for another head-to-head war on ice with our arch rivals. The rough-and-tumble Bulls are coached by Larry Mavety. The former pro player has led Belleville since they entered the league as an expansion team in 1981. The arena in the city has an even larger ice surface than the Memorial Centre, a 200-by-100-foot, Olympic size sheet of ice.

The battle for playoff positioning in the standings is heating up. We've played the Bulls several times this season and we really hate each other; making for an intense rivalry. The two, tough squads squared off in an ugly pre-game brawl earlier this season. The showdowns with the Bulls are played with grit and sandpaper, each inch of ice contested, and I expect this matchup will be no different.

Game on! Tonight has a playoff-type atmosphere. Goals by our physical right-winger Herb Raglan and Belleville's high-scoring

Stan Drulia has us knotted 1-1 after one period. Tempers flare for the two physically imposing teams early in the second when our captain, Jeff Chychrun, squares off, and fights Belleville's tough rookie Bryan Marchment. Mush, as they call him, is fearless and willing to fight anyone, even our rugged, six-foot-four, 200-pound, hard punching leader. Chych's fight changes the tempo of tonight's struggle, and gives me an extra boost of energy.

After a stoppage of play, there's a faceoff in front of our bench. I line up on my left-wing position beside Bulls' tough-guy Todd Hawkins. Hawk, as they call him, had famous run-ins with our own enforcer Marc Laforge, and I heard many stories about Forge's dustups with him.

This game is emotionally charged and I feel the energy. I am skate-to-skate, shoulder-to-shoulder with the lefty Hawkins when the puck drops. Crossing his path, he delivers a slash to my hand. The slash doesn't hurt but I want to stand up for myself. I blankly stare at him as we skate by the Belleville bench. I drop my gloves, and after giving me a menacing look, he does the same. Drifting into the corner face-to-face, I grab his jersey, and swing wildly. My first punch glances off his visor and I get ready to throw again. He grabs my collar and delivers one big punch – a left-handed bomb to the mouth; a literal punch in the mouth. My mouth! My legs go limp and I melt into the ice, dropping like a heavy sack. I am out! Unconscious! My eyes open, and I hear the muffled sounds of a roaring crowd. I feel the cool ice surface on my face. Where am I?

Hockey etiquette says if you get knocked out in a fight, get to the penalty box under your own power if you're able. I have to skate to the box, if for no other reason than to show everyone in this shitty, frickin' Belleville rink that I can take that punch. I get up slowly, gingerly skate over to the penalty box, and sit down. After being knocked senseless, it's good to know I'll be in here for five minutes because I'm in pain. I hear the public-address announcer call out the major penalties as action on the ice resumes.

My focus now shifts to my tingling mouth. I pull out my custom-made mouth guard and find it is full of blood. Unsure of what to do, I turn it upside down, dump the red saliva-filled blood onto the floor, and put it back in carefully, because my face is throbbing. The rabid Belleville fans behind me bang on the glass between us. I'm not coherent enough to deal with them right now; another time. Bloodied and woozy, I sit back and close my eyes. The home crowd is lit, loving the intense battle on the ice. Play continues. I serve my five-minute penalty and at the next whistle, skate back onto the ice. There are bitter feelings between the clubs and the crowd is rambunctious, just like it is when Belleville comes down the 401 to Kingston.

The next few shifts I skate with reckless abandon, crashing and banging, perhaps from the adrenaline or perhaps because I don't know where I am. The clock grinds down to zero to end the frenetic period of hockey. The jacked-up troopers return to the locker room and are buzzing. In all there are twelve fighting majors assessed. Tangling with a fighter like Hawkins gives me instant credibility in the room. Forge comes over to my stall, gives me a tap and says, "Go him again Sef!" Assistant coach Shawn Babcock, drafted by the Edmonton Oilers and a tough player in his day, enters the room, walks straight over, and gives me a pat on the leg along with an affirming nod of the head. It feels good to have the boys acknowledging the fight and supporting me. After examination, it is decided that I will not return for the third period. I'm not alert and have glassy eyes. I'm likely concussed.

The two teams finish another pugilistic fight-them-in-the-alley battle in their Leyden Division ice war. The eastern adversaries combine for a total of 180-minutes in penalties tonight. The Canadians lose a tight tilt 4-3 in front of 3,258 entertained fans and we drive back to the Limestone City after another classic Kingston–Belleville show.

The team arranges for me to see the dentist. His examination reveals that I need root canal therapy. I'm not sure what that is, but the good news is I will not lose my teeth. The bad news is I must spend two days in a dentist chair. My shadowboxing didn't prepare me for this. When I shadowbox, I never get hit.

Fighting has been part of the hockey experience for decades. Many fans enjoy watching a good fight. Fans are unlikely to run to the concession stand or go to the bathroom during a fight. In fact, almost all fans will stand up to get a better look. Of course, emotions run high in hockey and fighting can change the momentum in a game, and inspire teammates. It's playoff time!

The Canadians finish fourth-place in the Leyden Division with a respectable 35-28-3 record for 73 points; only three points out of second. After a three-year playoff absence, the local hockey fans are alive again. There is little playoff experience in our dressing room but we're confident and believe.

A first-round series with the Oshawa Generals is on deck. We lose Game One in Oshawa by a score of 6-4. Game Two in Kingston is the turning point in this series. We have a comfortable 4-0 lead as time expires on the clock at the end of the second period. The buzzer sounds, tempers on the ice boil over, and all hell breaks loose resulting in a line brawl. Wearing the series' emotions on their sleeves, all ten skaters square off in five separate toe-to-toe fights; five of our toughest guys and five of theirs. Chychrun, Laforge, Metcalfe, Verbeek, and Herbie Raglan, who hits opposing players like a Mack truck are involved.

The linesmen break up one fight at a time until only sticks and gloves remain on the Memorial Centre ice. The fans rise out of their seats, clapping, whistling, and shouting victory for their boys in these heavyweight bouts. The scraps energize the team, the fans, and the arena. Simply put, fighting elevates the emotion in the building and evokes a spirit on the bench out of thin air. The game ends with a decisive 6-0 victory, and the Canadians go on to defeat the Generals 4-2 in the best-of-seven series.

After the emotional victory versus Oshawa, round two is a peculiar round-robin playoff series set up by the league that sees Kingston, Peterborough and Belleville play a series of four games each; two home and two away. The top two teams after the round-robin will advance to the Leyden Division final series.

Stunning the Bulls 7-1 in Game One to a jammed Memorial Centre crowd of 3,608 boisterous fans starts us off. The show goes on the road for Game Two, and we lose a hard fought 3-1 battle to the talented Petes, setting up a pivotal Game Three in Belleville against the hated Bulls.

Game on! Trailing 3-1 after two periods, the never-say-die Canadians storm back with three unanswered goals in the third, two by Rags and one from Chych, to take a 4-3 lead. Reclaiming precious momentum, and sucking the life out of the arena, we're leading. Shortly thereafter, an innocent bounce off the boards in our zone ends up in the back of our net after a shot by Bulls' point-producing Stan Drulia, with a mere seven seconds remaining in regulation time. Tie game!

Sudden-death overtime begins and next goal wins. At 8:45 of the extra frame a hard, accurate wrist shot from the blue line beats our goaltender Chris Clifford. Feeling like our hearts have been ripped out, the devastating 5-4 overtime loss sinks in. Walking back to the dressing room, Kingston's teenage hockey soldiers battled hard for their city and each other. This one hurts! However, there is one more chance against the Petes. Time to regroup.

Trailing in Peterborough 3-1 in the third period, we rally to tie the game. In the end Marc Teevens scores at the 3:38 mark of over-time. The margin of victory in this strange, three team round-robin series is razor-thin. Peterborough and Belleville finish with four points each and Kingston with two, meaning the Bulls and Petes advance to play a best-of-seven Leyden Division final.

You may wonder what it means when players say, "I love these guys." I can tell you because I love these guys. What does it mean? I love coming to the rink. I love the comradery in the room, and I'll do anything for the boys. Sometimes the chemistry is just right, and the ups and downs of a long hockey season bring a team closer together. This all contributes to the inevitable heartbreaking disap-pointment when the hockey season ends, and especially, a season that ended too soon.

Draft Dreams

My rookie year is in the books and I decide to stay in town to finish school. Most of my teammates return home but that doesn't work for me because St. Jerome's back home uses a different school system which includes three terms of study. LaSalle is two semesters, so it makes sense to stay here with Mr. and Mrs. Stone. Besides, I've met a lot of new friends and feel comfortable staying. I'm not alone; local boys Chris Clifford, Teddy Linseman and Jeff Cornelius are still around.

I start to do things other teens do. I skip school on occasion to go down to the Lake Ontario waterfront and drive to the Picton Sandbanks on weekends to hit the beach. The weather is starting to get warmer, the ice on the lake is long gone, and Kingston is a great summer city.

I'm spending a lot of time with a girl named Lisa who I have classes with at LaSalle. One of the first times I knew I wanted to keep hanging around with her was after a game in March. Post-game, I had asked happy-go-lucky, Teddy Linseman, to drive me to her house. Teddy's a real character who keeps us in stitches in the dressing room. His legendary car can always be counted on for a ride across town. It's late but when you play hockey the night starts when the game ends. Keeping that in mind, Coach O'Donnell has set a curfew for us. On certain nights he checks, calling each players' billet home and the boys must be there to answer and speak to him directly.

Teddy drops me off on Lisa's quiet crescent and I walk up the sloping driveway. I'm not sure how I will get home but I'll worry about that later. My 10:30 p.m. visit is unannounced. I knock on the front door and it opens slowly. Looking into her eyes, I smile. With my wet hockey hair, dressed in my suit, and crooked tie I am sure I was quite the picture. She looks puzzled to see me at this late hour but thankfully invites me in.

Her parents are home and we sit in the living room watching T.V. After hockey games finish, I'm starving and want to eat. Post-game foraging or purchasing food is a high priority. Having said that, I mention to her that I may be hungry. She says, "Okay," and disappears into the kitchen. What now I wonder, peanut butter and jam, crackers and cheese, Kraft dinner? My stomach growls at the thoughts of food. I'll eat almost anything at this point. In a few minutes she reappears with the biggest ham and cheese sandwich I've ever seen, complete with all the awesome trimmings put on a large sandwich. Holy smokes! Look at that creation. I devour it quickly and think, 'I like this girl'!

It's May and my 18th birthday arrives. With school almost over, my focus becomes the NHL draft. The draft is scheduled for June 21st at the famous Montréal Forum. Hearing my name called on draft day would be a dream come true.

The hype is building momentum in the lead-up to the big day. I receive a letter from the New Jersey Devils that includes a questionnaire for me to fill out and return. Sam McMaster, director of scouting for the Washington Capitals, arrives in town and takes me out for dinner. The former GM of the Soo Greyhounds wants to get to know me as a person. The conversation is engaging and I can't help but feel like sticking out my chest just a little as we discuss hockey over dinner. Dining with an NHL scout; I like this.

Next up is a visit from David McNab, a scout for the Hartford Whalers. The former Wisconsin Badger has been employed as an NHL scout since 1978. He asks if I can suggest a place for our meeting. I sure can. We eat dinner at Gencarelli's, my favourite Italian restaurant in town. We talk hockey and life, and I find that he's an insightful man. The conversation is laid-back, as we discuss hockey, inspiration, goals, and dreams. I feel years removed from the OHL draft but in fact, it is less than one-year ago and here I am talking to NHL scouts.

I ask Lisa to the school formal (aka prom night) and she agrees. I rent a tuxedo for the night. I've never worn a fancy tux so Mrs. Stone adjusts my tie and takes photos before I leave. She has a wide smile on her face like a proud mother or proud billet-mother. She never had a son, having three daughters, and she visibly enjoys helping me get my affairs in order for this formal occasion. I'm equally happy she is here to help.

I arrive at Lisa's house and wait patiently for her to appear. She emerges from around the corner in the most dazzling, shoulder-less black dress I've ever seen. She looks amazing! Pictures are snapped by her parents and off we go to the waterfront. The formal includes dinner, a cruise through the Thousand Islands, and the dance. It is an awesome night and only confirms that my decision to stay for school is the right one.

I drive home to pack for the NHL draft. Rick Curran arranges travel for all of his clients to Montréal. Along with my parents, I board the train in Toronto as instructed by Rick. As we pull out of Union Station, I can't help but think about the historical Original- Six trips the Maple Leafs took from Toronto to Montréal for old-time hockey games against the Canadiens. Montréal here I come!

Arriving at Central Station, we take a cab to the hotel, which Rick has ready. His stable of clients are staying together downtown at the Sheraton Centre. Entering the lobby of the busy hotel, I receive an updated itinerary, and tickets to the draft. This weekend, Rick has a rooming list for his boys. I'm sharing a room with my Canadians' teammate, Marc Laforge. The hotel is buzzing with pre-draft chatter and excitement. It's going to be tough to sleep tonight. Time to set my wake-up call. I'll see you tomorrow on draft day!

Ghosts of the Montréal Forum

The day is here – June 21st – the 1986 NHL Entry Draft. It starts in a few hours. My eyes are open early this morning. I didn't sleep much, as expected. Forge and I are up and start getting ready. My mom helped me purchase a new suit for this special day; gotta look good. My friends, the Garibaldi family, purchased me a slim red-leather tie to complete my slick look. I shower and put on my new duds. This is my future, and my dream. I'm nervous and edgy as I descend in the elevator to the lobby. This is yet another step on this hockey odyssey. I think about all of the hard work: travel, games, tournaments, practices, workouts, bumps, bruises and on and on.

It's sunny and warming as I join my parents outside the bustling hotel. A collection of 18 and 19-year-old hockey players, nervous parents, busy agents, serious GMs, coaches, and scouts pass by on the streets. We walk slowly down to the Forum absorbing the sights and sounds. The draft venue is arguably the most famous arena in hockey. The Forum, or Le Forum de Montréal, is located near the city's downtown district. Home of the Montréal Maroons from 1924-to-1938 and the Montréal Canadiens from 1926-to-1996, this icon is home to 24 Stanley Cup victories; 22 by the Canadiens and 2 by the Maroons.

I remember as a boy watching the New Year's Eve classic between the Canadiens and the touring Soviet Red Army team. A 3-3 tie game played in front of an electric crowd involved NHL stars named Dryden, Robinson, Savard, Gainey and Soviet stars named Tretiak, Kharlamov and Petrov. Hockey pundits and fans still say it was one of the greatest hockey games ever played.

Legend has it that ghosts of hockey players past roam the halls of the decades old Montréal Forum. Legend or folklore, I'm about to find out. Standing outside the historic building, I look up and gaze at the façade. I can't help but think about stories of mythical hockey players like Maurice "Rocket" Richard, "the Stratford Streak"- Howie Morenz, Jean Béliveau, Guy Lafleur, and "the Pocket Rocket" – Henri Richard, not to mention Doug Harvey, Bernie "Boom Boom" Geoffrion, Jacques Plante, and others. Legends of hockey I admire and respect played here.

What a feeling walking into the building for the first time. It even smells like hockey! For a moment, I feel the ghosts of the Forum circle around me and fill my spirit. The home of the Canadiens is ripe with hockey history – photos, retired numbers, and Stanley Cup banners. This old rink has character, and a real pulse.

Looking at the draft floor, my impression is that this is the OHL draft on steroids. The space is filled with NHL general managers, coaches, scouts, national, and local media, and long tables representing the 21 league franchises. We find our reserved seats in the stands which are located alongside Rick's other clients, family members, and a deep pool of talented hockey players. The gathering crowd is quiet, and tension fills the air. Of course it does, this is the NHL draft. This moment in time feels like the pinnacle; the biggest stage of my life!

Player agents are able to establish what NHL managers and scouts are thinking about individual prospects. Rick has spoken to me about today and I have complete trust in him. An article in the Whig-Standard, written by Tim Gordanier, supports his thoughts. It read: "Rated in the seventh-round by NHL Central Scouting Bureau, but almost certain to be an earlier selection is Canadians left-winger Steve Seftel. The 18-year-old Kitchener native suffered a hairline ankle fracture on the second day of training camp and missed the first twenty games of the regular season as a result, but once he returned to the lineup and began seeing regular duties he excelled. "I think enough guys saw him at the end of the season to know what he can do," a scout said. "He just kept getting better as he got back into action after the injury. He is also a lot bigger right now than he was even when he was playing. Central has him rated in the seventh-round but he's going to go a lot higher than that."

My gaze takes me to the large stage that contains the podium where the all-important selections will be made. It is here, where players will walk up the stairs, onto the main platform, and pull an NHL team's jersey over their head for the first time.

One of the most impressive features is the large draft board. It stretches the length of the stage and has the logos of all 21 teams, along with round-by-round spaces where placards with selected player names will be inserted. I see nervous faces that reflect what I'm feeling. Players and parents sit quietly with their hands in their laps, some playing it cool, and some looking confident.

The first-overall pick belongs to the Detroit Red Wings. The Wings finished last season in last place with a record of 17-56-6 for a total of 40 points in 80 games.

The NHL president is John Ziegler. Opening the day with kind words for the hosts from Montréal, he invites the Detroit Red Wings up to the podium to make the first pick. Speaking into the mic, the Red Wings select blue-chipper Joe Murphy from Michigan State University. After the applause and handshakes, the second pick belongs to the Los Angeles Kings who select American-born scorer Jimmy Carson from the Verdun Junior Canadiens. The third pick by the New Jersey Devils is centre Neil Brady from the Medicine Hat Tigers.

I continue to watch the first-round proceedings from my seat in the stands. With the ninth pick, the New York Rangers select skilled defenceman Brian Leetch from Avon Old Farms High School in Connecticut. At the conclusion of the round only two players from the OHL are selected. Ken McRae, a centre from the Sudbury Wolves is picked 18th by the Québec Nordiques and Kerry Huffman, a smooth-skating defenceman from the OHL Champion Guelph Platers is selected 20th by the Philadelphia Flyers. The draft is unfolding and twenty-one names have been called. Round #1, with all of the cameras, interviews and photo ops, seems to take forever.

Moving on to Round #2, the first player off the board is last season's top-rated OHL prospect Adam Graves. The sure-fire NHLer will move to the Detroit Red Wings from the Windsor Spitfires. With the 32nd pick, my weekend roommate, defenceman Marc Laforge is selected by the Hartford Whalers. I'm happy for Forge as I watch him descend down onto the draft floor. The Kingston Canadians are off and running!

The second-round continues. The 39th overall pick belongs to the Québec Nordiques and they select right-winger Jean-Marc Routhier from the Hull Olympiques. The 40th overall pick is next. The Washington Capitals are summoned to the podium to make their selection. There is a pause and then the Capitals request a timeout. Yes, teams are permitted timeouts at the draft to collect their thoughts, or possibly complete a trade. The Capitals are prompted a second time by Mr. Ziegler to make their selection. Again, they pause and call a timeout. I feel like the temperature in the Forum is rising. Real or perceived, it's hard to tell. My mom says she's going to the concourse to buy a drink. Okay, I guess she's getting warm too. Perhaps it is getting hotter in here.

The Capitals are again called to the podium. My mind starts to wander due to the delay, as the Capitals representative steps up to the microphone. A voice calls out, "The Washington Capitals select from the Kingston Canadians…" 'Stop tape; this is me again.' In my mind I quickly do the mental math, okay, Forge is already picked and I figure this has to be me. Even though some of my teammates are present and still waiting to hear their names called, I think this is me. Start tape. "Left-winger, Steve Seftel." 'Oh my God, it is me!'

My dad reaches out to embrace me, and we're both busting at the seams. I rise, shuffle across our row, and walk down the stairs. Rick intercepts me and shakes my hand. Before reaching the draft floor, I see my mom rushing back from the concourse. She heard the call over the public-address system. She gives me a big hug. I turn, enter the floor, walk through the bodies, and make my way up to the podium where I shake hands with the Capitals' brass, and graciously accept that beautiful jersey they're placing in my hands. I carefully pull the jersey over my head and a giant smile grows on my face that will stay for quite some time. Standing on the stage, I look out and survey the entire arena. It is surreal. Dreams do come true!

I'm quickly whisked away by NHL public-relations staffers for photographs in front of the NHL shield both individually, and with my parents. I'm floating on cloud nine. Suddenly, the media appears. Some I know from Kingston – reporters from the Whig-Standard and local radio station CKWS, but other people asking me questions I've never seen before. I answer confidently, trying to contain my bursting insides and to act professional. It is a whirlwind and I'm spinning in it. It's as if time stands still, but beyond this chaos, names are still being called and the procession to the podium continues.

Taken to the Capitals' draft table, I shake hands with head coach Bryan Murray, assistant coaches Terry Murray and Ron Lapointe, general manager David Poile, and director of player personnel and recruitment, Jack Button. Jack is the former GM of the Pittsburgh Penguins. Before joining the Capitals' organization, he was the founder and director of the NHL's Central Scouting Bureau. Jack will become the man I lean on in the months following the draft. I will ask him question after question about hockey, and he always takes time to answer.

Today at the draft, after a firm handshake, he shares a story with me. "Do you remember the game in March versus the Marlies at Maple Leaf Gardens?" he asks. "I do," I reply curiously. I remember this game because, in front of family and friends, I was named second star. Jack continues, "Okay, that day I was scouting and watching you. I said to our goaltending coach Warren Strelow, next shift I want you to watch #12, Seftel on Kingston. Well didn't you go out on the next shift, score a goal and assist on another, after the shift, I asked Warren, Well, what do you think? He nodded and said, "What do you mean? He got a goal and an assist." I said to him again, I know, but what do you think? "Pretty good," he said. Jack looks at me with a big smile and says, "You made me look good that day!"

I spend the next chunk of time at the Capitals' draft table talking with the team's brass, and trying to soak up as much of the atmosphere as I can. It's all happening so fast but I want time to slow down. I want this day to last!

Names are still being called and players continue the march to the podium when my parents and I leave the Forum. I want to spend time with them. They've supported my dream, signed me up for hockey, drove me to games, practices, purchased all the equipment, and sacrificed their time and money for my journey. We spend the remainder of the day soaking up the sun in beautiful Montréal, eat on an outdoor patio and take in the sites of the historic city.

Unexpectedly, we cross paths with my old buddy Robbie Brown. My minor-hockey and lacrosse teammate was drafted today as well, selected by the Pittsburgh Penguins. We shake hands, and wish each other well in the future; the hockey world is a small one. Incidentally, he will go on to score 49 goals for the Penguins in the 1988/89 season.

Sunday, I return home to a hero's welcome. My Uncle Gery has put a sign in the front window of our house which displays the words: 'Future site of Steve Seftel's Donut Shop'. That is typical

Gerard humour and we all share a laugh. There's a buzz in Kingston and Kitchener as friends and family begin to discover the news. Within days there are newspaper articles with my name and picture, calls from the Kitchener-Waterloo Record, the Kingston Whig-Standard, draft lists posted in the Toronto Sun, and Toronto Star. A new phase of my life has started.

The draft was a memorable day that I think of fondly, but in truth it is only a step on a much bigger journey, a journey filled with highs and lows as I will soon find out.

Washington Capitals

In Canada, many kids dream of one day playing in the National Hockey League. During my younger years it's something I imagine on backyard rinks in the winter, or in the driveway shooting tennis balls at an empty street-hockey net. Without any association to a particular team, I see myself wearing my favourite team's jersey, or my favourite player's jersey. The NHL draft changes that and my dream has become clearer. I think about the future, and now I imagine my first NHL game wearing the jersey of the team that just said to the world, "We believe in you!"

The Washington Capitals joined the NHL as an expansion team for the 1974-75 season, owned by successful businessman Abe Pollin. He watched as the Capital Centre was built in suburban Landover, Maryland, as home to both the Capitals and the National Basketball Association's Washington Bullets. One of his first hockey decisions was to hire former member of the famous Kraut Line, Milt Schmidt, as general manager.

The Capitals' inaugural season was abysmal. They finished with far and away the worst record in the league at 8–67–5 and a total of 21 points. The eight wins were the fewest for an NHL team playing at least 70-games.

The Capitals turned their fortunes around in the eighties. In 1982, the team drafted Kitchener-native, and future NHL Hall of Famer, defenceman Scott Stevens, with their first pick, 5th overall. Then, the team hired up-and-coming David Poile as general manager.

As one of his first moves, Mr. Poile pulled off one of the shrewdest trades in franchise history on September 9, 1982, dealing longtime Capitals Ryan Walter and Rick Green to the Montréal Canadiens in exchange for defenders Rod Langway, and Brian Engblom, and forwards Doug Jarvis, and Craig Laughlin. This move turned the team's fortunes around, establishing Langway as the anchor of the improved defensive unit and earning him the nickname "Secretary of Defense" by Capitals' supporters.

The forward group was led by the scoring of dangerous centre Dennis Maruk, who scored 50 goals in the 1980-81 regular season and followed that up with 60 goals in the 1981-82 campaign. At the same time, speedy right-winger Mike Gartner and scoring-centre Bobby Carpenter were developing into dominant pro players. The result was a 29-point jump in the standings, and the organization's first playoff appearance in 1983 orchestrated by Mr. Poile, and head coach Bryan Murray. The Caps' dramatic turnaround inspired the increasing fan base in the D.C. area.

Turning the Capitals' fortunes around led to the team making the Stanley Cup playoffs for each of the next 14 consecutive seasons. The Caps, as they're often called, developed into a strong franchise with proven NHL stars like Langway, Gartner, Carpenter, Stevens, Bengt Gustafsson, Bobby Gould, Dave Christian, Larry Murphy, Kevin Hatcher, Al Jensen, and Pete Peeters.

In the 1997-98 season, the Capitals found themselves in their first ever Stanley Cup final appearance, only to be swept 4-0 by the Detroit Red Wings. The Caps' second Stanley Cup final appearance took place during the 2017-18 season. Captain Alexander Ovechkin led the team to a 4–1 series win over the upstart Vegas Golden Knights, and the Capitals claimed their first Stanley Cup championship.

After the draft, my plan is to attend my high school graduation at LaSalle but that itinerary quickly changes. I'm informed by Jack Button, that I, along with a number of other draft picks, will be travelling to Washington, D.C. for a few days of team-building exercises and meetings, to see the facilities, tour the city, and take part in formal introductions to the organization. This endless, summer whirlwind continues so I miss my grad due to the scheduling conflict but it's a worthwhile reason.

With a boarding pass in my hand, I step onto a U.S. Air flight from Toronto, and arrive in D.C. for a meet and greet at the hotel. It's a chance to connect with members of the organization's front office, the new draft picks, and others. I meet the Capitals' first-round pick, left-winger Jeff Greenlaw. He spent last winter playing for the Canadian national team under the tutelage of coach Dave King. Other players attending have been opponents in the Ontario Hockey League, some from the Western Hockey League whom I've never met, and still others are from the Québec Major Junior Hockey League, and U.S. colleges. Now, as a result of the draft, former enemies and strangers are friends and teammates, at least for this week.

Players are assigned two per room. In the morning, we jump out of bed early, eat breakfast in the downstairs restaurant, and assemble in the lobby awaiting pick-up vans. Gazing around, it's obvious to me that the Capitals' pipeline of talented prospects is full. Surrounded by a group of amazing athletes, I check my itinerary. Our scheduled morning session is for medicals at the Sports Medicine Centre. The afternoon session is for a review of the summer off-ice conditioning program with Terry Murray, followed by an evening group dinner with Mr. Poile and Coach Murray (Bryan) attending. The restaurant, located in Washington's southwest waterfront area, impresses me, and feels like the red-carpet royal treatment.

After a restful night's sleep, the prospects eat breakfast and prepare for individual interviews with Ron Lapointe and complete an Athletic Motivation Inventory Module with Jack. The modules are a sports-psychology personality test, evaluating mental toughness, leadership, character, and other traits. Jack says I scored well on these tests but I never see any results; they must be classified documents.

Before loading the bus for a ride to the Capital Centre, there's paperwork to fill out for Mr. Poile's administrative assistant, Pat Young. Arriving at the Capital Center, I discover the arena is quiet today. We're escorted to a large meeting room. I feel incredible sitting down in this rink for the first time. I want this to be my new home.

There is a time honoured mission in the NHL to win the Stanley Cup. The battle for the Cup is fought over several months, year after year. Each spring, a new army of skating soldiers hoists the prize, then in the fall, battle lines are drawn again to start another arduous grind to hoist the Holy Grail of hockey.

The boys take their seats at the prepared tables, and watch a video montage of the Capitals' previous season's goals, big hits, and fights. There is an abundance of highlights; a Capitals' version of "*Rock 'em Sock 'em Hockey*," that even Don Cherry would approve of. Played to theme songs from the movies *Rocky*, *Flashdance* and *Chariots of Fire*, it is motivating and makes my heart beat faster. There is footage of the hated Philadelphia Flyers, including our own Scott Stevens pounding on a Flyers' player with his fists behind the Capitals' net, highlights of scoring sensation Bobby Carpenter ripping a bullet slapshot past the Flyers' netminder, grinder Bobby Gould driving the net and scoring... Shot and a goal! The boisterous call fills the room. This famous tagline from the Caps' play-by-play man on Home Team Sports gives me chills.

I watch this sneak-peek video into life on the ice in the NHL, and blood surges through my expanding veins, goose bumps form on my skin. I look around wondering if the others are feeling the way

I am. However, the tables in the room are quiet, all eyes fixated on the large screen. The sights and sounds of the video instantly start the competitive juices flowing. In fact, in a room full of exceptional hockey prospects dreaming of one day playing in the NHL, the video is almost Pavlovian; the ringing of the dinner bell for the dogs! The sight of blood, goals, passes, hits and fights, awakens the competitor in me. In this moment, I have an instant hatred for the Philadelphia Flyers. The mere sight of their orange and black jerseys ignites an innate feeling to conquer, a subliminal message that these rivals are stopping us from winning. It ends with flashing photos of our ultimate goal. The stunning view of this Holy Grail of hockey invokes dreams of one day hoisting the league's greatest prize: Lord Stanley's Cup.

My saucer-sized eyes wander around the room and I think, 'maybe one of the boys in this room will help the Capitals win the Cup, maybe it will be me. It's possible that one of the guys sitting here might score the game-winning goal in Game Seven of the Cup final. That is the goal I've dreamed about since I was a young boy. The Washington Capitals have invited me to be a part of their dream, my dream, and our dream: the Stanley Cup!

Returning to earth, I discover Washington, D.C. in June is warm and humid. Being in the capital city of the United States of America, I feel a certain seriousness when walking around, seeing people hustling about, and doing their business. To the north is the State of Maryland and to the south, crossing the Potomac River, the State of Virginia. I'm not a Civil War historian but when I'm in D.C., I feel like I'm right on the line between the North and South, and there is a palpable feeling that goes with it.

The city is surrounded by the Capital Beltway, ring road I-495, which takes us anywhere we want to go, merging onto I-95 south over the river to Virginia. It is here where the Caps' practice facility is located, at a modest rink, not much bigger than Don McLaren back home. This is where the Capitals will hold training camp in a couple of months. On the flight home to Toronto, I review the provided twelve-week strength and conditioning program. It's clear and has instructions for each day of the summer.

These few days in Washington D.C. have given me a greater sense of purpose, a better understanding of the commitment required to develop as a hockey player, and it serves to stoke the fire in my belly. To be a successful professional, I need to continuously work hard, and commit to improving.

This Ontario summer feels different. I follow the Capitals' training regimen, pushing out reps on the bench press, building leg strength, doing squats, sprinting, foot work, and more. I continue my annual visit to Brigitte Wolf's power-skating school. I'm starting to carry myself with a swagger, not cocky, just confident. I'm no longer an OHL rookie, I'm a veteran. I'm drafted by an NHL team, and I will be attending an NHL training camp. I have to admit, at this moment I feel invincible!

At the end of summer, I report to Kingston to get in a few skates before leaving for the Capitals' main camp. The Canadians' training camp opens, and we play an exhibition game versus the Peterborough Petes. During this meeting, big, sturdy defenceman Luke Richardson, a future Toronto Maple Leafs' first-round pick, takes a poke at one of our rookies. I want to be a leader on our team, so I do the veteran thing and challenge Luke to a fight at centre ice. "Later," he says as he skates away. I'm not sure why he doesn't want to get it done now but whatever. Not too long after, a scrum ensues beside the Pete's goal. There is pushing and shoving going on as the players crash the net. Richardson and I are right in the middle of it. He looks at me and says, "Let's go." We drop our gloves, he pulls my helmet off quickly, and starts to get the upper hand as he lands blows to the top of my head. I throw my lefts while trying to dodge his barrage of fists. We begin to tire, are separated by the circling linesmen, and sent to our respective penalty boxes. Sitting in the box, I feel the new lumps on my head. I rub my hand over two protruding bumps. This fight serves as a wake-up call; my next stop is Washington, D.C., and the Capitals' training camp. Showtime baby!

The Stanley Can

Here we go! Attending a National Hockey League training camp is an honour. I feel prepared for Washington's camp and maybe oblivious to the task that lays ahead.

The Capitals cover each player's travel expenses to D.C. I'll fly in from Toronto along with other Southern Ontario boys. We're greeted upon arrival at Washington National Airport (now known as Reagan National Airport). A van delivers us to our hotel. The hotel is close to I-95 and the Woodrow Wilson Bridge that leads over the Potomac River to Alexandria, Virginia and the Caps' training camp facility.

I step out of the van at the hotel; it's hot, humid, and noisy from the busy traffic. The pack of wide-eyed rookies enter the lobby, exchanging handshakes and continue the march to the front counter where we will check in one at a time. A training camp itinerary is posted for all to see. I study the schedule for the first day, and see it's a full agenda. I'm starving, and need to find food. Eating is always a high priority. I'll wait a few minutes and locate my room first. Tomorrow it's on!

Being here in June with the rookies makes the surroundings, and the route to the rink, familiar and comfortable to my detail focused mind. Daily, the boys and I take the team shuttle van to the rink, watching the driver fight the busy morning traffic. There's nervous energy on the trip to the arena and few words are spoken. The Caps' veterans arrive in an array of sharp looking fast cars and sharp trucks. They will skate together after our practice and answer to Coach Murray.

Head coach Bryan Murray, a native of Shawville, Québec started his professional coaching career with the AHL's Hershey Bears in 1980. It didn't take long before he was elevated to the premier coaching position in Washington the next season. An intense coach with a passionate hockey spirit, when speaking he commands respect, and I listen and learn. He will go on to lead five NHL clubs over his exceptional career, coaching 1,239 games, and winning 620 of those contests.

The Capitals' veterans gear up in the arena in their regular dressing room. The rest of the boys in camp will find their equipment in trailers outside the rink. This is where my gear is waiting, complete with an individual folding chair to sit on. There it is, #45 Seftel.

Dressed in full and ready to go, I exit the trailer. Descending down the stairs into the sticky Virginia heat, I walk to the back door of the rink and enter. Camp is underway with a couple of high-energy practices. An elevated group of desks are set up on platforms to allow Capitals' management, coaches, and scouts good sight lines for evaluating players during practices and scrimmages. Every stride, shot, pass, and body check is observed, scrutinized, and evaluated.

An intra-squad tournament follows a couple days of practices. It is set up as a four-team round-robin to decide who will be the winners of the Stanley Can. The award is a blue, metal trash can with the words Stanley Can painted in white lettering. My team's bench boss is Caps' goaltending coach Warren Strelow. Warren is a big man, a jovial guy who always has a smile on his face. He has his serious side as well though and wants to win this mini-tournament in order to secure bragging rights with the other members of the competitive coaching staff.

Team Strelow's squad includes myself, and current Capitals' Bobby Carpenter, Larry Murphy, John Barrett, Lou Franceschetti and Bob Mason. The remainder of the team is made up of boys all trying to make the big club: Steve Leach, Ed Kastelic, Kris King, Dallas Eakins, Tony Kellin, Vito Cramarossa, Rob DeGagne, Patrice Lefebvre, Erin Ginnell, Rod Matechuk, and Alain Raymond. Coach Strelow makes it clear to the team that he wants to win this in-house tournament, no ifs, ands, or buts. Get 'er done boys, for Coach!

After a tournament full of energetic scrimmages, Team Strelow is victorious and awarded the dented Stanley Can. Proudly we gather at centre ice, surrounding our boastful coach for a ceremonial victory photo. Wrapping ourselves around the beat-up, blue trophy, we smile for the photographer. Team Strelow has won this year's camp tournament. He's very vocal with the members of the coaching staff, chirping away, knowing they're listening as he exits the ice, victorious and with a big grin. Bragging rights are Coach Strelow's this pre-season.

Training camp includes a unique off-ice experience: The Capitals invite Canadian-born professional boxer Donnie Poole to camp. The Toronto-native and welterweight boxer instructs the boys on how to defend themselves in a fight. Of course, boxing and fighting on skates have significant differences. Therefore, we work with Donnie on and off the ice in the art of self-defense. Off the ice, we partake in training sessions with the heavy bag. While working out with Donnie and fellow rookie Steve Hrynewich of the Ottawa 67's, a photographer from the Washington Post approaches us and asks for a picture for the newspaper. Donnie says sure but the photographer wants action, Donnie holds the heavy bag and asks me to punch it with the boxing gloves I'm wearing. I take up a boxing stance and put a serious look on my face. The Post prints the photo with the caption, "Boxer Donnie Poole, gives Capitals' rookies Steve Hrynewich and Steve Seftel pointers on the art of self-defense."

With the Stanley Can victory in the books, next up on the schedule is a series of rookie games. Rookie games involve players without NHL experience, usually draftees and younger minor-leaguers. They're typically physical affairs with the expected fisticuffs as guys try to make an impression on management. The Caps' rookies are scheduled to play the Philadelphia Flyers' rookies with home and away tilts. The two abrasive games are spirited, punchy affairs and I skate with self-assuredness. With each day that passes, my belief in myself is increasing.

Camp is sailing by and I feel sharp. On occasion I stop Jack, ask him to talk, and pick his brain about hockey. He's always accommodating, and patient as I quiz him. A wise hockey man, Jack has the ability to identify a player's character in a conversation quicker than you can say, 'The Original Six.'

With the rookie games complete, the Capitals prepare to start their pre-season schedule. The first game is at home in Landover on Saturday, September 20th versus Boston. Most of the players with junior eligibility have plane tickets for departure on Sunday. Friday night is quiet around the hotel as camp is winding down for the boys returning to junior and college hockey.

On a daily basis, lineups are posted in the lobby, along with other pertinent scheduling information. Everyone is anxiously waiting for Saturday's exhibition lineup to be posted. I enter the elevator and push the button that will take me down to the lobby. Just like every day, I confirm the posted camp details. The elevator doors open and I step out into the open hall. A couple of my mates wave me over, "Sef you're playing tomorrow," they say with youthful enthusiasm. The words sink in, and my mind shifts into overdrive. I walk over and check the list just to be sure, and yep, there's my name. Wow! On the outside, I act calm and cool but on the inside, I'm doing backflips. Hockey etiquette says to act like you've been there before even if you haven't and I haven't. I'm lacing up against the big, bad Bruins Saturday night. Time to buckle up!

Bourque's Corner

Ray Bourque played 1,612 NHL games for the Boston Bruins and Colorado Avalanche. The smooth-skating, intelligent blueliner holds the NHL record for career goals, assists, and points by a defenceman. He possesses tremendous offensive and defensive instincts. The five-time Norris trophy winner (NHL's top defenceman) dazzled hockey fans for many years. A legitimate, difference-maker on the ice. I watched and cheered as the dynamic defender helped anchor Team Canada in the 1981, '84, and '87 Canada Cup tournaments. A Stanley Cup champion, he was inducted into the Hockey Hall of Fame in 2004.

Saturday, or as we say back home, "Hockey Night in Canada", I'm pencilled in to play my first NHL exhibition game versus the

Boston Bruins. Therefore, I'll follow my regular game-day routine: a pre-game meal followed by an afternoon rest. Most players sleep in the afternoon hours but I can't so I call it a rest because I'm really just lying in bed trying to sleep. I get out of bed at 3:30 p.m. and change. I want to look sharp tonight. Descending to the hotel restaurant for a bite to eat, I think about tonight, the Bruins and the Capitals.

After paying my bill, I wait in the lobby for my ride to the rink. It's quiet and I attempt to clear my mind prior to the exhibition curtain-raiser tonight. Concentrating on the approaching task, my mind begins to wander. I refocus and feel a few butterflies in my gut. I'm uptight as we leave the hotel parking lot and merge onto I-95 N towards the Capital Centre.

The rink, a saddle-shaped arena, seats 18,130 people. Driving up, it appears that the Caps' home building is in the middle of nowhere and it is I suppose, being in this suburb east of the city. I love the address – 1 Harry S. Truman Drive. Sounds like a patriotic name, and makes me think of the stars and stripes.

Arriving in the sprawling parking lot, I survey the surroundings. I walk down the steep ramp leading to the back of the building where the players enter. Opening the door, I slip by a rink attendant. Walking briskly past the Zamboni, I see that to the right is the Caps' dressing room, and to the left is the visitor's dressing room.

It's intoxicating walking into the Capitals' room. I feel like I'm in a palace. There's a pristinely kept carpet, individual stalls with name bars, equipment ready to go, and clean home jerseys hanging. The stall is my space to prepare in this large, professional dressing room. There's it is – #37 Seftel.

Across the hall from the dressing room is the stick room where players craft their lumber. A torch is available and used if a stick blade needs to be heated in order to increase the size of the curve. Inside, players tape their twigs, check the flex, or just chat and chirp at each other. The boys are known to chew tobacco or sneak a cigarette in the workmanlike stick room. No matches are required as the torch is available for double duty. There is a player's lounge;

a place to hang out, talk, stretch, or find quiet time to mentally prepare for tonight's exciting affair.

It's time to get ready. I change out of my suit and into my Bauer blues. I put my equipment on way too early, and nervously wait in my stall for warm-up to begin. I watch the Caps' veterans as they prepare, each player executing their individual game-day routines. I was taught a long time ago to observe and learn from the pros.

Warm-up arrives, and the team walks single file to the ice surface. I step onto the Capital Centre ice for the first time and it feels both magical and exhilarating. The rink is bright from the overhead lighting. A massive scoreboard hangs above centre ice, complete with huge video-replay screens on all four sides. The warm-up music begins to blast and errant pucks bang off the glass like bullets.

Fans enter the rink and start finding their seats. Some stand up against the wobbly glass, and watch. Casual fans sip drinks, take pictures of their favourite player, or speak to each other in the subdued barn. Still more fans carry signs, wearing the jersey of their favourite Capital. I see a white #3 Stevens; a white #11 Gartner; a road-red #5 Langway. I don't see a #37 Seftel yet.

I do laps with the team, cut across the centre-ice line, and stare at the Boston zone. It's always good to know who you're playing against on any given night; it's part of the preparation. 'Oh boy, if I dump the puck into the Bruins' zone tonight, it may be in the corner of #7 Ray Bourque. Probably best not to dump the puck into Bourque's corner, with his eye-popping skill set, we may never get it back!'

I'm awestruck sharing the ice with a player like Bourque. I skate by #16 Rick Middleton and #20 Dwight Foster, the two players whose autographs I received at the Boston Garden with the Krauts. Kingston-native, #13 Ken Linseman, known as "The Rat", is in black and gold tonight. The challenge in my first exhibition action is to not watch these players like a fan, because in minutes, I have to skate against them and compete.

The buzzer sounds and warm-up ends. We retreat back to our room as do the Bruins. During this time players go about their own business, doing whatever it takes to prepare. I have a drink, sit in my stall, and repeatedly tap my left heel into the floor. My eyes are busy as I look around the room and soak up the big-league atmosphere.

Just before game time, Coach Murray enters, and the volume level decreases. This is Coach's time, for last-minute instruction and expectations. I look around and I'm starstruck by the sight of veterans Scott Stevens, Larry Murphy, Bob Carpenter, Mike Gartner, Greg Smith, Bob Gould, Bob Mason and Al Jensen. The first pre-game moments spent sitting in the same dressing room with the professionals I've only watched on television are surreal. Part of the challenge is to remind myself that I belong and have earned this opportunity to play on the big stage. That has to be balanced with the reality that I have a tremendous amount of work ahead. A coach once said to me, leave it all on the ice. Good advice!

It's game time! The clock on the wall ticks down to zero. We leave the dressing room as a tight unit, and walk down the runway to the ice surface. Fans start to cheer and lean over the rails as we appear from beneath the arena stands. "Bruins suck!" A loud voice calls out. "Let's go Caps!" shouts another, and one of the boys behind me chimes in, "Let's go fellas!" A fan rises and shouts, "Go get 'em Scotty!" I assume the excited fan is referring to Scott Stevens. He's a punishing body checker, and the kind of player the Bruins needs to be aware of when he's on the ice. I feel more confident from his physical presence. I like that he is wearing red, white and blue with stars and stripes tonight.

It's noisy as the tight troop steps onto the ice. The lights are even brighter, and the music louder as people stand up, clap and cheer! I do a couple hard laps like a missile! The buzzer sounds and I skate to the bench. The public-address announcer asks everyone to stand for the national anthem; *The Star-Spangled Banner*. It gives me chills hearing it. Players stand straight up, some rock back and forth on their skates, others stand with their eyes closed predictably thinking about what they're going to do after puck drop. I stare straight ahead, looking at the crowd that has grown to more than 10,000. The anthem is complete, the referee blows his whistle loudly, and the starting lineups move in for tonight's opening faceoff. The two opposing centres glide into the circle, the puck is dropped, and this game is on!

My first shift, I skate in aggressively on the forecheck and force a Bruins' defenceman to turn the puck over. The puck darts around the ice from the crisp, tape-to-tape, skillful passing. Later in the period, Bruins' five-foot-eleven, 190-pound forward Dwight Foster, picks up the puck in the neutral zone. The puck is stuck in his feet and he's struggling to get control. Ever since I was a young boy, I threw hard body checks and had a knack for knowing when to deliver them, likely from those long-ago lessons on the heavy bag at the Advanced Hockey Clinic. I never back away from physical contact. Foster gains control of the puck and is now skating across the centre red line. I'm coming in from the opposite direction with a full head of steam. I start to glide, and like a laser-guided missile, I set my sights on the target. Just as he raises his head to look and see where he's going, I arrive and deliver a shoulder into his exposed chest. He falls to the ice, lands on his back, and the crowd roars after the big open-ice hit. The explosion of sound from the noisy fans sends energy to my feet and I skate faster.

With about one-minute to go in the second period, a fast line change is executed and I'm up again. I hop the boards and dart into the offensive zone where one of my linemates and one of the Bruins are battling in the corner for a loose puck. As the one-on-one clash continues, I find a soft spot away from the Bruin defenders, and on the left inner hash mark. My linemate wins the battle and gains possession of the small black disc. Instinctively he looks up and fires a tape-to-tape pass onto my waiting stick. Without hesitation I rip a low wrist shot. The puck sails by the goalie's pad, catches iron, followed by a loud, tink, as it rings off the goalpost, and bounces out of the crease. The crowd releases a collective ooohhh! My legs start to shake and I briefly feel out of control of my limbs. Seconds later the loud siren wails to end the fast-skating period. Both teams return to their respective dressing rooms. I sit down in my stall and am quivering uncontrollably from the speeding adrenaline flowing through my body.

Third period. The scoreboard ticks down to zero to end regulation time, and the sixty- minutes played solves nothing as we are tied 1-1. In the end, we defeat the Bruins 2-1 in front of 10,734 fans at the Cap Centre. Mike Gartner's game-winning goal with twenty-one seconds left in the five-minute overtime period is the slim difference.

Post-game, I shower and change into my suit. Ready to return to the hotel, I am aware I have a plane ticket to Toronto for tomorrow. Before leaving the building, Jack informs me that I'm not going home just yet. "Steve you're not leaving. You're going to be playing in New Jersey." I love hearing those words. Another game; yes!

I have to change my plans and let my parents know tout de suite. The Capitals' second exhibition game will be on the road against the New Jersey Devils. The team assembles together at captain Rod Langway's restaurant, which is located in suburban Maryland, and is called Langway's Sports Bar & Grill, of course.

I arrive at the noisy restaurant, and make a collect call home from a pay phone to my folks, informing them that I will not be leaving tomorrow, and to discuss tonight's thrilling game. They're equally excited, but it's hard to hear them in the loud tavern.

Fellow rookie Billy Houlder will also be playing in New Jersey. The "Bill Man" will go on to play 846 NHL games. However, at this time, he's a key member of the North Bay Centennials and one of the funniest, down-to-earth guys I have ever met. I never tire of his humour, laugh, and side-splitting storytelling. Rooming with him on the road helps squash the nerves creeping into my busy mind. The "Bill Man" always makes me relax with laughter!

Waking up in the morning, I rush to get a copy of the Washington Post. I'd seen the reporters in the room post-game and I'm looking forward to reading about last night's tilt. A piece by Robert Fachet, accompanied by a photograph of Yvon Corriveau and Michal Pivonka, reads, 'Capitals score in overtime.' I scan the article and start smiling as I read a line near the end. Fachet wrote, "Rookies Pivonka, Jeff Greenlaw, and Steve Seftel impressed in their first Capital Centre appearances." At that moment, I feel like I'm on top of the world. Even though there is a long way to go, my hockey dream feels like it is right on track.

Flying from D.C. to Newark Liberty International Airport in Jersey, we arrive and check in at the hotel, located conveniently across the street from the rink. The Devils play at the Meadowlands Arena in East Rutherford. This is now unfamiliar surroundings. Playing on the road is a completely different animal. The Devils have a good club, led by Kirk Muller. He started his junior career with his hometown Kingston Canadians and later joined the Guelph Platers. The proficient scorer was deservedly drafted 2nd overall by the Devils in 1984 behind Mario Lemieux.

The team comes out fast tonight and takes a 4-0 lead after one period. Early in the second, grizzled, veteran defenceman John Barrett rims the puck around the boards. I corral the disc, and chip it off the wall into the neutral zone past the pinching Devils' player. A streaking Craig Laughlin picks up the loose puck and drives straight to the cage. He holds off a Devils' defender and skillfully buries a shot in the back of the net. I race up the ice to congratulate the boys in the typical hockey celebration.

Back on the bench, the public-address announcer chimes in with the scoring play, "and assisted by #37 Steve Seftel." With that, I've picked up my first exhibition point. I want this point to be the first of many. The Devils chip away at our lead but when the final buzzer sounds, we hold on for a 5-4 road win. Post-game Coach Murray is questioned about the New Jersey comeback by Robert Fachet of the Washington Post. "We played a lot of kids and they pretty much had their regular lineup, so I have to be satisfied," he said.

Post-game back in the visitor's dressing room, I'm taken aside for a discussion, and told that I will be returning to Kingston tomorrow. The Canadians are ready to start their regular season this Friday versus the Peterborough Petes. Jack informs me that Coach O'Donnell is asking if he can expect me back for the home opener. Jack tells Coach that I will indeed be there.

My first training camp audition with the Washington Capitals is complete and I take home many positives from the experience. Rubbing shoulders with the big boys during camp has helped me grow as a player, and I've taken a giant step towards my goal of playing in the NHL. However, sport doesn't always read like a fairy tale and the ending can be far different than the one you dream of! This journey is far from over.

Many are Drafted
Less are Signed

Returning home after camp, riding an emotional wave, I feel sharp mentally and physically. I'm composed, motivated, and own a strong sense of purpose. In other words, inspired!

The Capitals deliver this version of Steve Seftel back to the Kingston Canadians via a short flight to Toronto. I have a quick visit with my parents, and they present exciting news to me. Graciously, in my book, and perhaps reluctantly in theirs, they give me permission to use their 1979 Ford Pinto. I now have wheels! The two-door compact car is not fancy by any means. However, returning as a veteran player with an automobile means additional freedom to drive myself to games, practices, and movies, whatever. I admit, it feels good having this four-cylinder fire hazard at my disposal.

After their most successful regular season in five years, the Canadians open the 1986-87 schedule at home versus Peterborough. The team improved, just as we promised our loyal fans, and the organization is moving in the right direction. There's renewed optimism in town as we lay the groundwork for the start of the hockey season, building on the previous year's 36-point jump in the standings.

Glancing at the roster, there are ten returning forwards, five returning defencemen and overage goaltender, Chris Clifford, is coming back. Incidentally, last season, Cliffy became the first goalie in OHL history to score a goal. The shot came during a victory over the Toronto Marlboros in front of the home fans at the Memorial Centre – a 150-foot backhand into an open Marlie's net with twenty-five seconds left in regulation time.

The home opener of the new 66-game hockey season is here. Riding high, I want a more prominent role, and to be a leader. This is my sophomore season and, in my mind, I know I'm going to have a big game tonight. Real or perceived, after Caps' camp, I feel one step ahead of everyone else.

In front of an eager home-opener crowd of 1,940 fans, I receive a pass in the neutral zone, and skate up the ice two-on-two with veteran centre Andy Rivers flanking me. He occupies one defence-man while I dart to the right side of the ice. At the blue line, I dig my blades in, cut to the middle, wire a 45-foot wrist shot, stick side, along the ice, and into the net.

Later, on an offensive zone faceoff, I focus on the linesman dropping the puck. He straightens out the two centres and drops the disc. It bounces, I collect it with my stick and, without hesitation, drive straight to the net past a stationary Petes' defenceman, burying an 8-foot wrist shot under the goalie's blocker for my second goal tonight.

The only major penalties for fighting tonight occur in the third period when an unknown Petes' rookie confronts our toughest player. The new kid to the league challenges fearsome defender Marc Laforge, who is a physical player with Northern Ontario toughness, and a combative look in his eyes. Watching from the bench, a voice shouts sharply, "His name is Domi." "Who?" Says another. "Domi!" shouts the voice again.

This is Forge's third year in the league and opponents are aware of his physical reputation as he has dropped the gloves with most, if not all, of the league's toughest players and amassed 462 minutes in penalties in his first two seasons. Never one to turn down an invitation to dance, he willingly stands up for his teammates quicker than you can say old-time hockey!

The smaller Domi is chirping Forge before the faceoff. You don't need to hear the conversation; the body language says it all. Gloves off, it's on. The fight is short as they both fall to the ice; a draw by most accounts of the bout. It will not be long before we all know who the tough-as-nails Tie Domi is and the impact he will have on hockey. He will go on to play 1,020 NHL games and square off with many heavyweights including several notable bouts with legend-ary enforcer Bob Probert.

Back to the Memorial Centre, and tied 4-4, the boys notch three third-period goals to come away with a 7-5 victory. The opener is a win to the delight of the Canadians' faithful.

October leaves begin to change colour, and I receive a phone call from Rick. He has terrific news. The Capitals have revealed to him that they are offering me a contract. The Caps present a three-year entry level contract plus an option for a fourth. I'm captivated by this news that is music to my ears. An NHL contract! It's all hap-pening so fast. Two years ago, I was playing midget hockey for the Greenshirts and now the Washington Capitals are offering me a contract.

As a junior hockey player, I'm making $30 per week cash plus $10 per week set aside in the bank for the end of the season, there-fore I figure any amount of money offered up by the Capitals sounds good. I will not collect any salary until I turn professional or play an actual NHL regular-season game. Having said that, a signing bonus will be available as soon as I put pen to paper.

Mr. Poile sends the offer to the offices of Branada Sports in Toronto. Arriving as promised, Rick arranges a meeting for us. I'm being paid to play hockey! Hockey etiquette says don't gloat, be humble. I remember what Jack said to me in one of our many conversations, "It's easy to sign your first contract. The hard part is signing your second."

Rick reviews the contract details with me. I sit still and attentively listen. "Your salary in year one is $75,000 US and then $85,000 for the remaining years." The deal is loaded with performance bonuses. If the player wins any major National Hockey League award, the club will pay the player $10,000. There are bonuses for All-Star appearances, team wins, road wins, goals-against average... shutouts fetch us all $100, power-play percentage, penalty-killing percentage... $100 here, $750 there.

However, another important obstacle; to receive these team bonuses I have to be on the Capitals' roster and as of now I'm a member of the Kingston Canadians. My signing bonus is $55,000 U.S.: $35,000 guaranteed, payable over three years, $20,000 in 1986, $15,000 in 1987 and $5,000 in 1988. The remaining $20,000 is not guaranteed and is based on future games played.

The numbers sound good, and as I see it, any amount of money to play professional hockey is fair to my 18-year-old mind. I will have to pay Branada Sports 3% of my guaranteed signing bonus for negotiating the deal and 3% of any future earnings. All I want to say is, where do I sign? My mind darts from thought to thought as I take the pen and sign my name. Signing a contract in the fall of 1986 is a phenomenal feeling. However, what goes up must come down.

50 CCs

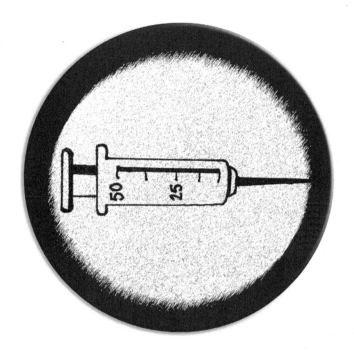

The gang packs their luggage and parks their cars at the Memorial Centre in advance of the annual Northern Ontario swing that, for this trip, includes Sault Ste. Marie and Sudbury. Loading the old iron lung, it's time to hit the road. The Greyhounds are the furthest geographical opponent we will face off against.

Carry-on bags are jammed with clothing, playing cards, music, magazines, and books. For this long trip we can wear tracksuits and lug our fancy suits in garment bags. I think about bringing homework; maybe one text book to read will do. The fully packed bus passes McDonald's, exits Division Street and rumbles down the 401 west for the eleven-hour journey.

The team is a little punchy to start the road trip and there's lots of chirping to be heard. A voice from the back of the bus yells, "Double up rooks." There are unwritten rules for these trips passed on from year to year, team to team. Coaches, trainers, and media members sit at the front, rookies sit in the next set of seats and may be required to sit together or double up. Veteran players claim their own space (or seat) as a permanent piece of real estate for the season. Card games take place in the rear rows. Often, we have Vern from Trentway-Wagar Coach Lines as our driver so it's a relaxing, familiar atmosphere. The big, silver coach is in high gear, and on cue, a voice calls out from the back, "Hold on to her Vernie, here comes the rhubarb." Vern chuckles, the boys laugh, and I smile, it's great to be on the road again.

Arriving in the Soo hours later, we all have a severe case of bus legs. "Stretch it out boys," we chirp while stepping onto the icy pavement at our modest hotel. The Hounds have a respected major junior history; I mean, Wayne Gretzky played here as a 16-year-old before moving on to turn professional at 17 with the Indianapolis Racers of the World Hockey Association.

The Friday night affair versus the Greyhounds is starting like any other; warm-up, national anthem, and puck drop. This spirited game is underway. Early in the first period, I score to break a 1-1 tie, with Mike Fiset and Daril Holmes drawing the assists. In the second period, I return the favour with an assist on a Fiset goal. The swift-skating centre Fisser is an energetic, Northern Ontario boy from Timmins.

Our line is flying, and my legs feel fresh. I collide at the blue line with my old nemesis, Dan Currie. The sharpshooter grew up in Burlington, Ontario. For the boys in Kitchener born in 1968, Burlington was our AAA minor-hockey rival from atom to midget. He was Burlington's most-dangerous player; a pure goal scorer. We both jumped to midget as bantams, and played two years at that level. In May of '85, we were both drafted by OHL teams. In June of '86, coincidence struck again and we were both drafted by NHL teams. This year, 1986, marks nine straight years of competing against one another and sets the stage for a burgeoning rivalry based purely on sport. This is how rivalries are born, developing over many winters of fierce competition, and tonight I've had enough of this guy!

The collision with him at the blue line is violent. In this moment, I feel like a savage. I glare at him, and he does the same. I'm raging, and my insides erupt. I throw down my gloves, he does too, and we go at it. The home crowd cheers their boy and jeers me, the enemy. "You goon!" Yells a fan from the home crowd. Not really, that's a line from the movie 'Slap Shot'. The circling linesmen intervene, separate us, and we're escorted to the sin bin; five-minutes each for fighting.

With that fight, I earn my first Gordie Howe hat-trick. In hockey, a Gordie Howe hat-trick is a variation of the scoring type of hat-trick, wherein a player scores a goal, records an assist, and gets involved in a fight all in one game. It's named after Mr. Hockey himself, who was well known for his adept skills at both scoring and fighting. Incidentally, years later I was introduced to Dan Currie while playing in the AHL. We shared a beer, a few laughs, and got along just fine.

After serving my major penalty for fighting, I leave the box and I'm back in the fray. I feel dialled in tonight. Hopping the boards with my line for a change on the fly, the puck is dumped into the Soo zone. Attributing my dogged pursuit of the puck to running down loose balls in lacrosse, I hustle into the zone, blow by the defenceman, collect the puck, and shield it with my body. The defender guides me into the corner and while transferring my body weight to my left leg, I maintain possession. I spot one my linemates. He's open, and I pass the biscuit quickly followed by, POP!

My leg goes limp, and I struggle to skate back to our bench. The period ends and I hobble to the dressing room. After an exam, the final answer from Pete is that I'm done for the night. My knee must be examined by a doctor. The Canadians double up the Hounds 6-3 tonight in front of 2,882 disheartened Northern Ontario hockey fans.

Post-game, I shower and wait for the boys in the poorly lit concourse. Slowly and carefully walking outside to the bitter Lake

Superior cold air. I'm pissed, and hoping my injury isn't too serious. I step up onto the bus and my knee slips awkwardly forward. That's an odd sensation! Something isn't right but I can walk so that's a good sign.

Back at the hotel, unaware of the severity of my injury, I feverishly try to convince Peter I'm okay. "Watch," I say, and I run down the hallway. Jogging back, I look at him and chirp, "See, I'm good." He's not convinced. Okay fine, time for bed. I tell Pete I'll see him tomorrow.

I open my eyes the next morning to find my left knee is swollen and stiff. Back on the bus we head east on the Trans-Canada Highway for the three-hour trip to Sudbury, and a game with the Wolves.

Arriving in the Nickel City in the early afternoon, the training staff takes the cold and wet equipment to the arena to hang up and dry. I need to find a way to the hospital to have my knee looked at but I'm not sure how to get myself there.

Hey, there's George Diamond! Who is George Diamond? He's a longtime Kingston Canadians' hockey fan who is along for the road trip with his brother Kenny. They have a car. "George, can you drive me to the hospital?" I ask. "Sure can," he says happily. I slide into the back seat and we drive to the Sudbury General Hospital.

The triage nurses attend to me and in due time, I'm seen by a physician. My knee is swollen, sore, and feels like it's going to burst. The emergency department doctor decides to drain the fluid pooling in the joint, to relieve the building pressure.

With my knee now in a tidy dressing, the doctor returns. "I withdrew quite a bit of fluid from the joint," he says. "Is that bad?" I inquire. "Draining the joint will make you feel better," he says. I thank him as he passes me the prepared documents. I scan the pink patient copy quickly. Only one clue jumps off the page – extracted 50 CCs of gross blood (about two-fluid ounces). 'Fuck!'

Later, after scoring three third-period goals in 97 seconds, the boys salvage a 6-6 tie with the Sudbury Wolves that I watch from the seats. Returning home, I have an appointment with the team's orthopedic surgeon. Arriving at the clinic, I'm still unsure of the injury I'm dealing with. The surgeon performs a battery of tests at his KGH (Kingston General Hospital) location. The verdict: a torn anterior cruciate ligament. I've never heard of this piece of the body before, nor do I know a thing about it.

He explains that surgery can be done to repair the ligament or I can strengthen the muscles in my leg through physiotherapy in order to support the joint and avoid surgical intervention. After discussion and evaluation, the choice is non-surgical and starting physio as soon as possible.

The next six weeks I spend in the physiotherapy department, riding the stationary bike, doing leg extensions and leg flexion exercises over and over and over. It's shitty to be on the sidelines again after a fast start to the season.

Jack challenged me to start dominating in junior hockey and I was on the right path. Reading the local paper only painfully reminds me of that fact. "Seftel had been playing extremely well prior to the injury," wrote Tim Gordanier in the Whig-Standard sports section.

Someone once said that what doesn't kill you, makes you stronger. I have to get through this. I attend games, but only as a spectator; scratch from your lineup #17 Steve Seftel. Yes, if you caught it, well done! I turned my back on superstitions and perhaps the hockey gods were not happy with me. I switched sweater numbers in my second year of junior hockey, dropping the #12 I had to take in year one for the #17 I wanted in year two.

The Capitals have me fitted and measured for a custom-made Lenox Hill knee brace. It's a cumbersome apparatus of plastic and steel; essentially, it's like playing hockey as the Bionic Man. It's designed to support my knee while limiting side-to-side movement.

I receive the brace, and try it on. This monster is fabricated with molded plastic foam, two steel struts, one-thick strap to tighten around your thigh, one-thick strap to tighten around your shin, two-thin straps that cross from front to back behind the knee, two buckles in front, one above the kneecap, and one below the kneecap. I try it out at practice. I'm supposed to skate with this forever? Alright then!

Saturday Afternoon's Alright for Fighting

After twelve long games on the shelf, it's time for me to start playing hockey again. I feel slower, less agile, and my left leg is strangled by plastic and steel. No matter, this is my new reality. A number of interested parties will be following my progress in the upcoming weeks, including Coach O'Donnell, Mr. Poile, Rick and my parents. For the first time in many months I have doubts about my health, my speed, and readiness. I feel obstructed, and restrained by the newly fashioned brace. Nothing I can do; suck it up buttercup. 'No one is going to feel sorry for you, better get used to it and get your ass in gear,' says my inner, prickly voice.

I return to the lineup in the nation's capital against the Ottawa 67's, our division rivals who wear red, white, and black, barber-pole looking jerseys, and play underneath Lansdowne Park at the Civic Centre. The Canadians score the first two goals tonight, but we lose 4-2 to the Brian Kilrea coached 67's. There are no points for me in my return game but I'm happy to be back playing.

The team escapes the city for a short road trip as the month of January winds down, playing three games in two-and-a-half days. Contests in Guelph, Kitchener, and Toronto are on the itinerary. Back on the bus, the Canadians will be absent from school Thursday and Friday due to the western roadie.

The short trip starts with a 5-2 victory at the Guelph Memorial Gardens against the Platers in front of 1,585 Royal City hockey fans. Post-game, a quick jaunt down Highway 7 to Kitchener follows for a Friday night matchup in my hometown. I'm looking forward to this one! The Canadians and Rangers are both stuck in the middle of their respective divisions making it an even game on paper. The boys pick up a narrow 6-5 victory at the historic Auditorium in front of 2,778 disappointed East Avenue Blue fans. Coach O'Donnell is pleased after tonight's win, telling the Whig-Standard, "I thought we had good speed and our passing was good too."

Post-game I have extra zip in my step, having collected a goal and an assist, being named second star, and receiving my Brut Faberge award. Feeling better about myself, the chest is puffed out more than normal when I meet my family and friends down below at the Aud. In fact, it's a relief for me too, because I'm extra nervous when I play in front of family. We have time for a short chat, and soon a voice loudly calls out, "The bus is leaving." It's time to go. The team boards the bus for our stay at a local hotel in advance of tomorrow's Saturday afternoon matinee vs the Toronto Marlboros.

One of the benefits of having the Marlies in our division is the four road games each season at Maple Leaf Gardens. Often we play them Saturday at 1 p.m. in advance of the Maple Leafs' game in the evening on *Hockey Night in Canada*. My parents will complete the weekend trifecta tomorrow and watch me and the boys play three straight days.

This winter, I watched the movie *Lethal Weapon*. Mel Gibson's character, Martin Riggs, is unpredictable and wild; unpredictable like junior hockey players. Waking in the morning, we have a fast breakfast, load the bus, and depart from Kitchener for the one-hour drive east to Toronto on Highway 401.

Here we are. It's a thrill playing at the Gardens. The bus stops outside the famous rink that Conn Smythe built, and the fellas file in through the side door with hockey bags hanging off their shoulders. One by one, we fill up the tiny visitors' dressing room, located around the corner from the renowned ice surface.

A primal feeling of boisterous, teenage testosterone swells in the room prior to warm-up after our big road wins the two previous nights. The boys stand, bounce, bend, pace, call out, and chirp like a pack of rambunctious wolves. The clock ticks down to zero and it's time for warm-up.

We walk towards the ice, following goaltender Chris Clifford. Moving single file, down the hall, turn left, then right, and there it is – the Gardens' ice. Cliffy is approaching the bench door when I look out and see the home Marlies already on the ice, stretching around the perimeter of their zone. There is a silent hockey code when it comes to warm-up: players don't dare cross the centre red line; not even with a toe. To do so is done at one's own peril, and every player knows it.

Cliffy steps onto the ice, makes the usual right turn towards his goal, where he stops promptly to prepare his crease. The Canadians follow in our bright, road red jerseys and matching red, blue and white trim Cooperalls.

Hamilton-native Mike Maurice can score goals, and throw punches. The overage forward cruises around our net and skates toward centre ice. Continuing his straight trajectory over the red line, he's now in no man's land, or Marlie turf. Deeper and deeper into enemy territory he advances. The boys are watching a stunning scene unfold. I've seen guys put their skate over the centre red line, but this… This is a stiff kick in the nuts to the Marlies.

As Mo starts crossing over his skates behind their net, a nervous twinge comes over me. He skates up ice towards our side of the rink. A few Marlies stand up, as now they've had time to process this unforgiveable turf violation. 'Ah fuck, hurry Mo, hurry, almost there, almost there, get over here.' Just as he closes in on their blue line, a player in a Marlie's jersey is in Mo's kitchen. I can see the foul words being exchanged, jawing back and forth as they approach centre. At that moment, Marc Laforge skates across the red line. One big unpredictable move, and smack, with one huge haymaker, Forge feeds the Marlie his big, red white and blue glove! The stunned player slumps to the ice, and all hell breaks loose. Players from both teams rush to centre, squaring off, with fists raised. The boys are ready to go and go they do!

Fans and ushers begin to scramble. Moms are screaming at the sight of the *Slap Shot*-like melee unfolding before their eyes, dads are shouting; it's chaos!

I hear the sound of cracking visors from fists. Looking behind me, my eyes catch a glimpse of six-foot-one, 205-pound Scotty Pearson firing hard rights off a reinforced I-Tech shield and the facial structures of a combatant. Jeff Sirkka, a good fighter from a tough Northern Ontario mining city, is going toe-to-toe and in fact, the Sudbury-native will fight twice in this pre-game donnybrook as will a testy Forge, who takes on two of the Marlies' biggest 19-year-old veterans.

Startled ushers rush down to the ice, and try to manage the out-of-control scene. I pair off with an opponent. Holding each other's jerseys, we push back and forth, staring, each waiting to see who is going to throw the first punch. Wrestling at the red line, we exchange the customary f-bombs while stepping over the sticks and gloves that litter the ice. Coach O'Donnell is shouting from the bench. It is difficult to hear; my heart is pounding. Pre-game brawls are frightening; no refs, no rules, free-for-alls.

The voices from the crowd continue screaming and shouting. I glance over, and past Coach's shoulder, I see my mom's concerned face in the crowd. A strange feeling comes over me and the brawl is suddenly less important. After several minutes the teams manage to separate and leave the ice to a continuous Maple Leaf Gardens buzz. It appears Saturday afternoon is alright for fighting!

Back in the room, in the aftermath of the free-for-all, the boys holler, grunt, groan, drop f-bombs, and bounce off the walls of our small room. Baby-faced, fast-with-his-fists, Sirk has one eye swollen shut after his pair of long bouts. It's obvious that Coach O'Donnell is annoyed. The referees summon Coach and after a few minutes or so, he returns to the room and sternly says, "I need three players on the ice to shoot on the goalies." The referees will permit both teams a short warm-up for the tenders and then we will start.

After playing the sixty-minute skirmish, we are bludgeoned 12–4 on this bizarre Saturday afternoon in Hogtown, in front of 3,741 fans who all have a story to tell their friends and family. Post-game, back in the tight dressing room, it's silent and subdued. Coach O'Donnell rips us in his controlled, professional manner. His feelings are visible on his strained face. The bus leaves the Gardens after the tired group grabs food at McDonald's for a long, quiet bus ride home after this unpredictable outing.

Following our infamous pre-game brawl with the Marlies, the OHL creates a new rule: on-ice officials must be present before the visiting team is allowed on the ice for warm-up. Unpredictable. Yes!

At the end of the regular season, the Canadians finish fifth in the Leyden Division with a record of 26-39-1 for 53 points. I finish my second injury shortened season with 54 games played, collect 21 goals and 43 assists for 64 points. The fifth-place finish sets up a first-round clash with the rival Belleville Bulls, who finished fourth.

The Canadians defeat the scrappy Bulls 4-2 and win the best-of-seven-series. Next up is the first-place Oshawa Generals. The powerhouse team is led offensively by the scoring of Scott McCrory and Derek King. Gord Murphy and Jim Paek anchor the stingy defence. After we win the first two games of the series, the high-flying Generals reel off four straight victories and take the series 4-2. Oshawa goes on to win the league championship and hoist the J. Ross Robertson Cup.

At the end of the tough series with Oshawa, my parents are waiting in the lobby. My knee feels wonky. I walk out of the dressing room in pain and with a noticeable limp. Hurting and gimpy, there is discomfort, but I dare not tell anybody. Surely it has to be better, and if it isn't, 'What can I do?' My bitter inner self tells me to eat the pain; that's the mantra!

I'll Write a Cheque

The Capitals find themselves erased from the 1987 Stanley Cup tournament by the New York Islanders 4–3 in the best-of-seven Patrick Division semi-final series. The memorable matchup is known as the Easter Epic after the Capitals play the longest Game Seven in franchise history. The incredible game ends at the 8:47 mark of the fourth overtime period on a series-winning goal by Islanders' speedy scoring-sensation Pat LaFontaine, and crushes the Caps' Stanley Cup dreams in a dramatic, painful fashion.

Capitals' GM, David Poile played his college hockey at Northeastern University in Boston. He started his post-playing career in the front office of the expansion Atlanta Flames in 1972. The intelligent hockey man departed the Flames to become GM of the Capitals in 1982, where he remained for the next fifteen seasons. Today, he has the title of the first and only general manager of the Nashville Predators. An astute manager, he's shown a willingness to make blockbuster deals, giving and gaining high-end talent in the process.

Draft day 1987 proves to be a pivotal moment for the Capitals' organization. Mr. Poile completes a trade with the Québec Nordiques for feisty centre Dale Hunter and veteran goaltender Clint Malarchuk in exchange for veteran forwards Gaétan Duchesne and Alan Haworth, and the Capitals' 1987 first-round draft pick (which is used by the Nordiques to select talented centre Joe Sakic from the Swift Current Broncos). Without a first-round pick, the Capitals use their second-round selection on defenceman Jeff Ballantyne from the Ottawa 67's. In the third round, the Capitals select left-winger Steve Maltais from the Cornwall Royals.

Post-draft, the Capitals invite the rookies down for the annual meet and greet. I join the group for a few days in the D.C. area. Jack informs me that I will be staying two days longer than the rest of the departing crew. An appointment to see the Capitals' orthopedic physician is on the schedule in order to evaluate my knee.

At the end of the week, the boys leave for home and the weekend begins. I'll be here alone until Monday, stuck in a suburban hotel alongside noisy I-95, with no car, and no money. I check out the quiet hotel lobby and empty snack shop. Being a resourceful young man, I go down to eat in the decorative hotel restaurant, not only because I'm hungry, but to pass the time that is going by at a snail's pace. I get to know the pleasant restaurant host quite well over breakfast, lunch and dinner. "Please charge it to my room," I say each time I visit. Incidentally, several weeks later I receive an invoice for these pricey meals from the Capitals' accounting department. Jack and I work it out based on the meal money the team would have provided for the extra days in the hotel. Whew!

Sunday afternoon, I receive a phone call from Coach Murray (the other Coach Murray – Terry). He must have received word that I'm alone, and he invites me back to his home for dinner with his wife and two daughters. I appreciate him taking the time to drive over and take me out for a few hours. The home-cooked meal and time spent with his family is just what I need. As I watch Coach interact with his two young daughters, I see a different man than the serious tactician and it makes me feel less stress and at ease.

Monday morning, I have my appointment with the orthopedic surgeon. He does his tests, takes notes and explains to me that my knee is stable and I'm given the green light to train as hard as I can. A quick flight takes me to Toronto and it's time to get back to the gym for summer conditioning work.

I hear Tom Cochrane on the radio and turn it up. He's the front man for the Canadian rock band Red Rider. His solo hit single *Life is a Highway* is a favourite song of mine, and as the lyrics say, "Life is a highway, I wanna drive it all night long." The only problem is, I don't have a car. The Pinto doesn't count as my car; it's still just a loaner from my parents. Like many players before me, the thought of purchasing a sweet, fast car is on my mind, especially with a signing bonus burning a hole in my pocket.

I want a car! My dream car is the Chevrolet Corvette, but that's a little too expensive right now. Plus, until I turn twenty-five, auto insurance will be extremely expensive. I know nothing about buying a car. Therefore, I ask my dad to give me a hand purchasing a vehicle, and we drive to the Pontiac dealership in Cambridge, Ontario.

I haven't even started shaving yet, and my boyish looks certainly catch the salesman by surprise when I tell him I want to buy a new vehicle. We take a slow walk around the medium-sized lot, and after a frank discussion with the salesman, and my dad, I settle on a brand new, V-8, metallic blue, Pontiac Firebird with a five-speed manual transmission.

"What about financing?" He asks inquisitively. I perk up and matter-of-factly state, "I'll write a cheque." "A cheque," he replies sharply. "Yes, a cheque," I say again. I'm not being arrogant; I have the money in the bank. He stares at me sideways as I pull out a personal cheque from my wallet and pay the total, which is just over $16,000. I calmly fill out the pertinent information and hand it over as he continues to stare with astonishment.

September's approach means a new hockey season is on the horizon. There is a buzz on the street. Capitals' management and coaches want a fast start to the regular season. That's the rumour! In order to achieve this, one of the strategies is to build the roster as quickly as possible. As a result, all of the players with junior eligibility, including myself, travel to Washington prior to the start of the main camp. There will be no exhibition games for the juniors, only practice, on and off-ice testing, conditioning, and then dispatch back to our respective teams before the main camp commences.

After a week in D.C., it's back to Kingston for year three and the 1987-88 hockey season. Buckle up! It is going to be a bumpy ride and I don't mean in the Firebird.

What Doesn't Kill You
Makes You Stronger

The German philosopher, Friedrich Nietzsche is credited with the phrase, "What doesn't kill you makes you stronger." Predicting what will transpire over the next several months would require me to own a crystal ball. It is a hockey season that is both memorable and forgettable; more likely the latter. Players grow as athletes each season from experiences, competition, adversity, challenges, winning, and even losing.

The Kingston Canadians finish the 1987-88 Ontario Hockey League regular season with 14 wins and 52 losses – 28 of those 52 losses in the last 28 games of the schedule.

The team sported a record of 14-24-0 before the monumental collapse began. Incredibly, we lose a mind-boggling 28 straight hockey games. It is an OHL record that remains unmatched to this day in the expanded version of the league.

How did this happen? Who is responsible? Why can't a team pick itself up off the floor? These are questions many people are asking at the end of the season in Frontenac County; at least the ones who are still paying attention. It is a demoralizing, challenging season for a wide-eyed group of teenage boys who all have hockey dreams, and for myself, the 19-year-old leader of the group. I suppose the entire organization needs to accept responsibility for the results. I'm going to expose facts that contributed to the historic streak, details, clues, stories, and the inside dope that led the Kingston Canadians to lose a jaw-dropping 28 games in a row to finish their hockey season.

The demise of the 1987-88 version of the Canadians is the consequence of a series of events and decisions, choices that impact a major junior hockey organization, its coaches, players, and staff. Truthfully, the collapse started in the summer of 1985 when general manager Ken Slater resigned. I was disappointed by the news; disappointed for selfish reasons but happy for Mr. Slater and his career goals. It's clear to all the boys that we lost a good hockey man, a man who cares about the organization, the city, and the team. He demonstrated a keen eye for identifying talent. The Vancouver Canucks got their man at the Canadians' expense, leaving a large void in the organization's front office.

More shocking to me at the conclusion of the 1986-87 season is Fred O'Donnell's resignation after just two years with the club. We lost another intelligent, respected hockey man; a calm, professional coach and leader. Furthermore, we lose the team's trusted assistant coaches Dale Sandles and Shawn Babcock. Both popular in the room, they are going to be missed. Dale is a smart man, and an excellent communicator. Babber, only a few years older than us, provides needed stability and confidence. The boys like his spirit on the ice in practice and in the room. These key departures are part of sports; the show must go on.

In advance of the season, the Canadians begin the search for replacements. The GM position is filled by the hiring of Gord

Woods, and the coaching job by the hiring of Jacques Tremblay. Coach Tremblay comes to the team via the Québec Major Junior Hockey League where he guided the St. Jean Beavers.

Drafting well is critical in major junior hockey. Teams must hit on draft picks to secure future success. Our ownership group believes they have a secure deal with 17-year-old Bedford, Nova Scotia native Steve Widmeyer when they use their first-round pick at the 1987 OHL draft to select the six-foot-two, 200-pound right-winger. Unfortunately for the Canadians, Widmeyer chooses not to report and never plays a single game for the organization. Instead he attends school at the University of Maine and plays hockey for the Black Bears. Incidentally, at the 1990 NHL draft, Widmeyer is selected in the 10th round by the St. Louis Blues after playing seventy-four games for the NCAA's University of Maine.

In the wheeling and dealing summer of '87, one of the first decisions made by the Canadians' new front office is to trade veteran rearguard Marc Laforge. The six-foot-two, 210-pound, Hartford Whalers' prospect is dealt to the Sudbury Wolves, in the process dispatching arguably the toughest player in the league. In a physical Leyden Division with future NHL heavyweights Tie Domi (Peterborough Petes), Rob Ray (Cornwall Royals) and Troy Crowder (Belleville Bulls), this trade is a head-scratcher. The move leaves a large hole on the Canadians' young blue line corps as we start the season with only one 19-year-old defenceman, tough leader Jeff Sirkka.

The Canadians' front office embarks on a dramatic overhaul of the lineup through a trading frenzy, including trades for purpose, and trades for the sake of trading. The revolving door never stops, roster changes continue, and as many as twelve players come and go. Departures include Forge, Alain Laforge (Forge's brother), Sloan Torti, Chad Badawey, Jamie Henckel, Peter Liptrott, and Brad Gratton, who is acquired in the summer and traded away in February. There are additions like Scott McCullough, Darcy Cahill, Frank Melone, Derek Langille, Dave Weiss, and Bob Leeming. From a team perspective, it's no way to build cohesion, and at times feels like a circus sideshow. My name is also floated about the league. The Windsor Spitfires are in town and I receive a phone call from Rick saying the Spits are looking to acquire me. He's confident the deal is going to being completed. I have butterflies all weekend waiting for the expected trade news. In the end, the proposed deadline deal falls apart and I remain in the city to see the carnage play out.

Adding to the bottom-dwelling squad's woes is the injury bug. Our top centre Mike Fiset is banged up and misses the final two months. Tough, spirited winger Scotty Pearson, is lost. Gifted, minute-munching defenceman Bryan Fogarty, is also on the shelf. Losing these dominant players leaves the gutted roster deep in it. Injuries can derail any team but particularly a group lacking depth and experience. We wonder aloud if things can get any worse. They're about to!

In January of 1988, Winnipeg-native Lou Kazowski is in talks to purchase the struggling franchise, and shortly thereafter he does. Rumours swirl in the strained local hockey community regarding Mr. Kazowski's intentions for the Canadians. Is he moving the team? The purchase of the fragile franchise ignites a brewing storm. There are times in your life, no matter how old, when you think you've seen it all, and then you realize, you haven't.

A home date at the Memorial Centre sees us hosting the Peterborough Petes. They're a dominant club, led by future NHLers Mike Ricci, Jody Hull, Tie Domi, and Dallas Eakins. They come out flying, hammering us. We're playing sloppy defensively and the Petes pepper our net. At the end of the dismal first frame, our frustrated new owner, a stranger to the team, takes matters into his own hands.

The second period starts and I'm in a state of shock to see Lou boldly standing behind our bench while Coach Tremblay stands silently, glaring at the ice. Lou will call the shots for this period of hockey. Here's how a reporter from the Whig-Standard captures the unusual events:

"After 22 straight Kingston losses, the Peterborough Petes would visit the Kingston Memorial Centre in front of just over 1,000 disheartened fans. The Petes put an early stranglehold on loss number 23. Kingston was out-shot 21-4 by Peterborough in the opening stanza and outscored 7-2. After the period, club owner Lou Kazowski, less than a fortnight into his proprietorship, sprang to his feet and stormed hell-bent-for-leather towards the Kingston dressing room. Once inside, in language that could strip lacquer, Sweet Lou was anything but sweet. He ripped everyone in sight, Coach Tremblay included, then moved behind the bench for the second period, leaving his lame-duck coach to change lines and twist in the wind. The Canadians responded with some energetic play in the second stanza."

As for me, on the bench, I watch and listen in disbelief as Lou stands behind us and barks out instructions. He lays anchor on the bench for the next painfully slow twenty minutes. Strangely enough we respond with inspired play. Our coach stands silently, arms folded, and face crumpled.

To start the third period, Lou retreats to the stands and his perch under the CKWS broadcast booth. He sits smugly in the crowd as the fans chant his name, Lou! Lou! Lou! On this cold, bleak night the fans appear desperate for a new voice to attach their collective hopes to.

The treatment of Coach Tremblay captures the lack of leadership in the rudderless junior hockey organization. A proud man, experienced coach, embarrassed and disgraced by the new owner in front of his players, fans, and colleagues, his tenure with the Canadians effectively ends during that fateful middle period of hockey versus the Petes, and that act of grandiose showmanship. Not surprisingly, post-game, Coach resigns from the team.

Having witnessed the abhorrent behaviour during the Petes' debacle, Peter Campbell also resigns from the club. Peter's decision is swift, and he is done! The Canadians' trainer since the day I arrived as a naïve rookie, he's become a good friend. I leave the rink that night a saddened hockey player.

An impromptu gathering at Pete's apartment with a few of the veterans allows for venting of frustration and anger. We're standing up for our coach, our trainer, and ourselves. We talk late into the night about our state-of-hockey affairs. We're sick of losing, and the spectacle we've become. We are now a punch line, a joke of the league. Living this drama has us all uncertain about the future. There's no bringing order to this mess of a season. However, like brothers, we're in this together, and feel a common bond.

The troop reports for practice and we exchange stories about the events of the last twenty-four hours. As Coach would often say, it's a scandal, a frickin' scandal! We realize one thing is clear, we're alone in the rink. There's no coach, no training staff, no general manager, nothing; an empty Memorial Centre for the team the organization forgot. The youthful unit is broken. At that moment, trust between the players and the front office responsible for our well-being and safety is severed.

The absence of leadership galvanizes the group of rebellious teens struggling to make sense of their new reality. In an abandoned dressing room, as happens in the tale of the *Lord of the Flies*, we decide to govern ourselves. It's a mutiny of sorts. If the organization doesn't care about us, we will run it. Inevitably, this attempt at governance fails as the room quickly plunges into chaos. Resentful, exasperated hockey players run loose and unsupervised in the empty arena.

Perhaps it should be assumed after such a dreadful streak of games that this ship is going to sink. Local radio and media are merciless. A song parody to Gordon Lightfoot's classic, *The Wreck of the Edmund Fitzgerald*, is heard on the airwaves. It's funny but not really because the young, weary Canadians are the butt of the joke. It's demoralizing and embarrassing to our competitive spirit.

There's no joy in Mudville as we lose, and lose some more. After the dust settles, still mired in a losing skid, the collapse continues with former Toronto Maple Leaf Jim Dorey assuming the interim coaching duties. Truthfully, with a few weeks left in the ghastly season, I don't care who they hire; this season is a wreck.

Firmly cemented in the league basement, prior to our last game, again versus the Peterborough Petes, and you guessed it, another loss, I feel ill and vomit a couple of times in the dressing room toilet before warm-up. It is likely a flu bug but it seems fitting that I want to puke at the end of this losing streak. However, I have to play. I want a complete 66-game regular season and I've made it this far; I may as well go down with the ship. Sitting in my stall and tasting the vomit residue on my tongue, I receive a tap, with a message that my billets want a farewell photo. I walk out slowly and step onto the ice. Larry says "Smile," and proceeds to chirp me, only the way he can. The Moran family, Larry, Janice, and their boys, have treated me like one of their own. They have endured this long season along with me and I'm thankful for their support.

I suffered a broken ankle my first year and a torn ACL my second. I had something to prove this winter and I set a goal to play every game in 1987-88 and prove I am durable. I accomplished that, along with leading the team in scoring with 32 goals, 43 assists and 75 points. These goals feel completely irrelevant now. As I said at the beginning, it's both a memorable, and a forgettable season. Mostly, it's forgettable as we finish in dead last, losing our last 28. Having said that, I will always remember the boys in the room who stuck together through a season that most will never endure. What didn't kill us, made us stronger, together!

In the Whig-Standard, as the dramatic season comes to a merciful end, a short clip in the sports section reads, "Canadians last game? Have we seen the last of the Kingston Canadians? After last night's 8-3 loss to Peterborough ended the season with a losing streak of 28 games, owner Lou Kazowski told Whig-Standard photographer Michael Lee that it was the last game for the Canadians in the "Canadians" uniform." In fact, it was! The following season, the team played under the name Kingston Raiders and wore black and silver uniforms, ending its long tradition and my chapter with the team.

I Have $50 that Says
You Can

The 1987-88 Washington Capitals finish the regular season tied for second in the tough Patrick Division with the Philadelphia Flyers, three points behind the first-place New York Islanders, setting the stage for a first-round playoff series with the rivals from Philly. Mr. Poile's bold move, trading for game-changing Dale Hunter, was completed in part to help push the Capitals deeper into the Stanley Cup marathon.

In fact, the trade pays dividends when battle-hardened Hunter scores a clutch goal on a breakaway in overtime of Game Seven versus the relentless Flyers, and sends the Capital Centre crowd into a mad frenzy. The series-winning goal instantly makes #32 the face of the franchise. Hunter's heroics propel the Capitals to the next round and a date with the New Jersey Devils. However, the good times are short lived. In round two, the Capitals lose a heart-breaking seven-game series to the Devils. The Stanley Cup still remains elusive for the hungry organization.

The day after my last game with the Canadians, the Capitals assign me to their AHL affiliate, the Binghamton Whalers, giving me an introduction to professional hockey life, and allowing me a chance to shed the memories of a difficult season. I receive a phone call early in the morning at my billet's house. It's Jack. He says I have to report to Binghamton and will be in the lineup tonight. "Where is Binghamton?" I ask Jack curiously. There's a pause on the phone, and Jack curtly responds, "Get a map."

Binghamton, N.Y. is located north of the Pennsylvania border on I-81 as I soon discover on my new road map. The team plays at the Broome County Veterans Memorial Arena. The Binghamton Whalers' logo is similar to the parent Hartford Whalers, however, the bluish coloured whale fin and wavy, green letter "W" are turned on its side, forming a tidy letter "B" to signal the club's Binghamton home. In the spring of 1988, one shoulder of the jersey displays the Hartford Whalers' logo and the other shoulder, the Washington Capitals'.

The talented roster is a combination of prospects from the two competitive franchises. During my stint in Bingo (the AHL city is nicknamed Bingo by the players), I make my professional hockey debut and suit up in three games for the club, coached by former Montréal Canadiens' centre Doug Jarvis. The boys call the calm, collected, soft-spoken skipper Jarvy. The three games I play are all losses. Yes, my personal losing streak, including my final days in the OHL, adds up to thirty-one games now. Stop smirking!

Hockey stories make the rounds even before the Internet, and as you might guess, the boys in Bingo are well aware of my unenviable games played losing streak. Suitably, they give me the nickname, Schleprock. Hmmm, Schleprock is a character on the cartoon, *The Flintstones*. He's known to carry a heavy burden due to his bad luck. This is well fitting for me at this moment in my hockey career.

Like many of the guys I've always enjoyed nicknames. Nicknames are part of the sporting experience and there are so many good ones. Some nicknames are obvious, while others develop from shared or individual experiences. A nickname gives teammates an emotional connection, builds team bonds, and the comradery athletes talk about. Nicknames say, we know you, you're one of us, and it signals acceptance by the larger pack. I've been given several nicknames over my playing career, and my teammates had many as well. Some of my favourite nicknames from squads I played on are: Babber, Bonzai, Chych (Chick), Farley, Peewee, Rags, Rocket, Stats, T-Bone, Top Gun, and Wheels.

The 1988 NHL Entry Draft is held in Montréal and the first-overall pick is Mike Modano from the Prince Albert Raiders of the WHL by the Minnesota North Stars. My brother from Kingston, Scotty Pearson is picked 6th overall by the Toronto Maple Leafs, and the Capitals use the 15th overall pick to select speedy winger Reggie Savage from the Victoriaville Tigres of the QMJHL.

The Capitals select point-producing centre, and Stratford-native Tim Taylor from the London Knights in the second-round. In the seventh-round, the Caps select two players I'm familiar with. The first is a former minor-hockey rival from Brantford, Ontario, Keith Jones, a power forward who is attending Western Michigan University in the fall. I'm even more excited to hear the Capitals pick my old Greenshirts' teammate, Brad Schlegel, from the London Knights. The smooth-skating defenceman with a high hockey IQ is preparing to play for the Canadian national team.

Time to get back to work. I begin the training regimen again and prepare for camp. An early summer trip to D.C. is on my schedule as well; the annual post-draft visit for rookies. This go-round we stay at the University of Maryland student dorms and spend a week training with Capitals' strength-and-conditioning coach, Frank Costello. He coached track and field at the University of Maryland for six seasons. The Capitals plan to teach us to be better athletes through Frank's expertise. For me, he wants improvement in my leg strength. Frank says I need a lot of work in that area. He says I have good upper-body strength but my lower limbs need attention, and I take that to heart.

I'm eager to start a new chapter in my life that includes hockey, and the additional bonus of being paid to play hockey. I start to stir when I think about moving to the United States. My passion for hockey is now my profession, a career, a job, a living.

Since I'm a Canadian citizen, and required to work, and live in the U.S.A., I need the appropriate employment paperwork to cross the border. Pat Young ensures each player has the required documents. In order for me to work in the U.S., the Capitals are required to file a petition on my behalf, with the U.S. Department of Justice, for non-immigrant worker status. Once confirmed, the approved paperwork will conveniently arrive at my home.

September rolls around and the new season quickly approaches. The boys assemble in D.C. for training camp. I will not fly as there is no need to return for junior hockey; it's time to turn professional. That's my plan at least; attend the Capitals' training camp, ultimately hoping to make the big club, but more likely carving out a spot on the Caps' new American Hockey League affiliate, the Baltimore Skipjacks. Going forward, the Capitals will send their top professional prospects to the AHL team. No more Bingo for the Washington boys.

Professional hockey is like an apprenticeship, and to make an NHL team as a 20-year-old is a daunting task. More likely, it is a path that includes development on a minor league team, learning your craft, improving hockey skills, and discovering what it takes to be a professional.

The Firebird is full, and I feel anxious as I leave my parents' home. I say my good-byes, and receive plenty of good wishes. It's time to go, and I depart for the ten-hour drive to D.C. I find myself once again overwhelmed by the magnitude of the situation. Similar to the junior experience three winters ago, I'm now going from being the big fish in the little pond, to the little fish in the big pond. Perhaps I'm feeling this way due to the disastrous final year of my junior career, but that's behind me now, or is it?

Driving through the Appalachian Mountains on Route 15 in the State of Pennsylvania, I have time to think about the hockey debacle last winter. My prickly inner self wonders if I'm ready for this change. I become fidgety and agitated. I desperately want to leave last season's memories in my rearview mirror.

Prior to training camp, Mr. Poile made a few coaching decisions. Bryan Murray remains coach of the Capitals. The Skipjacks need a head coach. He assigns Caps' assistant Terry Murray as coach in Baltimore, and hires former St. Louis Blues assistant coach Doug MacLean as the new associate to Bryan in D.C.

Training camp is underway at the Mount Vernon Ice Arena. It's my third camp, and I know the drill. Frank conducts the official off-ice testing. He told me to work hard in the summer on my legs to improve my explosiveness. I did, and I'm returning bigger, faster, and stronger. I now stand six-foot-three, 195-pounds.

A warm sun is beating down in the outdoor fitness testing area. I'm taking part in a short sprint that measures quickness and explosiveness. Each player gets three attempts, and we're being timed in the heat. My first two attempts I have a decent time. Jack is observing patiently off to the side of the black asphalt surface.

He keenly says to me, "What's your best time?" I tell him my results so far.

He pauses and asks, "Can you go faster?"

Like a young guy I shrug my shoulders and reply, "I don't know."

He moves closer and says, "I have $50 that says you can." I immediately perk up and stare in his direction.

"Oh, a challenge," says Frank.

"Are you up for it Steve?" he quips. "You'll need your best time."

"Yep, I'll try," I say. I can do this!

I line up in my three-point stance on the starting line and wait. Frank sets his stopwatch and says, "Ready, set, go!" I explode off the line, and it feels like my feet aren't even touching the ground. The zip line attached to my shorts flies off my backside, and stops the timer as I cross the maximum distance, which is only a few metres. I look back quickly, and see that Frank is staring at his stopwatch. He shows the time to Jack, and he nods. "You got it, Steve," shouts Frank, like a giddy dad watching his son win his first race. A big smile develops on my youthful face as I jog back slowly with a little extra hop in my step.

Later in the day, Jack passes me an envelope with a $50 bill and a note tucked inside. I hoist the greenback that features Ulysses S. Grant and read Jack's written message, which is loud and clear: 'This is a lesson about what is possible.'

Off the ice, I'm right on track, but on the ice, where it really counts, I'm struggling, and find it difficult to get going. I'm not sharp, and not even close to where I want to be as a player. I desperately try to turn things around. The Capitals hire a mental preparation coach to help the players with the psychological side of the sport, and I ask him for a meeting.

I arrange a time and we meet at the arena, but his wacky methods aren't working for me. He plunks me down on the bench in the dressing room, we exchange looks, he moves close to my face, stares into my eyes, and starts chirping at me, spewing a lot of different questions and comments. Some make sense, and some don't. Staring back at him, I'm unsure of my role in this activity. Like Bill Murray says in the movie, *What About Bob*, "Is this some kind of new radical therapy?" He begins to slap at my face, not hard, but enough to piss me off, and sting a little. I think to myself, 'What are you doing asshole?' Does he want me to play like an attack dog or a mad dog? I don't know, and I'm afraid to ask. Out of respect for him and the Caps, I pretend I'm okay with these quirky methods. I mean, the Capitals hired this guy, and he's here to help me, so this approach must work.

He does this strange routine again before a rookie game against the Flyers. I figure he wants me to play furious, angry. I go out and run around completely out of control, banging bodies with no regard for the puck. Crash and bang, crash and bang for sixty minutes. Post-game, I think about how I played, which was completely reckless. I don't know what this guy wants. Maybe it wasn't him, maybe I'm not ready for pro hockey. After all, I lost the last twenty-eight games I played in junior and incredibly, three more I played in Binghamton. Geez that's thirty-one losses in a row that I've frickin' dressed for, played in and lost. Thirty-one straight games! Teams talk about having guys who come from winning environments, because the players learn how to win, and what it takes to win. Suddenly, I'm questioning everything I've done. The residual effects of last season's fiasco infect my hockey mind like a disease. I become numb and frightful. Eat the pain!

A rookie game on the road versus the New Jersey Devils is on the schedule. We board the bus, and drive up the highway for the afternoon tilt. In tryouts, it's important to do something that separates you from the pack of competitors. There are a number of ways to get noticed: scoring goals, setting up goals, playing physical, blocking shots, and fighting, or better yet fighting twice in one night.

Game on with the Devils' rookies. One of the new boys is jousting with a tough, hulking player on the home team; an intimidating enforcer I know from junior hockey. This is an enormous guy to tangle with, six-foot-four, and 240-pounds. The one-sided fight starts like any other: square off, grab each other's jerseys, and go. This is followed by fist-to-face, fist-to-face, and fist-to-face. I can hear the clenched fists making contact with the bony facial structures. In quiet arenas like today you can hear the punches making contact. I hate the sound! The fight is short and ugly. They're both given five-minutes for fighting. Our guy leaves for repairs and doesn't return.

Post-game I shower, pack my bag, and find the bus. I step onto the motor coach, and after a quick look, I can see that the seats are mostly empty. About four rows from the front sits my new teammate, his head resting back on the seat. His eyes are black, his face is swollen, and his nose looks mangled. He sits quietly, so I walk past him to my seat. He looks awful, but at the end of the day, he's trying to earn a job, a contract.

Camp proceeds. There are no big-league exhibition games for me, only rookie games. It seems my own uncertainty about my play is also noticed by the Caps' brass who watch intently from the stands day after day. Nothing is handed out in the professional ranks; ice time has to be earned. I haven't played well enough to earn exhibition opportunities at this training camp.

The Capitals have talent up and down the lineup. There is an array of offensive weapons including, Mike Gartner, Bengt Gustafsson, Mike Ridley, Geoff Courtnall, and Dale Hunter and a talented defensive corps with Rod Langway, Scott Stevens, Larry Murphy, and Kevin Hatcher leading the way. Between the pipes, there are two quality veterans, Pete Peeters and Clint Malarchuk.

Camp comes to a close. After a rocky start on the ice so far, I'm assigned to the minors. Development in the American Hockey League will be crucial for my National Hockey League dreams. I'm sent down, and report to the Baltimore Skipjacks. I'm now a professional hockey player and need to continue the apprenticeship, honing my skills down on the farm.

What the Hell's a Skipjack?

Baltimore, Maryland is located forty miles north of Washington D.C. There's a history of professional hockey in the city, but by no means is it known as a hockey town. Instead, they're known for their beloved Major League Baseball team, the Orioles, the NFL's Ravens, and before that, the Colts.

Professional hockey history here dates back to 1944 when the Baltimore Blades skated in the Eastern Amateur Hockey League. In 1962, the American Hockey League approved an expansion franchise for the State of Maryland's largest city. The new team, known as the Clippers, was affiliated with the New York Rangers, part of the Original Six that also included the Boston Bruins, Chicago

Blackhawks, Detroit Red Wings, Montréal Canadiens, and the Toronto Maple Leafs. Perhaps the most famous player to wear the Clippers' uniform was legendary goaltender Jacques Plante, a hockey pioneer and the first goalie to wear a protective mask on a regular basis during games on the ice. A member of the prestigious Hockey Hall of Fame, his #1 jersey was retired by the Montréal Canadiens in 1995.

In 1981, a team named the Baltimore Skipjacks started playing hockey in the Atlantic Coast Hockey League. The following season, the Skipjacks shifted to the well-established American Hockey League.

Truthfully, I'm unsure what a Skipjack is, and soon find out curious hockey fans in AHL cities are equally confused. Many times, in future games, eager fans on the road will hold up signs with the probing phrase, "What the hell's a Skipjack?" I laugh each time because I didn't know what it was either before coming here. It turns out, a Skipjack is a small, sailing vessel used for oyster harvesting on the region's important Chesapeake Bay in the late 19th century. Baltimore is situated on the large coastal estuary, and was once home to many Skipjack vessels.

The eager, fan-friendly owner of the Skipjacks, Tom Ebright, is pleased to have the affiliation with the Capitals. The Caps will now send their top professional prospects to the AHL franchise for development. Terry Murray begins his new coaching assignment and directs the team. Home games are played at the Baltimore Arena, located near the waterfront in a redeveloped area downtown. The Maryland city proves to be a terrific location for the Skipjacks' players. A one-hour drive to Washington makes for easy travel back and forth when player movement is required.

The practice facility is located in Columbia, a bedroom community twenty-miles south of the city. Learning to be a professional requires me to fend for myself, which includes finding a place to live. My roommate, fellow rookie Tyler Larter, and I search for a place close to the mall hub, and not too far from the practice rink.

My new roomie Larts is a native of Charlottetown, Prince Edward Island and a former Soo Greyhound. He has a scoring touch and plays hockey on the edge. An agitator on the ice, his salty Islander mouth drives the opposition crazy. He's a master antagonist. Okay, he's a serious shit-disturber. He can chirp with the best – a trash talker extraordinaire. He is a classic on-ice pest with his stick, hits, pokes, slashes, elbows, and sharp-witted tongue.

We decide on an apartment in Columbia, in part because most of the boys live here, although some live in nearby Laurel, and Ellicott City. Fortunately, there is an abundance of apartment complexes, and there are many options in many price ranges. We're happy with our choice. The two-bedroom apartment comes at a price of $800 per month. Our first regular-season tilt is fast approaching and only days away. Navigating this professional hockey life is challenging and thrilling.

After practice downtown today, I have a good reason to smile, discovering my favourite band, AC/DC, is playing at the Baltimore Arena. Myself, defenceman Pat Beauchesne, a Saskatchewan farm boy with brute strength, and athletic Québec-raised, defenceman Alain Guay, purchase tickets to watch the iconic rockers.

Pat and Alain aren't as keen as me and decide to leave the loud rock concert early. However, there's no way I'm leaving. The night ends after a lengthy encore. Exiting the arena with a sea of people chanting and my ears ringing, I walk to my car. Finding the Firebird, I believe I can get to the highway but it's a little tougher now in the dark of night.

The minutes pass by and I completely lose my bearings. I'm driving through the twisting, turning, unfamiliar, downtown city streets and realize I'm lost. Motoring through the tough downtown roads in my sporty vehicle, I draw stares from the curious locals as I pass by. I have no idea where I am in this tall, concrete jungle. I'm becoming distressed as I continue to drive in circles. I have to get the hell out of here! 'Where's the frickin' highway 95?'

Wait, there it is, a sign directing me to the one highway I know, I-95. Shit, heading north on I-95, now west, then east. Do I hear I-95 south? There it is, thank-you, I speed down the narrow exit ramp and back to Columbia. This is another lesson to learn; how to navigate this big city.

Learning to be a pro, I need to manage time. Time can be both a friend and an enemy to a young player – a friend when there are minutes after morning practice finishes to take extra shots, to work out in the gym, to go out for lunch with the boys, to go to a matinee, and so on. However, if not managed properly, time becomes a young player's enemy – time spent with the wrong people in the wrong places.

Learning how to pay bills, buy groceries, cook, take care of my affairs, and at the same time focus on my career. It's a transition all young pro players have to make, and it can be intimidating at first. Driving around town with a laundry list of things to do, at times, this switch to pro hockey feels like a sink or swim endeavour.

For young pros who are barely out of their teens, eating properly is a hefty challenge. The hockey player's body and what it can do is their paycheck, therefore proper nutrition is crucial. Up to now I've had assistance with the task of cooking, preparing food once in a while for myself, but now I face completing this task every day.

It turns out that my cooking repertoire is limited, and lacks significant nutrition. I rely on easy recipes my mom made. I have success with shepherd's pie. I try boiling Oktoberfest sausage, and Shake 'N' Bake on chicken breasts. The results aren't bad, and my confidence is rising.

I set out to raise the bar, and invite a couple of the boys over, taking a stab at that timeless classic, meatloaf. My mom made it, and there's a recipe on the back of the onion soup box. I have skills. I can chop, I can slice, but I can't mince. Okay, who am I kidding?

Having said that, I can read and follow a simple recipe. I'm going for it! Following the instructions, I carefully assemble, and bake my meatloaf. Out of the oven, I dish it onto the plates. Have a seat boys! Banter and friendly barbs fly around the small dining table. "Not bad," says one, and another repeats the praise. It looks good, and tastes sort of like I remember. Not too long after dinner my stomach feels a little off. Okay, I feel terrible, as do the guys, and they tell me they have to go. It appears the meatloaf has put us all in the bathrooms. It has to be the hamburger! Can't be the cooking; no way. I think we will eat at the mall tomorrow. Note to self, scratch meatloaf from my recipe list!

Back to hockey. The Skipjacks are led offensively by Mike Richard who has a deep bag of tricks and the puck on a string, coupled with the lethal quick-release of winger Mike Millar, who played twenty-eight games for the Hartford Whalers last season.

Despite initial growing pains, I'm ready to start playing hockey. Coach Murray breaks the 80-game schedule into eight 10-game segments, setting goals for the amount of points the team needs to earn in each. Achieving the goal will enable us to take home small rewards like personalized shower wraps or shower shoes.

To begin the season, we have three games on the road versus the New Haven Nighthawks, Maine Mariners, and Sherbrooke Canadiens. The Jacks go zero and three. It's not the start we were hoping for. Coach Murray does not press the panic button but I'm starting to stress about it; thirty-four and counting. A win for me feels like my own personal version of desperation hockey! You know what I mean. That's our secret.

Pro hockey is faster and these guys are strong. No longer playing with teenage boys, I'm playing against men who are better athletes, better trained, and prepared. After a slow start, the fourth game is our home opener versus the Rochester Americans, and we get in the win column with a 6-1 victory to the cheers of the home Skipjack fans and me. A win! Halleluiah!

The 1-3 Skipjacks regroup under Coach Murray. He introduces me to a new facet of preparation: film study. More and more teams are watching game film. Terry rolls a T.V. and VCR into the room. Dressed in his tracksuit, wearing socks and shower shoes, he uses this teaching tool to review our opponent's break-out, power play, and penalty-killing tactics, along the way delivering reminders of his offensive and defensive schemes. Mistakes from previous games are pointed out to individuals and the team. He says I have to go to the net more. Our meticulous coach does not sugar-coat what he observes on tape.

I'm trying hard to acclimate to the professional brand of hockey. I have yet to score and I want my first goal. I need this monkey off my back, as they say. Five games complete, I sit at no goals. The sixth contest of the season is at the Hershey Park Arena, home of the Hershey Bears, the affiliate of the Philadelphia Flyers, and the Skipjacks' arch rivals. This is a geographic rivalry; the Pennsylvania town is ninety-minutes northwest of Baltimore. It's like when Kingston played Belleville, and the rink swells when the arch rival comes to town. The Baltimore Arena, which has an average crowd of around 2,500, can balloon to 10,000 when the Bears come to play us.

Tonight, the Skipjacks are behind the Bears in the third period, and I'm the trailer on an offensive rush. The puck crosses the blue line into the Hershey zone. I cross the line, and find open space. My centre takes the defenceman wide down the right wing. I settle into the slot, and yell for the puck. A pass lands right on my stick, and without hesitation, I rip a snap shot over the goalie's glove for my first professional goal at 10:47 of the third period. What a relief! It took six games but I finally score. The Skipjacks go on to lose tonight 6–3, but it still feels good to score my first. 'One less thing to worry about.'

Ups and downs this season rule the day. We have a few days off before our next game, and plans to have an informal rookie party are set. All the boys gather, and as is often the case with rookie parties, it involves alcohol. I feel uptight when I arrive. The party is underway. Beer, and shots of liquor are going down easier with each drink.

I begin to enjoy the goings on as my senses dull. The alcohol induced feeling turns into slurred speech, and stumbling around the house. Inevitably for me, the room is spinning, rolling; the sort of thing that makes me want to puke. Feeling my intoxication level rising faster, my head is ready to explode. In due time, I'm vomiting in the basement bathroom, and my night is over.

Sleeping it off in a basement bedroom, I'm somewhat coherent and relieved when my eyes open. It's morning. I've made it through to see the next day. Some will say this is boys being boys; some will say, it is team bonding; still others will say it was a great party man! Whatever it was, today, laying here, I'm woozy, and hung over. Practice is fast approaching, and I have to get up. Driving to the rink, my legs are like lead, my stomach aches, and my head is pounding. I have to get this done, power through practice, and get myself home to bed. Eat the pain!

As November arrives, we depart for a road trip: a three-game weekend excursion that includes Friday night in Newmarket, Saturday in Rochester, and Sunday back in Newmarket. The infamous three-games-in-three-nights; a minor-league tradition. The Toronto Maple Leafs' affiliate is the Newmarket Saints, whose arena is a one-hour drive from my hometown. A large contingent of family and friends will make their way to the game. Tickets are bought and paid for. I can't wait to see everyone and I'm sure they can't wait to see me play!

Road teams have their morning game-day skate around 11 a.m. Players loosen up and get their legs moving during this ice time. It gets us out of bed, and is an opportunity to prepare sticks, and focus mentally.

Coach Murray calls me over at the end of the short skate and tells me that I will not be playing tonight but will be a healthy scratch. I'm able to play but not in the lineup due to the numbers game. I'm crushed! I think about all the family coming to watch me play, and how disappointed they'll be. I feel like crap, like I've let them and myself down. I'm embarrassed but there's nothing I can do. The coach makes the decisions.

I call my parents and give them the shitty news. While I'm explaining my situation, I feel sick to my stomach. Controlling my restless emotions in these situations is not a strength. The contingent of family and friends arrives as planned, and I join them in the cramped rink. I'm not skating and performing for them, but standing in a suit watching like a spectator, and I hate the feeling. I want everybody to leave. I don't want them here. It's an awkward reaction. I want them here as Steve Seftel, the person but I don't want them here as Steve Seftel, the hockey player. I hope nobody shows up Sunday night for the return visit. It's a long night that seems to go on and on, and I just want it to end. I want out of Newmarket.

Post-game we drive to Rochester, N.Y. I wake up thinking there will be no pressure tonight because nobody will be here to watch. Saturday night against the Americans I'm back in the lineup. Of course. That's part of the ups and downs, and growth for rookies. Post-game we drive back across the border to Newmarket. I'm in the lineup Sunday night against the Saints. Being a healthy scratch is part of the learning curve as a pro player, and it sucks!

Penalty Shot

The team returns to Maryland and practices downtown. I shoot my mouth off with one of the vets this morning. I sense he's bitter and realize that perhaps I've crossed a rookie redline. I can see animated, bitchy rumblings amongst the veterans.

At the end of practice, I'm walking on eggshells as I make the long hike to the dressing room. I begin to take my gear off but my senses are on high alert. I'd be lying if I said I wasn't nervous about what I envision is coming next. Yep, here it comes. I'm escorted out to a quiet area, and carefully shaved in all the appropriate places. I only hope the boys have steady hands. The hair on my head remains, but that's about it. My rookie initiation is unceremoniously complete.

Thanksgiving in Canada takes place during the month of October. It was a special day for me growing up because the annual K-W Oktoberfest Thanksgiving Day parade takes place on the holiday Monday. Every fall, we parked at my grandparents' home and walked to King St. to view the big, two-hour parade.

In the United States, Thanksgiving takes place on the fourth Thursday in November and starts with the televised Macy's Thanksgiving Day parade from New York City. Adding to my obsession with this holiday is the generosity of the people. Americans know how to throw a party and celebrate. My first Thanksgiving in the minors, I'm invited to the home of one of the Skipjacks' team doctors to join him and his wife and two children. I accept the invitation and feel grateful for their hospitality and company.

Thanksgiving in the U.S. also includes one of my other passions – football. Watching football all day before eating a feast fit for a king is a slice of heaven to me. My new friends have this holiday right. Year after year I will enthusiastically celebrate American Thanksgiving, and still do today. My Canadian family and friends look at me sideways when I get excited about Thanksgiving in November. Thanksgiving twice a year? Why not?

Back to the ice. The Skipjacks have a mediocre first three months of the season in the win-loss column. I've had a less than spectacular start. It's a difficult first half for me and I find myself in and out of the lineup. The pro hockey road has been bumpy so far. I have to keep working hard, stay healthy and keep improving.

Struggling on many days with anxiety, the pressure to perform can get the best of me. Before and after hockey games I'm in knots. I feel like I'm being chased by a tiger. I'm in constant combat with my inner voice. Never mind, shut that voice up now. I have to focus. Remember the mantra, eat the pain! It may not be a good mantra but it's the only one I know.

Christmas break is short in pro hockey, therefore, it's difficult to visit family or travel too far. Typically, we get December 24th and 25th off. This December we play in Utica, N.Y. vs the Devils on the 23rd and then at home versus the Hershey Bears on the 26th. We usually play our closest opponent on the day after Christmas to limit travel time after the holidays.

Happy New Year! It's 1989 and in the month of January I'm earning extra ice time from Coach Murray. I've gained his confidence with my play recently, and he's giving me a regular shift. The season is long, and that's another lesson to learn. The junior hockey regular season is 66-games, while a professional one is 80-games.

Longer, tougher seasons, also mean more travel, and sleepless nights on buses. Sleeping on the bus is difficult. I place my head on the inner armrest under a pillow, and my legs lay on the headrest of the seat across the aisle. There is still poker at the back, euchre in the middle, movies on the small T.V. screens, and fast-food while we drive to the next city. The rigorous schedule is taxing on the body. Three-games-in-three-nights as we say and do or four-games-in-five-nights; it's a grind!

As the season wears on, I've shed weight, and become pale from the busy schedule. Entering the final game of the season on April 2nd in Glens Falls, N.Y. versus the Adirondack Red Wings, the Skipjacks are not in playoff contention. Tonight, we're trailing in the third period when an opposing defenceman intentionally closes his hand on the puck in the Wings' goal crease, and the referee signals for the appropriate call, a penalty shot. He shouts to the bench, "Need a shooter!" Coach Murray calls out my name for the pressure-filled penalty shot. I've never taken one before, and in the end, this will be both my first and only professional penalty shot. At this time in the sport, we still have ties folks; no shoot-outs yet!

I'm nervous as I hop the boards. I stand on the blue line with my stick on the ice. The referee places the puck on the dot at centre, takes his position, and blows his whistle. I've decided while waiting that I'm going to shoot, blocker side, over the pad. I want no indecision at the net.

I skate to the puck, and continue toward the goal. I cross the blue line and skate closer, making eye contact with the goalie as I skate in with my head up. At the hash marks, I dip my helmet, and make one strong move with the puck to the left. The goalie goes down. I fire an accurate wrist shot over his pad. The red light goes on; goal!

I raise my arms and let out a huge roar. Skating up the boards, I hand out high fives to the boys on the bench. When the final buzzer sounds, the season ends with a 7-6 road loss to the Red Wings.

After a rigorous schedule, the Skipjacks finish the season with a 30-46-4 record for 64 points, and miss the Calder Cup playoffs. I, along with a few others, are recalled by the Capitals to be a part of the taxi squad.

The taxi squad are boys added by the club to provide depth during the Cup run and to gain valuable big-league experience.

The Capitals finish first-place in the Patrick Division with an impressive 41-29-10 record for 92 points. However, they quickly lose their first-round best-of-seven playoff series to the Philadelphia Flyers 4-2 as the pesky Flyers avenge their Game Seven loss of a year ago. The season is over for the Capitals and Skipjacks. Back to the drawing board! But hey, now you know what a Skipjack is!

Is that the Hanson Brothers?

The Capitals are active on the trade market in 1989 as Mr. Poile deals fan favourite, and sharpshooter, Mike Gartner, along with high-scoring defenceman Larry Murphy, to the Minnesota North Stars in exchange for tenacious, goal-scoring winger Dino Ciccarelli, and steady, stay-at-home defensemen Bob Rouse. It is a high-profile blockbuster trade that sends shock waves through the organization.

On the coaching side of the ledger, Mr. Poile adds Regina-native Rob Laird as an assistant to Bryan Murray. A former Pittsburgh Penguins draft pick, Laird was the twice-named IHL (International Hockey League) coach-of-the-year previously guiding the Fort Wayne Komets.

At the 1989 Entry Draft, the Caps use their first and second-round picks to select highly-touted, future goaltenders Olaf Kolzig and Byron Dafoe. Incidentally, Olie the goalie's birthplace, is Johannesburg, South Africa, and he will play 714 NHL games. Byron Dafoe's birthplace is Sussex, England, and he will play 415 NHL games.

My rookie season is under my belt, making this my sophomore season. I have to be more prepared; bigger, stronger, and faster. I want to add weight to my lanky frame. Moving my summer workouts to Gold's Gym, I follow the Caps' rigorous training program, play summer hockey, and return to the guru of the blades, Brigitte, for power skating.

To promote growth, I ingest protein powder and eat, and eat, and eat. I need quicker, more nimble feet. Keeping that in mind, I work on agility drills, and complete sprinting routines at a local track. Squats, lunges, leg presses, leg extensions, and leg flexions; the results are easy to see. It surprises me to find expanding stretch marks appearing on my upper body as my muscle size increases.

My legs are lean; skinny some say. My back goes up when people call me skinny. I prefer the term lean. At the end of last season, I weighed 191-pounds. Today, as I prepare to leave for Capitals' training camp five months later, I'm popping out of my shirts, and my weight has ballooned to 214-pounds. Earlier this off-season I was tipping the scales at 218. I've never played hockey at this weight. It's heavy, but I like the idea of being big and strong.

Training camp for the Capitals will be a special one because the organization is taking the show on the road and will be touring Sweden and Russia. The plan is to have a portion of camp in Sweden, and then to conduct an exhibition-tour of Russia. Joining the team is the reigning Stanley Cup champion Calgary Flames. Each club will play four games against Soviet National League teams with contests scheduled in Moscow, Leningrad, Kiev and Riga.

Having said that, not every player attending training camp will make the long trip overseas. Mr. Poile and his coaching staff will take the Capitals' players, along with a group who are deemed to have a legitimate shot at making the big club. Since it's my sopho-more season, I want a shot at the trip and playing with the big boys against the Russians. In my heart, I believe my name is in the dis-cussion. Each September at camp, I analyze the organization's depth chart. Performing the mental math, I can easily see the deep competition for precious NHL jobs.

The training camp itinerary is communicated, and I discover my name is not on the Russia list. The news is disappointing. Staying home sends a clear message that I have more work to do. I need to become a more consistent two-way forward. I will remain in Maryland with the boys not going across the Atlantic. In their absence, we will participate in a mini-camp at the Columbia Arena. There are enough skaters for two teams; all young pros, free agents, and draft picks. Capitals' scout Barry Trotz will lead the on-ice activities. The former coach of the University of Manitoba men's hockey team cut his teeth in the Caps' organization, starting as a part-time scout, and moved up through the coaching ranks. Trotzy makes sure the remaining players toe the line while the Capitals are away.

It's an unusual camp with the Capitals' players and coaching staff absent. However, this is still a tryout, and surely notes on performances will be observed and communicated by the remain-ing coaches and staff. Trotzy reminds us of this important fact whenever the intensity level of scrimmages, or practices, doesn't meet his expectations.

Off-ice fitness testing is today and, feeling like I'm in peak physi-cal condition, I boldly march into the evaluation area. The first measuring stick of the day is the bench press – 175 pounds of free weight, pushing out as many repetitions as possible. I desperately want to improve my previous year's total, which was in the teens. I'm ready to show off my newfound strength, most notably, the 175-bench press.

A few eyebrows go up when the boys see my new larger size. One of them curiously looks at me and says, "Sef, you look bloated." "Did you just do curls all summer?" "No," I reply sharply. Bloated my ass? 'Not bloated, just big; 214-pounds big as a matter-of-fact.' I position myself on the flat bench, start throwing the barbell around, and push out twenty-eight reps of the steel bar and plates, smashing my previous mark. All my off-ice strength tests are much improved over last season.

Next up is the on-ice tests. We step on the ice, and I find I'm slow. Through the sprint tests, and endurance tests, I make no improvements. 'Shit!' Am I too heavy?' Whatever it is, I can't change it today.

Camp is long while we wait for the Capitals to return from Russia. Scrimmaging against the same guys day after day is getting stale. The hotel in Columbia is comfortable and a convenient two-minute drive from the rink. Let's go to the mall for lunch boys. My favourite spot has an awesome Philly cheesesteak sandwich with thinly-sliced pieces of beefsteak, melted cheese, and onions. The cheery guy on the counter always asks if I want hot peppers, and I answer, "No." He then turns around on cue, and shouts at the busy cook, "Hey José, steak and cheese, no hots!" I love hearing the call every time.

The well-travelled Capitals cross the Atlantic, returning from Russia. Mr. Poile whittles down the roster to a manageable number. We're split into two groups. After an underwhelming camp, I'm starting the season back in Baltimore. It's year two with the Skipjacks, and we're scheduled to play an exhibition game versus the Boston Bruins' AHL affiliate, the Maine Mariners. It's a home date for Maine but will be played at a neutral site, Johnstown, Pennsylvania, the home of the ECHL (East Coast Hockey League) team, the Johnstown Chiefs.

Many hockey fans will know that portions of the movie *Slap Shot* starring Paul Newman were filmed in Johnstown, Pennsylvania. In fact, the movie's fictitious team, the Charlestown Chiefs, used the city's Cambria County War Memorial Arena as their home. Numerous scenes from the iconic hockey movie were filmed in town, and at the old arena.

I'd seen the flick countless times; it's a staple for long bus rides, and even longer road trips. Laughter rings out whenever the famous hockey film is played on the VCR. The boys memorize lines from the cult classic, and shout them out on cue. Of course, any hockey fan who has seen the movie is familiar with the infamous trio of players known as the Hanson Brothers. The notorious Hanson's play old-time, Eddie Shore hockey, and accompanying fisticuffs against the likes of Ogie Ogilthorpe, Tim "Dr. Hook" McCracken, Ross "Mad Dog" Madison, and Clarence "Screaming Buffalo" Swamptown.

When our boys enter the barn in Johnstown, I scope out the concourse. In my mind's eye I can see Paul Newman as Reg Dunlop in his brown leather jacket and gaudy matching pants. The old building is just like I remember in the movie, and I soak up the vibe in the War Memorial.

Warm-up begins and we walk down the short tunnel to the ice surface. The crowd starts to fill the rink. Perhaps it's the mystique of the movie or the thought of Ogie Ogilthorpe suiting up for the Mariners, but the energy in the rink is as ramped up as any game I've ever played.

After warm-up, we return to the dressing room, and receive last-minute instructions. Game time is here and we hit the ice for puck drop. I gaze around the rink. It's jammed with people all loud and enthusiastic. The arena is buzzing as the crowd rises for, *The Star-Spangled Banner.* I look down the bench for Reg Dunlop or Dave "Killer" Carlson. "Dave's a killer, Dave's a mess!" A classic line from the movie replays in my head.

The referee drops the puck to start us off, and the Mariners dump it into our zone. Our quick defenceman hustles back after the loose biscuit. A Maine forward crosses our blue line, barrelling in like a runaway locomotive. I can see the play developing from the bench; their aggressive forechecker wants to deliver a strong message with a huge hit. The message about to be delivered is, you guys are in for a long-ass night! Our d-man picks up the puck along the end boards, and is wallpapered by the crashing forward. The crowd roars with excitement. The message is delivered, and this competition is on.

Do up your chin straps boys, play hard, and keep your head on a swivel. The battle continues, and we fight for every square-inch of ice. The crowd hollers after every hit, and stands for each fight.

'You goon!' shouts a voice from our bench, and it's hard not to laugh out loud.

Thinking back, it was a lively, fun game to play, and gave us a story to tell friends down the road. Each future road trip when the movie *Slap Shot* is inserted into the VCR, I'll remember my one and only visit to the Cambria County War Memorial Arena. My only regret: I didn't get to meet Reg Dunlop, or the Hanson Brothers that night.

Guns, Drugs, or Pit Bulls

The Capitals open the new season on October 6th at home versus the Flyers. The Skipjacks' open the AHL season the same day on the road versus the N.Y. Islanders' affiliate, the Springfield Indians.

I'm off to a slow start, and trying to find my game that has gone missing. Days on the calendar are passing by, I'm goalless, and struggling to get on track. I'm determined to turn my fortunes around. There's all kinds of advice hockey players receive when play on the ice isn't going well: keep it simple, don't try to do too much, prepare better, back to basics, and so on. I need to do something. Finishing checks is a strength of mine; a way to contribute to the team when an offensive game is struggling.

A matchup versus the Utica Devils is scheduled today at our arena. Early in the game, a loose puck is along the boards to the left of the home bench. A Devils' player is digging at the biscuit, and I circle into the area. 'Finish your check, be physical to turn this shit around.' The internal message fires from my brain to the nerves and muscles in my legs, and upper body. I close in quick. I recklessly make contact, and my opponent is launched face first into the boards. It doesn't sound good and I hope it's better than I imagine. He's hit his face on the protruding ledge. Pushing and shoving ensues. The referee assesses me a five-minute major penalty, and one of the linesman escorts me off the ice. I'm out of this game, with a major infraction and a game misconduct.

Everything is a blur as I walk back to the dressing room past our home fans. Shaking, I sit down in my stall. I stand up, press my open palms into my head, bend at the waist, and grunt aloud, "Ahhh!" I begin pacing the empty Skipjacks' dressing room, like the caged black bears I watched as a boy at Waterloo Park, back and forth, back and forth.

Inside the training room, I can hear muffled voices while our team doctor is working on the Utica forward, and I ask our trainer how he's doing. He shakes his head, and tells me he's getting a lot of stitches, and has lost some teeth. "Fuck me," I reply. It's the first time I've inflicted this kind of damage on another player, and it leaves a pit in my stomach. Mentally, I'm replaying the split-second hit over and over, wishing I'd taken a different angle, or not hit him at all. Sinking like a stone into a deep, depressing hole, I feel shitty! My turbulent thoughts haunt me. It continues for days, more days, and turns into a twenty-five-game goalless streak; the type of streak I've never experienced in my hockey life.

Plunging mentally and making matters worse, my luck off the ice is no better. Due to my own procrastination, I resist putting Maryland license plates on my Firebird. I'm not going to do it plain and simple, and continue to drive the car with my Ontario tags.

Practice one quiet Sunday morning is downtown in the city. Driving with my roommate Steve Maltais beside me in the passenger seat, we travel north on I-95. It's early and the roadway is wide open so I drive faster to fill the open space. I continue to accelerate, and fly by a carefully covered state trooper. I catch a glimpse of the cruiser, and quickly press down on the brake pedal, holding my breath for a moment as I glance in the rearview mirror. The cruiser quickly pulls out, the lights on top of the vehicle churning and clearly visible. The trooper slowly closes the gap between us, and I pull the car over. I roll the window down as the burly trooper approaches and willingly cooperate as he asks for the pertinent documents. He walks slowly back to his car. "This sucks," I mutter to Malts.

After a few minutes, the grim-looking trooper approaches my window again. "Step out of the car please," he says sternly. Malts and I slide out of the vehicle, and stand side by side facing the Interstate. We glance at each other with that "now what" look. My Ontario license plates and driver's license have the testy trooper convinced we're delinquent Canadians in a rush to get home. The trooper looks at me with suspicious eyes and disapprovingly says, "When I see you Canadians heading back to the border at that rate of speed it makes me think you're smuggling guns, drugs, or pit bulls!"

What? I peer down at the dry ground, and think for a second, I don't own a dog, and I've never held a gun. I've held a joint but I'm not a drug smuggler. Okay, tell him the truth. Yes, tell him the truth. "No, no sir, we live here, we play hockey, for the Baltimore Skipjacks."

Hopefully that will smooth things over. The now puzzled trooper stares at us inquisitively; the "we play hockey" line is having little or no effect on him. He likely thinks hockey is the sport where Canadians hit each other over the head with sticks, and fight on slippery, icy surfaces. Or maybe he could care less about hockey and delinquent hockey players. "Wait here," he asserts and returns to his car.

He slowly walks back with a serious face, hands me two tickets, and a blunt explanation. He issues me a $40 speeding ticket, and a $250 ticket for driving with out-of-state license plates while being a resident.

Some time later, a security advisor gives the boys a presentation. He's an experienced lawman who leads a frank conversation on the perils that exist out on the streets. He provides guidance to young, easily influenced athletes. Players can be duped financially, hustled by questionable characters, or just plain fall into the wrong crowd. Opportunities to invest money come without warning or credibility. We listen to an informative discussion covering the pitfalls of alcohol and drugs, not to mention gambling, and in particular, gambling on sports, especially the one you play.

Once he has all ears tuned in, we listen to a presentation on the risks and hazards involved in drinking and driving, and then he suggests a demonstration. He asks for one volunteer to consume a few cans of beer in short order while he continues his lecture. Calmly he speaks and observes the goings on in the room as his volunteer drinks the provided pints. Once the beer is gone, he asks his student to indulge him in basic tests that will be performed if an individual is suspected of drinking and driving. I watch curiously as my teammate fails the sobriety tests miserably. "See what I mean? And never say, I just had a couple," he adds.

After a home game not long after, and with good feelings swelling in the room after our win, I hit the bar and have a few drinks. I leave the watering hole and walk to my car, then start down the highway in my Firebird to complete the thirty-minute drive to my apartment. I exit the highway and proceed into Columbia, past the mall, a mere half-mile from my destination. Suddenly, I see quickly approaching red flashing lights from a police car in my rearview mirror. Alarmed by the sight, I pull over slowly and stop. A police officer approaches on my left, and I lower the window. He tells me I have a burned out headlight. 'Shit.' "Have you had anything to drink tonight," he asks. "Just a couple," I say without thought. 'Fuck!' He proceeds to shine a light in, and says, "Step out the car please."

Now, his partner has joined in, and asks me to walk to the back of the vehicle. My heart is racing. I'm panicky. 'No, this can't be happening. Stupid headlight.' "Can you walk in a straight line heel-to-toe?" says the sullen officer. My body is shaking, and I struggle with the simple maneuver. Things are looking bleak. This can't be happening. How can I walk a straight line when I'm so nervous? "I'm really nervous," I implore to the two policemen. There is no response from the serious officers.

"Can you recite the alphabet?" he says. "Yes, I can." I do it. 'That was okay.' I did it, this should be good now. "We're going to have you blow into a breathalyzer," he says. 'What? 'No, no, I'm fine.' They escort me to the back of the cruiser, and I sit and wait. What have I done? I take a deep breath and bury my face in my sweaty hands. When asked, I blow slowly into the small unit. The officers step away. My heart is now pounding. 'What will I tell my family, the coaches, and the team? What if I'm charged? I'm screwed!' Agonizing minutes pass and they return. This is it! 'I'm fucked.' "You can go," one of them says. They say nothing else. I get out of the cruiser, slowly walk to my car, and drive two-minutes up the road to my apartment.

This is rock bottom and it's abundantly clear I have to change. The first three months of this hockey season I've been distracted, I'm drinking too much, I'm too heavy, I'm not taking care of my body, and I'm not focused on hockey. Learning hard lessons and admitting to myself that I need to change is a step. This season had promise, and it's by no means over.

My mind is a train wreck! I need to think, and make changes before I buckle under my self-inflicted pressure cooker. I need to repair myself because my hockey career depends on it. Keep it simple: the four Ds – desire, dedication, determination, discipline. Perhaps there is a light at the end of the tunnel that will allow me to salvage this season.

Musical Coaches

Fortunes can change in a heartbeat in the sporting world, including hockey. Look at the story of New York Yankees' first baseman Wally Pipp. He told Yankees' manager Miller Huggins he was suffering from a headache and couldn't start, so Huggins replaced him with Lou Gehrig. Gehrig, nicknamed, "The Iron Horse," didn't miss a game for almost 15 years and 2,130 straight ball games.

I've had my share of troubles over the last few months and I'm suffering from a crisis of confidence. Honest soul searching has me hungry to prove myself as a hockey player. I need a jump-start. I need a goal! My fortune turns around one night in December in Halifax. Bursting up the ice, I drive the net on my wrong wing, and a semi-breakaway. A Citadels' defender closes in on me. I protect the puck, lean towards the net, make a quick move, and tuck it between the goalie's legs. I look skyward, realizing the puck has crossed the goal line, and my goalless drought is finally snapped. It truly feels like the weight of the world has been lifted off my shoulders, providing a moment of maximum relief. One step forward, a fresh start; it has to be. That single goal against the Citadels helps me rediscover my scoring touch and lost confidence.

Events off the ice turn January 1990 upside down. The Skipjacks are playing well under Coach Murray. Terry has guided the well-balanced team to a 26-17-2 record through the first 45 games of the schedule. Our talent-rich, character-filled unit is led offensively by a potent one-two punch: gifted puckhandler Mike Richard – we call him Rocket due to his prolific scoring and playmaking ability; and former Montréal Canadiens' first-round draft pick, Alfie Turcotte, who has both speed to burn and an equally quick stick. Added to the mix is a trio of talented rookie forwards: lamp-lighting Steve Maltais; hardworking centre Tim Taylor; and the soft, skilled hands of John Purves. Montréal-native Jim Hrivnak is solid in goal along with savvy veteran Bob Mason. The deep defensive unit is the real strength of the crew and provides a tonne of leadership, loaded as it is with skill, and players who can skate for miles: Chris Felix, Mark Ferner, Dennis Smith, Alain Cote, Brian Tutt, Kent Paynter, and defensive stalwart Billy Houlder.

Change strikes like a bolt of lightning in the organization, and a startling game of musical coaches commences. Mr. Poile fires long serving coach Bryan Murray, (who had been the Capitals' head coach since 1981.) He's replaced by his brother Terry. I'm sure this will make for interesting dinner conversation at future Murray family events! We're on the road in Newmarket when the news breaks. Terry is scrambling around the modest Ontario rink as the announcement sinks in. He has no time to waste, and disappears, on his way back to the capital city to start his new position.

I'm happy for Terry, getting his first shot at a head coaching position in the NHL. Not unlike the players in the minors, coaches are also looking to move up to the next level. Terry is an intelligent hockey man, and a detailed coach. A draft pick of the California

Golden Seals in 1970, and a veteran of 302 NHL games, at times in practice he looks like he can still play. Leaving us in Newmarket, he looks prepared and focused for his opportunity in the National Hockey League. Meanwhile, the Skipjacks need a coach to fill the void left by his departure. The game of musical coaches continues, and Mr. Poile assigns Capitals' assistant coach Doug MacLean the coaching responsibilities in Baltimore for the remainder of the season.

This dizzying turn of events cause ripples throughout the organization. The wild card for me, and the Skipjacks, is Doug MacLean. The Prince Edward Island native with a master's degree in educational psychology is a breath of fresh air, and exactly what I need to keep myself on point. A new start with a new coach; a clean slate. It's time to reset, and earn his trust.

Coach MacLean is a players' coach who is approachable. Mac, as we call him, possesses a great sense of humour, accompanied by an infectious laugh that I never tire of. I enjoy when the boys tell him jokes so I can hear his exuberant laugh that dissolves any stress building in my head. Beyond the humour, we know that when it comes time to work, Mac knows how to put his game face on, and prepare us to play inspired hockey. Speaking with a reassuring voice of confidence, he makes me believe in myself. A passionate hockey man who knows how to get the most out of his players, I love playing for him! He's a coach I will run through walls for. On his watch, my game is turning around through hard work, and determined play. Earning his trust on the ice leads to valuable shifts. The timing is perfect as my first-half slump is replaced by on-ice success, and confidence in me from Mac.

In the winter of 1990, I make another significant decision and purchase an engagement ring for my best friend Lisa. Through word of mouth, I discover a jeweller in New York City who sells wedding engagement rings to pro hockey players. Boys on the team have purchased from him. I inquire around the dressing room, and I'm able to find the phone number of the ring whisperer in the Big Apple.

I phone him, and explain the size, colour, and clarity of diamond I want. He promptly sends me three rings via registered mail, and

I choose the one that best suits what I'm looking for. I return the others, along with a personal cheque. It so easy!

My plan is to give Lisa the ring at Toby's Dinner Theatre in Columbia. She flies down to Maryland to visit and I purchase two tickets to *It's a Wonderful Life*, the Jimmy Stewart classic. The ring sits tucked in my sock until I can muster the nerve to pop the question. Why in my sock? I don't really know but it is an obsessive-compulsive thing. I finally ask, she says, "Yes," and we're engaged.

Rejuvenated and reestablishing myself with newly fashioned determination, I'm thriving under Mac, and this leads to more ice time, and responsibility. On the road again, and with Coach MacLean behind our bench, the boys prepare to play the Sherbrooke Canadiens at the Montréal Forum. It's a thrill to skate on this historic sheet of ice, and I can't help but look around for the storied ghosts of the Forum. I stare at the banners marking Stanley Cup victories, and retired jerseys, marveling at the history now as much as I had when I was here earlier in my career on draft day. A modest Montréal crowd watches today as a late goal by Sherbrooke breaks a 1-1 tie and we lose a nail-biting 2-1 game to the Northern Division leaders, led by Mark Pederson and Benoit Brunet.

The Skipjacks finish the regular season with a 5-2 win over the rival Hershey Bears. Mac guides us to a 17-13-5 record down the stretch, and we finish third in the Southern Division and only two points out of first. The Rochester Americans finish in top spot, led by forwards Mike Donnelly and Donald Audette. Can our talented lineup win a Calder Cup? It's been a long time since I've hoisted a championship trophy.

The upbeat, confident finish sets up a first-round playoff series with the defending Calder Cup champion Adirondack Red Wings and a post-season encounter between future NHL coaches Doug MacLean and Barry Melrose. The teams are separated by a razor-thin two points in the final league standings. Hockey pundits consider the Skipjacks underdogs entering the series. Adirondack is led by the silky passing of centre Murray Eaves, and the timely goal scoring of Dale Krentz.

I used the last thirty-five games to earn Coach MacLean's trust and have managed to turn my hockey season around. Entering the best-of-seven series, I'm skating on a line with rangy, veteran centre Doug Wickenheiser, and hardworking, physical right-winger Robin Bawa. Wick was the first-overall pick of the 1980 draft by the Montréal Canadiens and played 556 NHL games. Robin Bawa played 61 NHL games. Entering the series, we're the designated shutdown line, and Mac gives us the task of keeping the Eaves line off the scoreboard. Couple that with our two scoring lines, and we believe in ourselves.

The squads split Game 1 and Game 2 in Glens Falls, N.Y. We win Game Three at home 5-1, before the Wings deliver a Game Four overtime dagger, and we lose 5-4. Responding in Game Five on the road, we double up the home team 6-3, setting up a date in Baltimore to clinch the bitter series.

The local hockey fans are hungry for a series win; they haven't tasted a playoff victory since 1985. The home troopers come out flying in front of an electric home crowd at the arena. As expected, this crucial battle is full of piss and vinegar, and is a chippy affair. The intense game is heating up and about to boil over when Adirondack coach Barry Melrose engages in a fiery discussion with Mac through the wobbly pane of glass separating the benches. Angry as hornets, the verbal jousting between the coaches is full of barbs and salty playoff language, as is expected in a hard-fought series. The exchange causes the skaters on both sides, and the Skipjacks' fans, to join in the shouting. Our passionate fans bang on the glass separating them from the Wings' bench boss, attempting to further infuriate the seething Adirondack coach. An angry Melrose pounds with his fist on the glass partition separating the two teams, dislodging it, while he continues to berate our coach. Mac, never at a loss for words, gives it right back as our animated fans continue to holler. Cooler heads prevail, Melrose is given a game misconduct, and tossed out by referee Lance Roberts.

A desperate Red Wings' club press hard to even the score but the minutes tick down on the board above centre ice. The final buzzer sounds and the series is clinched with a 5-3 victory, propelling the

Skipjack faithful into another hockey orbit. After the game, Coach MacLean heaps praise on his boys, and my line, which he calls his checking line. "Seftel, Bawa and Wickenheiser totally shut down the Eaves line. That was the key to the series," Mac said to Hockey News reporters Mike Kane and Bill Picket.

After a thrilling series, the semi-finals are up, and a date with the Rochester Americans, the Buffalo Sabres' affiliate. Here we go! The Amerks win Game One and Game Two at home. The parent Capitals recall truculent winger Nick Kypreos. The energetic, power forward plays a heavy, physical game. Kyper's energy is contagious and his absence will leave a hole in the lineup, meaning the boys will have to step up.

We bounce back winning Game Three and Game Four at home. The series is tied two games apiece, setting up a crucial Game Five back in Rochester. Meanwhile, in the Stanley Cup playoffs, after defeating the New Jersey Devils 4-2 in the best-of-seven first-round series, the Capitals are playing the New York Rangers in the next round.

In the last game with New York, Capitals' tough left-winger Alan May suffered a leg injury, and is expected to miss the next game at home. The team is finishing practice at the arena prior to Game Five, and the eight-hour bus ride to Western New York. After practice, I return to the room and have a seat in my stall. Mac calls out. He wants to see me in his office. He tells me to have a seat, and I do. He says I'm going to Washington. "You've been recalled by the Capitals for tomorrow's playoff game." I'm beside myself with the news. The hard work I put in over the last few months has paid off, and the Caps have noticed. I haven't even played an NHL game, and my first action will be a Stanley Cup playoff game vs the Rangers at the Capital Centre. The boys load the bus and drive to Rochester since they play tomorrow too. I drive back to my apartment and phone home with the news. "Is the Capitals-Rangers series on *Hockey Night in Canada*?" I ask.

Game day: the Stanley Cup playoffs. I arrive early for the morning skate, park my car in the enormous lot surrounding the arena, walk down the ramp at the back of the rink, open the door, move into the Zamboni area, and turn right to the dressing room. I've walked this route before but there's an eerie calm in the silent arena before the Stanley Cup storm.

I enter the dressing room and stop to chat with a few of the former Skipjacks, Tim Bergland, Nick Kypreos, Rob Murray, and John Druce. Drucer has sweet hands, accompanied by an accurate shot. The former captain of the Skipjacks is on fire these days, inspiring local media and fans to coin the catch phrase, 'Druce on the loose.'

I inspect the room, looking for my stall. Captain Rod Langway walks by. The six-foot-three, 220-pound physically imposing, quintessential d-man oozes charisma. He's the master of defensive body position and one of the last players in the league to play without a helmet. There's Dale Hunter, Scott Stevens, and Mike Liut. This is the real deal!

Players are getting treatment from the trainers due to battles won and lost in previous games. Others are in the stick room heating up their blades, enjoying playoff banter, and a big dip. I change into my Bauer blues and dress to my waist. I look at the clock on the wall over and over and it appears the minute hand is barely moving.

It's go time and I walk to the surface. I step onto the white ice and Coach Murray passes by, greeting me with a hello. "I've heard good things about your play Steve," he says as he glides by. It feels good to hear those words from Terry. He blows his whistle and leads the enthusiastic group through a crisp, short morning skate.

I'm nervous, but bloody excited! I hit rock bottom earlier this season, and now I'm skating with the Capitals, preparing for a Stanley Cup playoff game. With hard work and focus, fortunes can change fast. There are so many ups and downs on this journey. At the end of the skate, I'm able to determine that Al May, whom I'm replacing, is now a game-time decision. Therefore, my appearance tonight is tenuous at best. I stay on the ice until all the players leave, and peer around the empty arena.

Both the Caps and Jacks have important games tonight. I step off the ice, and walk to the dressing room. Coach Murray asks to see me. Okay here it comes. He calmly explains that Al May is going to play, and therefore, they have decided to fly me up to Rochester to play for the Skipjacks. "They can use you," he says. Truthfully, I want him to say, 'You're playing tonight Sef or you can stay here tonight, and perhaps we will need you later in the series.'

I want this bad! I was so achingly close to playing tonight. Now that I'm in "The Show", I never want to leave. The Show is a slang term guys in the minors and junior use when referring to playing in the NHL. As a result of the last-minute change, I hustle to undress and shower. A Capitals' staffer drives me to Baltimore-Washington International Airport for a flight to Roch. I arrive about 3:30 p.m. and take a cab to the hotel.

At the Greater Rochester International Airport, I pick up the local paper, the Democrat and Chronicle. I search the sports page, find an article about tonight's all-important Game Five with the Americans, and receive an instant energy boost as I read my name. The article, written by Kevin Oklobzija, says: "Baltimore meanwhile, was weakened as the Capitals recalled Hrivnak and gritty two-way winger Steve Seftel. Seftel may return today because Alan May (leg cramps) is expected to play for Washington tonight."

I feel poised and energized entering tonight's critical game. Having said that, the game day routine is shot, and I need a pregame meal. Arriving at the hotel, I walk over to a nearby restaurant to scarf down a quick dinner and meet the bus out front. We have a big tilt to play tonight.

The arena is hopping, and the crowd is noisy. The Americans skate on the ice to the song *Freeze Frame* by the J. Geils Band, and it always gets me fired up. The puck drops and the game is fast. I play loose and score a goal to keep it close. The troops battle hard tonight, in the end suffering a gut-wrenching 5-4 overtime loss in the pivotal fifth game. Back home we go. The next game is three days away on Saturday afternoon.

Playing messy defensively, we give the speedy Amerks the wide-open hockey they're looking for in Game Six. We come up short losing 8-5, giving Rochester the series-clinching win. Meanwhile, the Capitals defeat the New York Rangers 4-1 in their best-of-seven-series. This marks the first time the Capitals emerge from the battle-hardened Patrick Division and move on to the semi-finals, against the Boston Bruins.

Before locker clean out finishes at the arena, I learn from Mac that I, and a few of the guys, have been recalled by the Capitals. We will join the team for the Stanley Cup playoff push. As I daydream about the past few months, I think about the New York Yankees' Wally Pipp, Lou Gehrig and how quickly your sports career can change.

Catching a Cab with Grapes

Don Cherry was born in Kingston, Ontario in 1934. He is a true Canadian-hockey icon. The graduate of the OHA's Barrie Flyers had a lengthy professional playing career including stops with the famed Hershey Bears, Springfield Indians, and Rochester Americans. During the 1971-72 season, he was hired by his former club in Rochester as head coach. After leading the Amerks for three seasons, he was signed on as head coach of the Boston Bruins to start the 1974-75 season. Following time spent with his big, bad Bruins teams, he finished his coaching career in 1979-80 with the Colorado Rockies. The, tell-it-like-it-is storyteller is a staunch supporter of Canada, its amazing people, Canadian hockey, and its amazing players.

The taxi squad and I report to practice at the Capital Centre. I had an opportunity last season to experience life with the "Black Aces", as Don Cherry calls us ready-for-battle depth players. The band of extra hockey soldiers practice, travel, eat, and if needed, dress and play for the team. In case of injury, suspension, and the like, we're here to add support in the gruelling Stanley Cup marathon.

The Prince of Wales Conference final series starts in the warming month of May. Games One and Game Two are in Beantown at the historic Boston Garden. The Campbell Conference final sees the Edmonton Oilers hosting the Chicago Blackhawks at the Northlands Coliseum. With only four teams left in the race, we're well aware that one of these clubs will hoist the Cup.

Flying out to the passionate city of Boston, we arrive at Logan International Airport. The boys settle into our downtown hotel, where I'm rooming with Malts. The busy Massachusetts city is a great sports town – Celtics, Red Sox, Patriots, and Bruins. I'm eager to see this final-four series get underway.

The Capitals and the taxi squad take the morning skate at the Garden in advance of Game One. Skating around the ice at Coach Murray's lead, I spot the *Hockey Night in Canada* crew quietly standing on the bench observing our spirited practice. I glance out of the corner of my eye each time I pass by to catch a glimpse of Bob Cole as he intently watches the on-ice activities. This is the big time! I've watched Mr. Cole on T.V. Saturday nights, and now the famous Canadian play-by-play man is standing right in front of me. Where's Don Cherry and Ron MacLean? Grapes talks about the taxi squad on *Coach's Corner*. Maybe he'll mention us tonight during his segment on CBC.

The visitor's dressing room at the Garden is plain and nothing resembling today's palatial standards. The Caps have the main room in the old barn, and the taxi squad has the smaller, tight space in back. After the skate, we return to the hotel in order to refuel with a pre-game meal that is fit for kings, or hockey players in pursuit of hockey's Holy Grail.

With stomachs now full, the troopers begin to disperse, returning to quiet hotel rooms for pre-game naps. Even though I'm not playing, I go through my regular routine: Attempt to sleep, up around 3 p.m., dress, and down into the lobby.

Malts and I stroll out of the hotel, and attempt to wave down a cab for a ride to the Garden. Attentively looking out at the busy street, I sense the front door of the comfortable hotel opening behind me. I hear faint footsteps and all of a sudden, a familiar sounding voice, "C'mon boys, let's get a cab!" We turn around and it's Don Cherry! It's Mr. Cherry! It's Grapes! He's making his way down to the Garden as well. The famous Original Six arena is another home for him. Grapes flags down a cab, and the three of us pile into the back seat. I can't believe it; Don Cherry!

I stare and listen closely to him for the entire ride. He tells us candid story after story, and we don't get a word in edgewise. We just nod a lot, agree, and laugh. I mean, he's the master storyteller and an outing like this may never happen again. The cab arrives. Grapes keenly says, "I know how much you guys make in the minors. I'll pay for this one!" Nice! Again, we nod and agree. "Thanks," I call out. With that, we three hockey brethren walk into the famous rink together, Mr. Cherry walking one way as we step towards the dressing room. What an amazing chance meeting! I will listen to Don Cherry many Saturday nights in the future on *Hockey Night in Canada* and always fondly remember the cab ride with him to the famed Boston Garden.

Chatting prior to Game One of the series, and spending a chunk of time in the media room, the taxi squad has Jack's ear. Quizzing him about hockey and draft prospects, he speaks about a generational-type player, an offensively-skilled player and physical specimen who is projected to be a star in the NHL. The up-and-coming new kid's name is Eric Lindros and he plays for the Oshawa Generals. "Is he as good as they say?" I ask Jack curiously. He calmly nods an affirming yes. As a matter of fact, Eric Lindros will be the first-overall pick of the 1991 NHL Entry Draft by the Québec Nordiques and play 760 games while collecting 372 goals, 493 assists and 865 points.

On the ice, the Capitals drop the first two games with the Bruins by scores of 5-3 and 3-0. Post-game we bus to the airport, and take a charter flight back to D.C. I stretch out in a quiet row of the plane. We eat and talk about the other ongoing series. In the Campbell Conference, the Blackhawks and Oilers split the first two games and are knotted at one game apiece.

Returning to Washington for Games Three and Four, there is a feeling of desperation in the air with the Caps down two games to none. The noisy home crowd isn't enough, and the boys drop the next two fast-paced games by scores of 4-1 and 3-2. The tight-checking series is a sweep for the Bruins, and the Stanley Cup dream ends again for all of us. For selfish reasons, I'm disappointed. I'd watched in the past as taxi squad players hoisted the Cup. Even though I haven't been with the Caps for the season, I'm here now, and we're four wins away from playing in the championship series.

In the end, the Edmonton Oilers defeat the Boston Bruins in five games, and win the Stanley Cup. For the Oilers, it's their fifth championship in seven years, and their only one without Wayne Gretzky, who was traded on August 9, 1988 to the Los Angeles Kings.

The players clean out their lockers after the season-ending loss and prepare to start the off-season. Exit meetings – much like a review and planning session – take place with Mr. Poile. These meetings offer a one-on-one opportunity to speak with the GM directly about where he thinks you are as a player, and where he expects you to be in September. The meeting I have is positive, but it's the last words he says to me that ring in my ears. "I want you to do whatever you have to do to get prepared for next season because you're going to have an opportunity to make this team."

Is that a Pelican?

I'm beaming and have an extra bounce in my step as I walk to my car after my sit-down meeting with Mr. Poile. He wants to see me back in D.C. next season looking like an NHL-ready player. Okay, let's go!

Rushing back to our two-bedroom apartment, it's noontime. The plan is leave for home first thing in the morning. The boys are ready to go their separate ways for the summer months. It's a pleasant 75-degrees outside, and people are out soaking up the Maryland sun. We hook up at the apartment, go out for a lazy dinner, get back, hang out, and clean up. Spring days are getting longer, and we sit around exchanging stories about the season that was.

The sun is setting and it's getting darker. Continuing to talk, it is now 11 p.m. and we're all wide awake when one of the eager fellas says, "Why don't we just leave now?" Looking at each other, we nod in unison. "Let's do it, let's go!" The decision is made; we're leaving. Scrambling about, we recognize there is one problem: we haven't packed our cars. Getter done fellas! Up and down the stairs to and from our third-floor apartment we rush. Packing our vehicles to the brim takes about one-hour and though my enthusiasm to leave fades, it is strong enough to get me and the others into our automobiles.

Now we're closing in on midnight. Despite the time, we depart in our convoy, barking, and howling like a pack of excited wolves. The thunderous music in my Firebird picks up my spirits. I'm tired, but whatever. Let's go home! Canadian border here I come! Speeding up I-95 N, traffic is light, and our roaring cars get to the city limit where half of the convoy continues on, north towards Montréal. I honk as I peel off, following Malts to I-83 N headed for Harrisburg, Pennsylvania.

The highway is familiar. We cross the Maryland State Line. Arriving in Harrisburg in a flash, we cross the bridge over the Susquehanna River. The capital city of the State of Pennsylvania is not a big place, but Harrisburg looks similar to many blue-collar communities in the Keystone State. Ninety-minutes into the drive, we're a short distance away from the chocolate capital of the world, Hershey, PA.

Malts and I merge onto I-81 N, knowing that the Canadian border will appear in about seven-hours when the highway conveniently ends at the Thousand Islands Bridge. Now, at 1:30 a.m., the energy I experienced departing Columbia has left my body, and I'm fading fast. Aside from a few transport trucks, the Interstate is empty, quiet, and dark. To my left, I can see an outline of the Blue Mountain Ridge in the Appalachians. The mountains surround us for a period of time as we move closer to the New York State border, however, that will be a few hours yet.

The darkness makes my eyes heavy. I focus on Malts' red taillights. Minutes pass by the dozens, and the humming V-8 engine of my Firebird places my mind in a trance. I hit the seek button on the radio, and it scans the Cumberland Valley for any signs of musical life. It stops, but I don't like the song so I let it continue until I hear a tune that makes my toes tap. Raising the radio's decibel level, I increase the bass, and the car's interior vibrates. Roll the window down, I say with my inside sensible voice. A few songs pass, and then the music acts as a mild sedative. My eyes are heavy, and I want to close them and sleep. 120-km, 125-km, 130-km, 135-km... Maybe drive faster, and arrive faster. I pass Malts and take the lead for a while to mix up the monotony. He passes me again, and we start a decent into the valley ahead. I'm tired, I'm so tired, and I'm, zzz!

My subconscious self-nudges my insides, or maybe a guardian angel named Jerome gives me a poke. My eyes quickly spring open, and I see a large bird in the middle of the Interstate. A pelican! It's a pelican! I instantly slam on the brake pedal, and thrust the clutch of the Firebird to the floor while desperately reaching for the manual stick shift. 'A pelican! Is that a pelican?' 'Is that a fucking pelican? Can't be. You fell asleep, snap out of it.'

I slow down, and cruise in the right lane as I regain my composure, and wait for my heart to settle back into my chest, because it's firmly lodged in my narrowing throat. I look in my rearview mirror for any signs of a pelican. Peeling my white knuckles off the steering wheel one at a time, I try to clear the cobwebs and settle my firing nerves.

The light of day starts to inch up on the distant horizon, and helps my weary mind. About 5 a.m. we arrive in Binghamton, N.Y. I flash Malts, and we stop for gas and breakfast. We need to rest. "That seemed like a good idea when we left," I chirp. Malts laughs and gives me a smile, the kind of smile that says, 'what were we thinking?' He doesn't have to say it; I can see it on his fatigued face. I tell him my story about the creepy pelican, and we share a laugh that turns into tired giggles, the kind of giggling that develops because we're giddy from exhaustion, and wondering why we agreed to leave at midnight.

Once we finish breakfast, the sun is up and the Canadian border is only three-hours away. We exit Bingo, and merge back onto I-81

N. Rejuvenated by food and light, the fatigue is gone. The drive through New York State leading to Syracuse is quiet, and lightly travelled. We cross over the Thousand Islands Bridge, hit the border and clear Canadian customs.

The cool air smells cleaner in the Great White North. Crossing into Canada always feels good for my spirit. I lower my window, and wave to Malts as he hits the 401 E headed for a stop in his former junior stomping grounds, Cornwall, Ontario while I merge onto the 401 W. I reach Kingston, and visit my old billets Larry and Janice Moran. It's finally time to sleep. As I drift off, and with an entire summer to prepare, I think about Mr. Poile's words to me in my exit meeting. Showtime baby!

Lake Placid

In the summer of 1990, a compelling transaction takes place in the Capitals' ranks. After eight-seasons in Washington, all-star defenceman Scott Stevens, a restricted free agent, is moving on. The dominating, versatile leader is offered a contract by the St. Louis Blues. As a restricted free agent, the Capitals have the choice to match the offer tabled by the Missouri team in order to keep him in D.C. but Mr. Poile chooses not to match, instead settling for the compensation owed for the signing of the coveted veteran blueliner.

In other moves, the Capitals make adjustments to the coaching staff. Coach Terry Murray is joined by new assistant, John Perpich, the former coach at Ferris State University. Former Capitals' bench-boss Bryan Murray finds a new home as the Detroit Red Wings' coach and GM. Popular Skipjacks' coach Doug MacLean departs the organization and joins Bryan in Detroit as an assistant. I learned a lot from Mac, and, maybe more important, he helped me relax, and put fun back in hockey. With Mac gone to Detroit, Rob Laird is assigned by Mr. Poile as head coach in Baltimore. His assistant will be Winnipeg-native and former member of the WHL's Regina Pats, Barry Trotz, who sets aside his scouting role to become a coach in the professional ranks.

I receive an end-of-summer phone call from Jack. He says the Capitals need a few players to instruct at their hockey school prior to the start of training camp. The Caps will provide hotel accommodations, and I'll earn $500 US per week. Jack informs me that he has also invited Malts, and he's accepted. I enjoy teaching hockey schools so this seems like a reasonable plan. Once the hockey school is completed, training camp will begin.

After winning their first Patrick Division championship, last spring, the Capitals kick off the 1990-91 season in Lake Placid, N.Y., a timeless hockey locale, and the site of the famous "Miracle on Ice", a men's medal-round game played during the 1980 Winter Olympics.

In the first game of the medal round, the upstart Americans were matched up against the highly skilled Soviets. Trailing 3-2 entering the third period, the scrappy U.S. team scored two unanswered goals to take the lead, winning 4-3, and stunning the shocked Soviet squad and the hockey world. Following the game, the U.S. went on to clinch the gold medal by defeating Finland in their final game of the tournament.

The victory became one of the most iconic moments in hockey history. Equally historic was the television call of the final seconds by legendary sportscaster Al Michaels. He famously declared, "Do you believe in miracles? Yes!"

Well, Lake Placid is the perfect backdrop for training camp. Last spring Mr. Poile gave me his endorsement, and challenged me to get it done and make the Washington Capitals. This is my third-year of pro hockey. Feeling more mature, and ready to make a statement, there are higher expectations bearing down on my shoulder as camp begins.

Players report for physicals in D.C. Once the medicals, routine paperwork, and housecleaning are complete, the team, coaches, and trainers board a plane for Lake Placid. All training camp activities will take place at the Olympic Arena facilities in the village.

Arriving in Lake Placid, I discover it's a small, quiet town. The community is situated on a lake of the same name, and in New York State's picturesque Adirondack Mountains. Many shops, restaurants, and old hotels are located along the main drag. Here, a car isn't necessary; everything is within walking distance. The remnants of the 1980 Winter Olympics are visible, including the enormous ski jumping hill, and the nearby arena.

Camp starts and I feel prepared, ready, and in a good place mentally. Scrimmages, on and off-ice fitness testing are right on track, and I feel fast and strong. 'Keep it going, one day at a time, I can do this.'

Between scrimmages, skate and stick reps make the annual visits to secure agreements with players to use their products. I'm a committed Bauer skate and Koho hockey stick client. I listen to the reps from the other companies as they try to promote the advantages of their products. I order a stick pattern from the Victoriaville rep, and a pair of Daoust skates. However, in the end I stay loyal to my preferred brands.

After tough scrimmages today, a group of us leave the rink, and walk to a nearby restaurant for lunch. Beside the rink is an old, concrete track, and I see Capitals' larger-than-life captain Rod Langway doing laps wearing his newly fashioned rollerblades. I watch Rod when I can during camp. He commands respect. His self-confident presence and leadership qualities leave an impression on me and I learn by observing the esteemed veteran blueliner. Needless to say, I'm impressed by the extra work being done by the Capitals' grinding leader.

The boys are enjoying a hot tub in the hotel after dinner tonight. We'll hit a movie later on, in the only theatre in town. The Capitals' pre-season schedule is starting, and I nervously wait for the line-ups to be posted in the lobby. The first two games on the schedule will be against the New York Rangers: September 14th at the

Baltimore Arena, and the next night in Albany N.Y. The lineups go up and I see I'm scheduled to play both. I have to make the most of this opportunity. It's time to make an impression on Mr. Poile and Coach Murray.

We depart the Lake Placid Regional Airport on a flight to Baltimore. Arriving at BWI, the team loads the bus and rides toward the Inner Harbor. Checking in to our downtown hotel, we discover it's a short, familiar walk to the arena.

Game time is here. The puck drops. The pace is fast, up and down the ice. I rip a shot on goal, but not a dangerous one. 'Giveaway, ah shit!' I return to the bench, and from behind me I hear, "C'mon Sef, you gotta make the safe play there. Coach is right and I know it. I have to be better next shift. The game flies by: 5-4-3-2-1, the buzzer sounds, and it's over. The team gathers around our goaltender, and we walk back to the room. I sit down, and replay many of the shifts in my mind. Shit, not enough tonight. Tomorrow I have to be better!

Post-game, I find food to eat, and return to the hotel. We fly to Albany the next morning for back-to-back games versus the Rangers. I'm feeling more pressure as puck drop approaches. There are only so many chances to impress Mr. Poile and the coaching staff when you're trying to crack the lineup, and take a veteran's NHL job away.

The puck drops in Albany. I fly around the ice, hitting my maximum speed. I'm looking to make a statement. Streaking across the Rangers' blue line, I have a big hit in my sights. Their defenceman is skating towards me. I come in square for a massive collision, and at the last moment, my wiry opponent senses my presence, makes a quick dodge, and I only get a piece. Once again, the tempo is fast, passes are hard, and on the tape. The game moves faster at this level. Good players are able to slow the pace down, and make plays on their terms. I never feel comfortable on this night, 5-4-3-2-1, the buzzer sounds, and it's over. They say stay positive, but this is not enough. My two-game audition did not separate me from the rest of the hungry pack.

Next up on the Capitals' exhibition schedule is two meetings with the Hartford Whalers on September 16th in Norfolk, Virginia and September 19th at the Hartford Civic Centre. Post-game, I'm informed that I will be flying back to Lake Placid for two rookie games versus the visiting Montréal Canadiens, instead of going on to Norfolk. My suspicions about my play are confirmed. I needed to do more, and apparently Mr. Poile agrees. The Skipjacks' new bench-boss, Rob Laird, will direct the crew in Lake Placid against the visiting Canadiens' rookies.

The pace is slower in the rookie games, and I receive loads of ice time in the pair of tilts against the Baby Habs. I see playing time on the power play, and penalty-killing units. I need to be a force on this rookie team, a pacesetter, and a professional. I need to keep working hard and take on a leadership role! Perhaps I'm not that far from the dream after all.

Packing up camp, we return by plane to Washington. Settling in to our D.C. hotel, I see I'm pencilled in for a game in Richmond, Virginia. The crew travel by bus for the two-hour drive to play the New Jersey Devils. I play loose tonight, not feeling the same pressure I experienced in the Ranger games. 5-4-3-2-1, the buzzer sounds, and it is over. As we always do, we gather around our goalie and walk together back to the dressing room. I pause, and think about my play. I'm pleased with the performance, but worried I'm not where I need to be on the Capitals' depth chart.

I'm assigned to the Skipjacks for the start of the season. On the positive side, Rick calls to say that Mr. Poile is offering me a new contract. The Washington Capitals' now vice-president and GM David Poile is sending the paperwork by way of registered mail.

I'd earned my second contract from the Capitals, and Mr. Poile; a one-year deal, plus an option. My NHL salary is now $110,000 U.S., with a guaranteed minimum salary of $30,000 for both years. There is no signing bonus this time, however, on my 40th game played I will earn an extra $10,000 and after my 80th game, I will earn another $10,000. It feels good to have Mr. Poile's confidence in my development. This is positive news and an act of faith in my ability. I'm getting closer to my dream. Another step in the journey!

Road Trip

Training camp is complete; I'm assigned to the AHL. It can be deflating, being sent down to the minors, but I'm choosing to stay positive, slap on a brave face, go down, and work hard to earn an NHL job. That's my style; be respectful of the decisions made and the developmental process. It's time to show I can consistently produce in the minors. I feel poised for a breakthrough season. My personal goals are to score 25, be a leader, and play a grinding 200-foot game – responsible in both ends of the ice.

The Skipjacks hired Kenny Albert last season to serve as their play-by-play man. He's the son of legendary sportscaster Marv Albert. The elder Albert is famous for his calls of New York Ranger games, regular season and playoff NFL games, and much more.

When Marv comes to check on Kenny and his new job calling minor-league hockey in Baltimore, I take the opportunity to introduce myself. Kenny tips me off to his dad's location. I seek him out, and find him sitting quietly with his wife in the upper deck of the arena. "Hi Mr. Albert, it's nice to meet you," I say cautiously. I feel like I'm meeting sportscaster royalty as I introduce myself, and shake hands firmly with the famous game caller. "I've listened to you for a long time," I say eagerly. Marv is polite and soft-spoken. We engage in a short conversation before I move on, not wanting to wear out my unannounced welcome. I wanted to meet Marv and I did. Mission accomplished. Incidentally, Kenny Albert has supplanted his father as one of network television's top voices in sports. He currently does play-by-play for all four major-professional sports leagues including the NHL, NBA, MLB and NFL. Even sportscasters move from the minors to The Show.

Coach Laird encourages me to take on a leadership role with the Skipjacks. I want the coach to lean on me, and truthfully, I'll take the responsibility and pressure that goes along with it. Wearing a letter again feels good and I crave that duty.

The squad starts the season at the Hershey Park Arena versus the Bears. Early in the fast-flowing affair, I rush in on a 2-on-1. With my eyes, I direct my linemate to the goal. He breaks hard for the post, gaining a step on the back-peddling defenceman. We cross the hash marks, and I slide a hard, backdoor pass behind the defenceman's legs for an easy tap in goal. The boys are off and running. The Jacks win their opener tonight. Road wins in Hershey feel good for a couple of reasons: One, they're our bitter, arch rivals, and two, it's a tough rink to earn two points in. The old-school arena was built in 1936. Their boisterous fans are loud and let us know often how much they dislike the Skipjacks from Baltimore.

I said I was going down to the AHL to work hard, and earn an NHL job. I'm seeing valuable time on the power play and penalty-killing units. Coach Laird wants me in front of the net on the power play. I'll stand in there and take the punishment from the opposition for the opportunity to play special teams. A good start to this season is a must!

The team is led offensively by playmaking-centre Alfie Turcotte, sophomores Steve Maltais, and Tim Taylor, and newly added rookie Reggie Savage. I play on the grinding, checking line with heart-and-soul centre Rob Murray and six-foot-two, 225-pound, two-way winger, Jeff Greenlaw. The Skipjacks' defence is once again led by a group of veterans including talented rearguards Mark Ferner and Chris Felix. Kent Paynter adds a cannon slapshot to the mix. Goaltending duties go to steady Jim Hrivnak, former Soo Greyhound, and Gloucester, Ontario native Shawn Simpson, and Olie Kolzig. Olie blocks out the sun, standing six-foot-three, and weighing 225-pounds.

We head into ten games in the month of October, seven of those at home in the familiar confines of the Baltimore Arena. Post-game at home, we're asked questions by laid-back Baltimore Sun sports reporter Jim Jackson and his energetic, protégé Nestor Aparicio. This comfortable start to the new season inevitably leads to a busy November rife with road games. Road trips are a good time for players to bond and build team unity. Fifteen games are slated for the month of November with eleven on the road, including the annual trip to the Canadian Maritimes.

The Maritime roadie includes contests against the Halifax Citadels, Fredericton Canadiens, Moncton Hawks, and Cape Breton Oilers. An AHL presence has existed in the Maritimes for many years leading up to my time in the league. For a team largely made up of Canadian-born players, the Maritime trip is anticipated with extra eagerness.

Per diem or meal money will be converted to Canadian dollars for this excursion. I'm looking forward to returning to my home country, and walking around the streets with other Canadians, in Canadian cities. I expect to hear fellow Canucks say that oh so familiar eh? Maybe I'll say eh at the end of a sentence, and get an approving nod from an Acadian who understands. Eating at Harvey's is always on the to-do list. I'll buy a couple bags of Hostess salt and vinegar chips, which I can't get in the U.S. I anticipate reading the local papers with the extensive hockey coverage on the front of the sports section. Hockey will be centre stage in the Canadian newspapers. Real hockey highlights on TSN will jump off the T.V., not be featured as short clips at the end of the hour, like on ESPN. Hockey matters in Canada, and it feels good, and the way it is supposed to be.

We fly from BWI to Halifax to start us off, and as the plane begins the descent into the Maritime city, I stare out the window at the coniferous forest that spreads as far as the eye can see. Cone-bearing, needle leaved trees create a green ocean of life below; we're in Canada now. We hit the customs desk, and I'm asked my citizenship to which I proudly reply, "Canadian." The customs officer responds, "Reason for your visit?" I sharply tell him I'm a professional hockey player, and after some chit chat, he says, "Good luck!"

The first game of the road trip is in Halifax, followed by one in Moncton, and two in Fredericton. As the trip progresses, the grind of the schedule wears on the team. Puddle-hopper propeller planes, bus rides to small hotels, fast-food, and then faster-food all take their toll. There is another tilt against Moncton, followed by a short flight to Sydney, Nova Scotia for a game against the Cape Breton Oilers. Afterwards, we return to the hotel. It's quiet and the lights are dim. We arrive just before the restaurant closes, and are told we're too late to order food. We plead our case, and the polite manager agrees to cut us a break; the dining staff will serve us. We work, or play if you like, during the typical dinner hour for most. Our hockey schedule is not typical, and meals come at unusual times.

I'm tired as the road trip is getting closer to completion: tired of fast-food, of living out of a suitcase, of hotel beds, and flat hotel pillows. Pre-game skates, meals, meetings, and wake-up calls, are not met with the same vigor the longer the trip stretches. To be a professional, a hockey player needs to find the reserves to play, and focus mentally under these conditions.

Eight-games-in-thirteen-days are down but we still have two more to play: in Halifax, and the final one back in Cape Breton. Halifax has the largest rink in the Maritimes, and is located downtown. I like playing in this cold Nova Scotia community. The Québec Nordiques' affiliate plays here, and will square off against us tonight.

After the game against the pesky Citadels, the boys discuss having a team-building night. There has been enthusiastic banter about the clubs in downtown Halifax, and the fact that closing time is 3 a.m. There is Canadian beer: Labatt, Molson, and Maritime famous Moosehead; beer with a higher alcohol-volume per bottle than the watery beer in the U.S. We walk the short distance to downtown. The bar is loud, and the beer tastes good. The hours pass, 12 a.m., 1 a.m., 2 a.m., another round?

I continue to drink and decide a switch to Moosehead is in order to support the local economy. I stare at my greenish beer bottle, and wonder how it became empty so fast. I'm really not drinking now; I'm just pouring beer down my throat. Anyone else need a beer? At 3 a.m. the lights come on, and the bouncers start to push the patrons out like herding cattle. We delay while we drink our last beers, and negotiate with the large round-faced bouncer. "We promise we'll leave in 15-minutes," I chirp. "No, you have to go now," he says, determined to make us move our feet towards the exit door. Reluctantly, we walk to the front with the others closing the now bright with light club.

I know the hotel is down the street; no turns, just walk straight. This proves to be easier said than done. The bone-chilling winds off the Atlantic plow through my suit as I stumble down the sidewalk. Back at the hotel, I put in my wake-up call, fall asleep, and in what seems like minutes, I hear, Ring! Ring! Ring… Fuck! The sound of the phone pierces my ears. As the Irish Rovers say in their song *Wasn't That a Party*, "my head is like a football, I think I'm gonna die." That's accurate, and I'm paying the price for my behaviour last night.

Walking to the rink, I'm hung over and hurting bad. Back to bed after practice to sleep it off is my plan as the gang disperses for the free remainder of the day. My roommate on the road is my roommate at home, Malts. We share a lot of laughs but I'm not laughing much today. I get out of bed and we walk down the street for dinner. Malts and I pick a downtown restaurant. I'm still woozy. I sit in my chair, order and, feel a rumble in my stomach. This hangover is far from over. Our waitress disappears into the kitchen. Maybe it's the thought of food, or the images of barley and hops. Whatever it is, I look at Malts and announce, "I gotta go!" Quickly I stand up and rush out of the restaurant leaving Malts to eat alone.

There's not much time, and I know it as my brain says, "Reverse gears!" There's an alley beside the restaurant. I run over to gain privacy, and vomit at the side of the building during rush hour in Halifax. Throwing up at 5 p.m. the next day after a hangover; that's a first for me. Not a good first, but a first. Oh Canada!

Rink rats: Ron and I.

Kitchener Bauer Krauts.

Sumperk tournament champions 1984.

Looking good on Prom Night
with Lisa 1986.

Kingston rookie. Cast on my leg.
Wearing running shoes and not skates.

Photo op with Mom and Dad at the Montreal Forum.

Interview with Kingston play-by-play
voice Jim Gilchrist.

Final game for the
Kingston Canadians 1988.

Home game at the
Baltimore Arena.

Post-game Capitals vs
N.Y. Islanders
with Jeff Rimer.

My best friend Lisa.

My best man Scotty Pearson.

Some of the boys. L to R: Shawn Simpson, Jeff Greenlaw, me, Brad, Steve Bisson, Steve Herniman, Jim Hrivnak.

Fan Appreciation Night at the Baltimore Arena.

Malts and I.

Teaching passing on backyard ice.

Father-son game with Nicholas.

A father-son moment
with Calvin.

Coaching Waterloo Wolves Minor Peewee Black. Thanks boys!

Super Series of '91

One of the perks of playing pro hockey is practicing in the morning for two hours, and having the rest of the day free. In afternoon hours, I can work out in the gym, attend matinees in empty theatres, and do errands in half-empty stores. There's plenty of time to take care of business, and to get things done.

It's also a good time to get a haircut. Even in the midst of the mullet craze, haircuts are necessary. The eighties' hair bands still dominate the day as does longer hair or hockey hair. This hairstyle is easily cut short on the sides and front while left long at the back. I've bounced around from place to place and today I decide to check out the hair salon across from my favourite grocery store at the local strip mall.

Opening the door and stepping in, I look around. The salon is a good size with seven haircutting stations, and the all-female staff is busy cutting away. I survey the room, wondering how long the wait will be, and wondering if I should have made an appointment. There's one available chair where a woman with straight platinum-blonde hair stands and is sweeping the floor from her previous cut. She looks at me curiously, "Can I help you?" She says probingly. "Yes, I'd like a haircut," I reply. "I can help with that. Have a seat, and I'll be right with you," she calls out assuredly.

When prompted, I sit in her chair located in the tidy workstation, and discover the confident woman's name is Helen. We engage in polite conversation about my hockey hair or mullet. "Don't take too much of the back," I say calmly. The friendly conversation moves on to regular hairdresser-client talk and I'm able to ascertain that Helen owns this salon. "Are you off today?" she asks. "No," I answer. "What do you do?" she inquires. "I play hockey for the Baltimore Skipjacks," I say boastfully while trying to impress her with my Canadian charm. Helen can see right through my cocky hockey-player bravado, and she's a straight shooter who calls it the way it is, as I will soon learn to appreciate. Upon learning I'm a hockey player for a team she's barely heard of she replies in her Maryland drawl, "Isn't that the game where y'all hit each other over the head with sticks?" Okay, he we go, I've been down this road before with my American friends. "Well, that's one way to put it, but yes," I counter. No need to puff the chest out, this woman barely knows a puck from a curling rock. It appears that she is unfamiliar with life north of the border, especially the passion for hockey. She is intrigued as I explain the professional-hockey process, and the affiliation between the Skipjacks and Washington Capitals. At least she's heard of D.C.'s Capitals. Okay, we're making progress.

Hockey is foreign to my new Maryland friend, but that's not unusual in this state south of the Mason-Dixon Line. Helen speaks with the traditional local accent. She's divorced, and her daughter Tracy works at the salon. Tracy is about my age, and in time, I think Helen sees me as a wide-eyed, naïve Canadian boy who needs to be taken under her motherly wing to survive down here in the land of the free and home of the brave. But that's getting too far ahead.

Today, as Helen raises a mirror to show me the back of my head and new haircut, I invite her to watch a Skipjacks' home game. Hockey tickets can be useful for bartering. Always looking for a deal, I suggest to Helen that perhaps I can give her two free tickets to the next game at the arena in exchange for a haircut. After a brief negotiation, she agrees to my proposal. Living just north of the city, and not too far from the arena, she determines that a trip down-town to watch a hockey game sounds sort of interesting, and not too inconvenient. We have a deal!

Three hockey clubs from the Soviet Union tour North America in what is known as the 'Super Series of 1991'. The teams, CSKA Moscow, Dynamo Moscow and Khimik Voskresensk, play a 21-game exhibition tour – meaning every team in the National Hockey League will play one game against one of the touring Russian clubs.

Game One of the series is December 3rd, 1990 in Los Angeles, and the Kings defeat Khimik Voskresensk 5-1. The Washington Capitals are scheduled to play Dynamo Moscow on January 8th, 1991 at the Cap Centre. Prior to the game, the Caps recall me and a few of the other Skipjacks to play the visiting Soviets. It isn't a regular-season game, but it is a paid NHL day, a chance to put on the Capitals' jersey, and to play the Russians. Furthermore, it will be an opportunity to leave an impression on Mr. Poile, and Coach Murray.

Preparing for this game, like any other, I drive down to Landover for the 7:35 p.m. start. It feels great walking into the Caps' dressing room again. They're dressing veterans Kevin Hatcher, Calle Johansson, Nick Kypreos, Peter Bondra, and Mike Ridley among others.

Here we go! Veteran linesman Ray Scapinello and Mark Vines take their positions, and the Russian referee drops the puck to start this challenge. The Soviets are fast, move the puck quickly, and play at a rapid pace. After one period, the scoreboard displays a 1-0 lead for the visiting Dynamo club. At the end of two, the faithful fans in attendance are encouraged by the 2-1 lead for the team in white. I'm playing on a line with Ukrainian-born, Caps' centre, Dmitri Khristich, and my Skipjack linemate, Jeff Greenlaw. At 13:39 of the third period, Dynamo knots the game at 2-2 to the groans of the home crowd.

With less than two-minutes remaining in regulation time, my line hops the boards, and hits the ice flanked on the defensive side by, hulking, six-foot-four, 232-pound Kevin Hatcher and newly acquired Mike Lalor. Scooping up a pass from Khristich in the neutral zone, I skate down the left side towards the Dynamo blue line, sail by the bench, fake the defenceman inside, and cut to the outside. He hesitates for a fraction of a second, and in that moment, there is enough time for me to gain a step. I drive hard to the net. An explosive Greenlaw is skating to the back post. Powerfully built Greenie is arguably the fastest skater in the organization, and I know his blinding speed will get him to the net first. The only thing between us is another defenceman. I see Greenie's stick arrive at the crease as predicted, and as I do, I slide a pass across, and he directs it into the net by the sliding goalie. He scores! The familiar Caps' siren wails! With only one-minute remaining, we have a narrow 3-2 lead. It's a frenetic finish; the crafty Dynamo Moscow boys press hard for the equalizer. The final buzzer sounds to seal the win. The crowd is up on their feet to celebrate the victory. We hop the boards, and the boys mob River in his crease.

We leave the ice to the cheers of the remaining fans. Back in the dressing room, my equipment is soaking wet and beads of sweat fall off my nose. I consume the energy inside, and the fantastic feelings that exist after a win. I'm growing into the player I need to be in order to play in the National Hockey League.

Returning to my apartment, I discover Helen is ready to take me up on my offer to attend a Skipjacks' home game, and says she will be accompanied by her boyfriend Tim. I leave two tickets at the arena box office, and ask if they can stick around and meet me afterwards. Experience has taught me that hockey is a sport much more entertaining live; television doesn't do it justice. Many people that are introduced to the sport in the live setting are immediately hooked by the speed of the game, and the combination of skill and physicality.

Post-game, I meet Helen and Tim in the lower concourse with my wet, hockey hair and dressed in my suit to say hello, and to see what they're thinking. Helen introduces me to her gentle silver-haired boyfriend. I firmly shake his hand. He's a warm, down-to-earth man, who speaks softly and with a Maryland accent. Helen and Tim are definitely intrigued by this unfamiliar game called hockey.

"Well, good game eh? Did you like it?" I ask the pair inquisitively.

Helen looks at Tim keenly and says, "Eh? Eh? I told you Tim, he's always sayin' eh!"

Tim speaks up, "Y'all really whack each other with those sticks! Doesn't it hurt?"

"No, we're covered in equipment from head-to-toe, and you get used to it," I tell him matter-of-factly.

"Why do y'all punch each other in the face?" quips Helen devilishly in her Southern drawl. "Geez doesn't that hurt?" she asks.

"It can hurt," I reply calmly. However tonight, I don't feel like explaining fighting, scrums, and face washes to them. Maybe next time, if they want to watch again.

Helen leans in, stares at my face and says, "Are those your real teeth? I hear you hockey players are all missin' teeth!"

"Yes, they're mine. One is dead from a root canal due to fists and pucks but they're mine," I reply and smile displaying my pearly whites to her.

"My question for you is, do you want to watch another game?" I ask eagerly.

"For sure, eh!" Says sharp-witted Helen, as she quickly winks at me and gives me a big smile.

"Yes I heard it," I heard you say, eh?

With that, Miss Helen and Tim are hooked on hockey, and will become my trusted, dependable friends, opening up their homes to me, sharing meals at restaurants, sharing famous Maryland blue crab parties in the off-season, and of course, free haircuts. Helen becomes a sort of surrogate mother to me. Interestingly, without encouragement, she often calls me Steven. Only my family members call me Steven.

The Goon from Baltimore

The Skipjacks hit the road and travel to Portland, Maine to play the Mariners. I like playing in this picturesque New England city, situated on the shores of the Atlantic Ocean.

Post-game, after a nice road win, Coach Laird calls me out of the dressing room. He wants a sidebar. I follow him into an adjacent room with sweat beads still on my face and steam rising off my head. He looks at me and says, "Congratulations, you're going to Washington, for a game Tuesday in Detroit." I'm overwhelmed by the news and all I can spit out is, "Thank-you." My mind starts darting from thought to thought. "Any advice?" I ask. "Play your game," he replies. Immediately I have butterflies as I think about the promotion. I turn and slowly wander out of the room and think, this is it. My dream!

First things first however, we have to get home from Portland. The pack loads up the iron lung, and drive south on I-95 for the eight-hour ride home. Word spreads that myself and skilled, puck-moving defenceman, Mark Ferner have been recalled by the Capitals.

Monday morning, I call everyone back home to share my incredible news, and I ask my parents if they need tickets. Detroit is a three-hour drive from their home in Waterloo. I think about the locations they can reasonably drive to for a game: Toronto, 1-hour; Buffalo, 2-hours; Detroit, 3-hours, hmm too far, maybe, maybe not. It's a Tuesday night, not a weekend, likely too far. I hang up the phone and I'm disappointed as I digest the news that my parents will not be attending. There will be other chances. I'm planning on staying in D.C., or at least coming back to stay in the future.

The excitement is difficult to contain, but there's no time to relax, I have to get to practice. I drive down to the Capitals' Virginia practice facility. Yes, I'm driving south on the always busy I-95 today, and not north. That's what I want; south means The Show.

I walk into the dressing room like I belong. I've been in the organization for a while now, and know these guys, some better than others. Exchanging hellos and handshakes, I play it cool. I'm at the peak of the hockey summit.

I bump into happy-go-lucky, athletic-therapist Stan Wong. He's a familiar face, having been around since my first camp in '86. Stan always calls me Stevie. I like that and it eases my juiced up nerves. I locate my stall after consulting with friendly, always-eager-to-help, equipment-manager Doug Shearer; another familiar face. Players slowly filter into the room. Dale Hunter enters with his son Dylan. Geez, Hunts is married with children!

The change room is across the hall. I switch into my Bauer, cotton long underwear, and short sleeve shirt. Players needing treatment for injuries are in the trainer's room with Stan, while others stretch before practice to loosen up, and work on crafting their sticks. The minutes pass by, and everyone is ready. The routine chirping continues. Staying out of it, I stand and listen to the sharp-tongued barbs flying around. It's go time!

One by one, the boys step onto the ice to begin practice. Coach Murray sharply blows his whistle to start us off with a warm-up skate and shots for the goalies. Now with the blood flowing, he instructs us to line up for a 2-on-1 drill. At my end, I wait at the front of the line on the left side. My partner on the right side is fierce, hardworking Dino Ciccarelli, a point-producing machine.

Coach Murray blows his whistle to start the drill, and the talented winger takes off like he's shot out of a cannon. Boom! I move my legs as fast as possible so I can keep up. We race up the ice, attacking the backward skating defenceman. Man, Dino is fucking flying. The play ends at the net with a shot on goal, and we file back in line. At that moment, I realize how hard these guys work in practice. I understand the intensity, work ethic, and commitment required to stay in The Show. Dino, my unpaid tutor, taught the rookie on the other side of the ice a valuable lesson, and demonstrated what it takes to be a professional in the NHL. The education is swift. It's wise to be a quick learner surrounded by these cagy veterans. Coach Murray keeps us on the ice for a brisk fifty- minutes. We don't practice long, but skate as hard as we can for the entire time on the ice. Lesson learned!

Post-practice and after eating lunch at a busy restaurant, we drive to the airport for a commercial flight to Detroit. There is no charter flight this time. I love charter flights; it's an awesome way to travel.

The plane touches down in the Motor City later that afternoon, and we check in to our hotel, located down the street from Joe Louis Arena. Nervous excitement fills my chest, and I want to play right now. Tomorrow, we will be facing the Detroit Red Wings, coached by former Capitals' bench-boss, Bryan Murray, and assistant Doug MacLean; my coach just a few months ago. Both men are well respected in the league. Their presence certainly adds an element of drama to the big tilt ahead since they're still well connected to their former employers and the players in Washington.

This contest will be the third meeting between the Murray brothers this season. Bryan's Red Wings and Terry's Capitals have already played each other, on October 6th in D.C., and November 19th in the Motor City. When the brothers' teams feuded back in October, it was the first time since 1977 that brothers opposed each other as NHL coaches. Brotherly competition aside, there's still a hockey game to play and my first appearance in The Show for those keeping score at home. It's so freaking awesome! Now that I'm here, I never want to leave.

The Red Wings are a good hockey club, led by captain, Steve Yzerman; the awesome speed of rookie Sergei Fedorov; and the presence of enforcer Bob Probert. Probert is considered the toughest player in the league by many, and he is in my book. He possesses a nice set of hands for a big man, and scored twenty-nine goals for the Wings a couple years back.

Tuesday, January 22nd, 1991 I awaken early for breakfast. My game-day mental preparation starts the moment I wake up. The unit assembles at the Joe for the traditional morning skate. Since this is my first NHL game, this is my first game-day skate, and another piece of the preparation. These skates are usually less than forty-five minutes, depending on the schedule; some longer, others shorter, and still others optional for some. The home team skates first, and the visitors second.

Undressed after the skate, I return to the hotel for the prepared pre-game meal and nap that follows in preparation for tonight's huge tilt. My roommate, Mark Ferner, can sleep, but not me. I can't sleep on normal days so forget it today. I lay in bed and go through a mental tug-of-war in my head. Flipping and flopping, I need to relax but that's easier said than done because my mind is in overdrive. Having said that, I will go through the routine of laying here, and trying to rest.

Game time is 730 p.m. My usual arrival time is two-hours to two-hours-and-fifteen-minutes before puck drop. I walk into the rink today at 430 p.m.; three-hours early. It appears I'm the first one here, and the dressing room is completely empty and silent.

Since I'm here extra early, I scan the press notes and analyze the rosters. The information about tonight's matchup fills my obsessive appetite for names, statistics, scores, standings, and streaks. Tonight, the Capitals are missing shutdown defenceman Rod Langway; speedster Peter Bondra; hard-nosed defenceman Neil Sheehy; and skilled defenceman Chris Felix. Mr. Poile acquired Al Iafrate and his clap bomb slapshot from the Toronto Maple Leafs in exchange for Peter Zezel and Bob Rouse, so this lineup tonight will have a new look.

Continuing to read the press notes, I study information about Dale Hunter, Mike Ridley, Dave Tippet, Kelly Miller, Kevin Hatcher, and Calle Johansson. I spot individual and team streaks for the Red Wings. There is information about Yzerman, Fedorov, Probert, Keith Primeau, Gerard Gallant, Rick Green, Rick Zombo, and Tim Cheveldae, who appears to be starting in goal tonight.

Surveying the still quiet dressing room, I find my stall. The training staff make sure our equipment is hanging, and ready. Ignited nerves create a queasy feeling in my stomach. It doesn't happen every game, and I'm thankful it doesn't. However, when my nerves strike, I like to know where the nearest bathroom is.

Keeping in step with my normal pre-game routine, I prepare for warm-up. I stop and stare at my jersey hanging with my equipment again. I'm here! I stretch and make sure my sticks are ready. I put on my equipment no differently than any other day but this seems different and, in fact, it is. Soon I will be stepping onto the ice with the best hockey players in the world and playing in the best league in the world: the NHL.

The clock on the wall counts down to the start of warm-up. The ice soldiers become restless. Time for battle boys! One by one guys stand, giving encouragement, riding a rising tide of emotion, but not too high as this is only warm-up. Walking down the runway to the ice, we step into the largely empty arena, as most of the fans have not yet arrived. Onto the ice, turn right, and skate towards our goal. Strangely, I feel like I'm skating on ski moguls; like over little bumps and hills. 'How can this be?' I ask myself, 'It can't be, because it's not. This ice is flat, just like every other ice surface. Relax, the ice is fucking flat!' I take a few deep breaths, and confirm, in fact, the ice is flat. That's encouraging news. Perhaps it's the awe-inspiring aura of this world-class league. Maybe it's nerves, or overexcitement. Okay, I'm nervous. Why wouldn't I be nervous? This is only my first NHL game; my dream!

I survey the ice, and see Hunts calmly skating; big Iafrate unloading his cannon slapshot; smooth-skating Yzerman; speedy Fedorov – geez he looks fast; heavyweight Probert – his hometown is across the river in Windsor. The respected enforcer has fought most, if not all, of the league's toughest players. I'm a left-winger and he's a right-winger so we may line up opposite each other tonight.

The competitors on both sides execute the standard warm-up. Skating another lap, I cruise towards the Detroit bench. I see a familiar face. My old coach Doug MacLean is standing behind the bench curiously watching. My old coach… Perhaps a little banter with him will help loosen the firm grip my nerves have on my shaky legs. I know, on the next lap, I'll talk to Mac. He'll see me, congratulate me on my recall, and my first game. After all, I gave him everything I had, and he was instrumental in my development. I loved playing for him, and he'll be happy to see me in The Show.

Completing a quick lap, I start gliding across the centre red line towards the Detroit bench. Mac and I make eye contact. Here's my chance. I move closer, and closer. He'll say something like, "Way to go kid – you did a great job getting here, good for you bud, congratulations!" Mac begins to speak, and I lean in to listen as he's about to say something profound to me. "Hey Sef, I told Probert you're the goon called up from Baltimore!" You said what? I continue gliding up the boards and do a quick double take. Are you kidding me? What the hell? He has to be kidding. He's screwing with my head. Yes, just head games, that's Mac's sense of humour. On the next lap, I stay away from the Detroit bench, and my old coach. We can talk hockey later.

Returning to the dressing room after warm-up, thinking about Mac's comment, I try to convince myself he's only messing with my noodle. Coach Murray enters the room. He reminds us about tonight's game plan, and calls out the starting lineup. "Hunter-Seftel-Druce up front." Wow, I'm starting with Hunts and Drucer.

The digital clock on the dressing room wall counts down to zero. Now the voices in the dressing room are a little louder.

"Here we go boys."

"Let's go, Hunts!"

"Big start boys."

"Go hard Kyper!"

"Finish your checks boys."

"One shift at a time fellas."

"Short shifts tonight."

"Let's go chum."

"Goalies first!"

"Weather the storm boys!"

It's time, and the troop begins to filter out of the dressing room. One by one, we make our way down the runway toward the ice. The 20,000 seat Joe Louis Arena is now almost full as goalies Liut and Beaupre lead us out. Both teams are flying around their respective zones at Mach 2 speeds, creating an internal vortex at each end. The public-address announcer has final messages for the anxious crowd and then says, "Ladies and gentlemen, please rise for the playing of the national anthem." I glide over to the blue line, and stand straight with my teammates. I remove my helmet, and *The Star-Spangled Banner* begins to echo through the jammed Joe Louis. Oh say can you see…

It's always good to know who you're up against on the other side. Since I'm a left-winger I know I'll be matched up at the opening faceoff with Detroit's starting right-winger. I stare across to the Detroit blue line, and I see #24, Bob Probert!

He's six-foot-three, 225-pounds. I think back to last season. He was visiting the Capital Centre, and I watched as he fought my former Skipjacks' cohort, Yvon Corriveau. 'Geez, maybe Mac did tell Probert I'm the goon called up from Baltimore.' Well if he did, it's one way to make the TSN highlight package tomorrow. Oh boy! One shift at a time, one shift at a time, I repeat over and over.

The national anthem is ending… and the home of the brave! The referee blows his whistle with authority! Both teams line up for the draw. Skating to the centre circle, I put my stick down, and notice that directly off my left shoulder stands the big, physically intimidating Bob Probert. Our Father who art in heaven…, okay, enough, play hockey. Play your game! Hey you can go down in a blaze of glory! Play your game, play your game. Coach Laird's advice was, 'Play your game!'

I line up beside Probert; shoulder-to-shoulder, skate-to-skate, stick-to-stick, and the puck drops. The pace is quick, and the puck darts from stick to stick. The disc is dumped into our zone, and our pivoting defenceman rushes back for the loose rubber disc. Without hesitation, he rips it around the boards to my wing. One of my strengths is being strong on the wall in my own zone. You know, take a hit to make a play. I rush back to the hash marks on the left circle as the puck is sailing around the dasher. I've done this many times. It's a routine skill for wingers, and not as easy as it appears. I corral the puck as Probert crosses the blue line towards my position. Instinctively, I chip it off the wall as Probert lowers his shoulder into mine. 'If Mac was serious, I'm going to find out now, either with a slash, a face wash, or worse.' There's nothing; the play moves up the ice. Wow! No glove to the face, no whack, no chirping. I guess Mac was yanking my chain!

This battle is fast and lively, and at the end of one period it's scoreless. Nick Kypreos is sent off for roughing twice; once with swift-skating defenceman Yves Racine and once with tough Joe Kocur. At the end of two periods, we're still scoreless!

Early in the third, Capitals' dependable-defenceman Calle Johansson opens the scoring and gives us a slim 1-0 lead. Moments later, big Probert receives a five-minute major penalty for high-sticking and a game misconduct. To add to the drama, Capitals' physical Al May and d-man Mike Lalor each receive roughing minors on the same stoppage. It's an intense period in Hockeytown. Adding to the penalty parade, scrappy Hunts also receives a five-minute major for high-sticking and a game misconduct. Regulation time ends in a hard-fought 1-1 tie, and forces a five-minute overtime period.

The crowd is buzzing as extra time starts, and with seconds on the clock evaporating quickly, point-producing centre Mike Ridley rips home a shot and scores at 3:08 of the extra period, to seal the victory for us. A quiet Detroit crowd moans as they realize their team has lost. I fly over the boards, skate into the Red Wing zone, and jump on the expanding pile just like one of the boys, the team, the Washington Capitals!

The Spectrum

Leaving the Joe after the win over the Red Wings, the boys go out to eat in downtown Detroit. Kyper leads the way to a restaurant in Greektown. He's a spirited guy who spent a portion of last season with me under the guidance of Mac and has now earned a spot in D.C. I'm on cloud nine after an exciting road win, and having my first game under my belt. We eat, share stories, and hearty laughs. Following the meal and with stomachs full, it's back to the hotel room to try and get some shut-eye. It's difficult to sleep after I play because I'm still replaying the game in my mind. I'm wide awake, and tomorrow we hit the road again. Our next stop is the City of Brotherly Love; Philadelphia.

After a short practice in suburban Detroit, we bus to the airport for a commercial flight to the Pennsylvania city, so the Caps and Flyers can renew acquaintances tomorrow night. The on-ice enemies compete with extra grit and sandpaper. The Patrick Division rivals have combined to play many memorable grind-it-out hockey wars to loud jeers and wild cheers of avid fans in both cities.

The Spectrum in Philly was built in 1967 to be the home of the expansion Flyers. It's the arena where, in 1976, the touring Russian Red Army club infamously left the ice in the middle of an exhibition game after being roughed up by the host Flyers, who were known as the 'Broad Street Bullies' for the way they played on the ice with truculence and an abrasive style. They used this influential, physical brand of hockey to win back-to-back Stanley Cups in 1974 and 1975.

I'm looking forward to playing at the arena which seats 17,000 plus; the rink has character and history. Through Stanley Cup victories, Captain Bobby Clarke, Reggie Leach, Bob "Mad Dog" Kelly, Bill Barber, Bernie Parent, Barry Ashbee and others played here for the hometown Flyers.

The digital clock on the Spectrum dressing room wall counts down to zero. I stand up in my stall and start to shift my weight from leg to leg. I adjust my elbow and shoulder pads; a nervous and game-time superstition. "Here we go boys," shouts a voice. It's go time!

The Spectrum crowd tonight is loud and boisterous. They're known to be a passionate fan base. The game starts with the drop of the puck, and we're on our heels. After five-minutes we're down 2-0. The pace of this game is quick. At the end of the first period we're outshooting the Flyers 13-9 but still trail on the scoreboard where it counts most.

Period two gets underway and we're taking it to our tough opponents. Kyper scores to cut the lead in half. We're skating better as a team and peppering the Philly net. Dynamic goaltender Ron Hextall is making save after save to keep us off the scoresheet. The Flyers respond for their hot goaltender by scoring two unanswered goals and grabbing a 4-1 lead.

The loud arena turns into a powder keg. All we need is the flicker of a match and boom! Tempers are flaring now with the three goal Philly lead. No-nonsense Al May drops his gloves with Flyers' enforcer Craig Berube. Five-minutes each for fighting are assessed by referee Bill McCreary. The confrontational period ends with competitive centres Dale Hunter and Ron Sutter fighting immediately after the puck drop in the Philly zone. The linesmen pull Hunts off Sutter and separate the two warriors. We outshoot the Flyers 17-5 in the second period but Hextall is sharp tonight.

Period three starts and the Flyers' big-gun Rick Tocchet scores a power-play goal. The nastiness of the rivalry continues and tempers boil over again. Strong on his skates, Al Iafrate dukes it out with Berube. That's Berube's second go-round. Kyper and combative Scott Mellanby square off and fight in the third period. The late altercation sends a message to both benches about what can be expected the next time we play. Like the Hatfields and the McCoys, scores will be settled in future games. The rivalry will continue even though the players may change.

Flyer fans rise to their feet and clap as the clock ticks down. Their team is going to win tonight and they appreciate their boys' effort. The buzzer sounds and the Flyers take the win and the precious two points.

In the end, it's a disappointing outcome. The Flyers' physical, hardworking Tocchet scores three goals tonight, and smooth-skating Pelle Eklund adds four assists in the 6-1 win. The game is completed in front of an announced crowd of 17,322 of the Flyers' faithful and others. A feisty affair between the Patrick Division rivals results in 90-minutes in penalties being handed out by referee McCreary; a typical Capitals-Flyers rivalry night.

I'm more comfortable in this spirited game, but due to all the penalties, PP and PK units see a lot of ice time. As a result, my time takes a hit. I'm still adapting to the increased speed, and pace of play. The speed requires that decisions with and without the puck be made quickly while under constant pressure from the pressing opposition. Mistakes made can quickly end up with a puck in the back of our net and an unhappy Coach Murray.

For the Caps, this is four losses in the last five. The only win in the last five outings was the overtime victory two nights ago in Detroit. Losing hockey games, and especially too many, too fast, causes coaches and managers to scrutinize everything and everybody.

We exit the Spectrum with a loss, and return home for two upcoming home games: tomorrow night versus the Minnesota North Stars, and Sunday afternoon versus the N.Y. Islanders. Philly isn't too far from D.C. so we bus home. The bus rolls south on I-95 for the two-and-a-half-hour trip. It's a quiet ride after a loss. There are no movies, no music, no laughing, and no having too much fun.

Sitting there, I replay the game in my mind. I think about the plays I should have made to avoid mistakes and simple opportunities for improvement. These guys are strong and difficult to out-muscle. I have to play fast and smart. I drift off to sleep on the humming motor coach, and awaken as we're passing the Inner Harbor in Baltimore. I stare out the window at the familiar, lit city surroundings. Hopefully I won't be back here for a while; I want to stay in The Show.

After a few days on the road, the Caps return home for their traditional Friday night home date – Friday 8:05 p.m. in Landover at the Capital Centre. The crowd is buzzing as warm-up commences. It's a completely different atmosphere playing at home versus on the road, and it feels good to be on our ice. The energy from the fans soaks right into my legs, and gives me endless sources of reserve power. Capitals' jerseys are visible throughout the seats. Many fans are cheering, standing, holding up homemade signs, or holding out programs in the hopes of getting an autograph. It's an infectious feeling.

Warm-up music echoes in the arena like a rock concert, with fans and players preparing for the opening puck drop that is only minutes away. Playing hockey in front of 18,000 plus screaming fans who are on your side is an incredible adrenaline rush, and under these conditions, motivation is not a problem for me.

Back in the room after warm-up there is a review of tactics from Coach Murray, and strategies on how to limit the attack of the

North Stars' offensive weapons, speedy Mike Modano, playmaker Neal Broten, and goal-scorer Brian Propp. The digital clock on the wall counts down to zero, and the boys start to stand. It's go time!

We walk down the runway from the dressing room to the ice surface and a thunderous roar from the crowd gains strength as the squad comes into view. A large decibel meter is situated on the upper wall, and the gauge continues to climb as the crowd noise increases. The players step onto the ice, quickly skate out to the blue line, back around the net, digging their blades in hard to make the turn. Helmets are straightened, equipment adjusted, and jerseys tugged. Nervous twitches, and individual superstitious rituals are performed as each player prepares for the puck drop that is only moments away.

The home crowd is lively tonight as referee Dan Marouelli drops the puck for the opening faceoff to start this match. Hardworking Caps' winger Nick Kypreos stirs up the crowd by duking it out with North Stars' big bruising-defenceman Mark Tinordi. A brisk first period ends with roughing penalties for scrappy Al May and Stars' defenceman Neil Wilkinson. The scoreboard reads 0–0 as the two teams leave the ice for the intermission and flood.

At the start of the period, the pace picks up. I'm cruising through the neutral zone when Stars' high-energy leader Brian Bellows darts for open ice. I reach out and grab at his jersey; anything to slow down his speed. He stumbles. Quickly referee Marouelli's arm goes up for a delayed penalty. North Stars' goalie Brian Hayward skates to the bench for the extra attacker. Once we touch the puck, Marouelli sharply blows his whistle to stop play and signals for me to skate to the penalty box. He skates over, makes the call, and penalty sign; two-minutes for interference. I step into the home penalty box. 'That was a lazy penalty. Get your feet moving. Shit, please don't score while I'm sitting in here or Terry will be pissed. He's likely sour already since I took a lackadaisical penalty in the neutral zone.' At this moment, I feel like I'm sitting on the designated hot seat. The boys kill off my minor offense. I race out of the box, and hustle back to the bench. No damage done. Powerful-skater Al Iafrate scores a highlight-reel goal on a beautiful rush, Ulf Dahlen replies with a goal for the North Stars, and the period ends tied 1-1.

Stars' sniper Brian Propp and Caps' puck hound Dino Ciccarelli chip in with third period goals for a 2-2 tie at the end of regulation time. A five-minute overtime solves nothing, and each team receives one point to add to the standings.

I feel good after tonight's game. Showering and leaving the rink, the parking lot is largely empty. I drive home to the apartment and eat. We have practice tomorrow and the New York Islanders are in town on Sunday afternoon.

Operation Desert Storm

The dramatic and surprising invasion of the small country of Kuwait by Iraq on Aug. 2nd, 1990 is the catalyst for the start of the Gulf War. Within seven days, 15,000 U.S. troops arrive in Saudi Arabia to participate in the new conflict.

Operation Desert Storm launches on Jan. 17th, 1991. The combat phase of the war, led by the United States and supported by thirty-five coalition countries, begins in response to the rapid, unexpected offensive.

The thoughts of war are on the country's mind, and have settled into its collective conscience, including mine. A war of this large size and broad scope is new to me. Up to now, I'd only studied about large-scale wars in history classes. Living near the capital city of the United States only heightens my concerns and anxiety, as well as that of the on-edge citizens of Washington, D.C.

A swell of patriotism consumes the supportive country during the month of January, as Americans rally behind their loyal troops, and the branches of the military forces. Declarations of allegiance, encouragement, and national pride are on display throughout the awakened, unified fifty states. Having said that, it is chilling watching reports on the news night after night. The network news anchors encourage citizens to be vigilant, and watch for any abnormal, suspicious activity. However, for all of us, even in the midst of conflict, life still goes on, including hockey.

Today is a scheduled 2 p.m. matinee versus the New York Islanders, and I'm up early. Arriving at the rink, I feel the influence of the Gulf War and Operation Desert Storm. A buzz exists in the Capital Centre during this uncertain time. It is clear to me that the citizens want the men and women of the military to know they are unequivocally supported. We all do!

The digital clock on the wall counts down to puck drop, and the fired-up crew begins to stand as the seconds tick away. It's game time! Hitting the ice, and with the opening faceoff moments away, the public-address announcer asks everyone to stand for the national anthem. He states, "Today there will be a special ceremony for the military troops participating in Operation Desert Storm, followed by *The Star-Spangled Banner.*" The crowd enthusiastically applauds the men and women of the U.S. military, and supporting coalition forces. The game-day voice then asks everyone to stand for Lee Greenwood's song, *God Bless the U.S.A.*, and the rink goes silent as the music starts and the fans absorb the song's inspiring words...

If tomorrow all the things were gone
I'd worked for all my life
And I had to start again
With just my children and my wife
I'd thank my lucky stars
To be living here today

Cause the flag still stands for freedom
And they can't take that away
And I'm proud to be an American
Where at least I know I'm free
And I won't forget the men who died
Who gave that right to me
And I gladly stand up
Next to you and defend her still today
Cause there ain't no doubt I love this land
God bless the USA
From the lakes of Minnesota
To the hills of Tennessee
Across the plains of Texas
From sea to shining sea
From Detroit down to Houston
And New York to L.A.
Well there's pride in every American heart
And its time we stand and say
And I'm proud to be an American
Where at least I know I'm free
And I won't forget the men who died
Who gave that right to me
And I gladly stand up
Next to you and defend her still today
Cause there ain't no doubt I love this land
God bless the U.S.A

The patriotic song concludes. The inspired crowd is chanting, cheering as the national anthem follows, and begins to bellow through the delirious arena. In this moment I feel 12-feet tall. With the sounds of *The Star-Spangled Banner* winding down, the crowd noise is deafening, and it's hard to hear the players and coaches standing beside me. Goose bumps cover my body from head to toe. My insides quiver as I listen to the crowd getting louder, and louder, and still louder. The fans don't want to sit down. The thunderous Capitals' faithful continue standing, clapping, and chanting. It's an arena sent into a frenzy! A giant wave of patriotism consumes the Capital Centre, and for a moment, the hockey game isn't as important.

In the capital city of the United States, playing for the Washington Capitals, seeing and hearing this visible show of public support for the troops is beyond moving. Throughout the country a nervous energy is in the streets, and yet in the arena, standing together, there is a sense of security, and strength that rises up from the voices in the crowd of loyal hockey fans.

But there's still a game to play. I have to get into this one early with my adrenaline pounding, get an early bump, and get my feet moving. It's a frantic first period, and Kevin Hatcher opens the scoring on a long slapshot to give us the lead. However, as the buzzer sounds to end the period, the Islanders are in front 2-1.

The second period is underway, and I want to make a statement, do what I do well, create havoc on our aggressive forecheck and finish my checks. In the middle of the frame, the puck is dumped into the Islanders' zone, and I skate in at top speed with no waste in my strides. My heart pumps faster to assist in delivering valuable oxygen to my legs. An Islanders' winger picks up the puck on the hash marks, and is attempting to make a clearing pass. I see his head is down, and he's standing still; an easy target. I start to glide and, as he looks up to make a pass, I deliver a stiff open-ice shoulder check to his chest, launching him up and over onto his backside. The crowd roars with approval, and the energy goes directly to my legs.

The puck clears the Islanders' zone, and our defenceman wires the disc deep into their end of the ice again. We regroup outside the blue line. I am soaring. I skate straight for the defenceman retrieving the puck, he picks it up, standing still with his head down. I cut across the ice in front of Isles' goalie Glenn Healy. The d-man pivots directly into my path, attempting to pass the puck around the dasher. In that moment, I deliver another stiff shoulder check along the wall that sends him reeling backwards onto the ice. The crowd roars again. I'm shaking as I skate to the near bench for a line change. Big hits can change momentum and these have. I sit back on the bench gasping for air for my burning lungs, and basking in the moment. The crowd is feverish; they want a Caps' victory.

A testy melee sends six skaters to the penalty boxes. Al May stirs it up with veteran Gary Nylund. They're assessed fighting majors, and joined by Caps' tenacious Steve Leach, mammoth Ken Sabourin and the Islanders' shifty Ray Ferraro and gritty Brad Lauer. There are scoring chances, scrums, and big, bone-crushing hits. Ciccarelli scores, followed by a goal from superstar Pat LaFontaine and sharpshooter Derek King for the Isles. At the end of two periods, the visiting Islanders lead 4-2.

There's still time, and we need a response in period three. Two unanswered goals by veteran-leader Kelly Miller and Sabourin tie the game up at 4-4, forcing sudden-death overtime for the third time in four games for us.

At 4:21 of overtime, Miller scores again, blowing the roof off the arena as the fans erupt. The Islanders leave the ice slowly, and the boys pour over the boards, creating an expanding mob around today's hockey hero. Sports can bring communities together during difficult periods in time, and today it has! This win feels like a win for the capital city, Washington D.C., the troops, and its patriotic citizens.

The dedicated fans linger as they savour the Sunday afternoon victory, and bask in the feelings of patriotism. Capitals' television host Jeff Rimer requests my presence for a post-game chat. The remaining fans listen to my first home interview. I peer up at the giant scoreboard, and see Jeff focusing the microphone in my direction. I answer his questions carefully and confidently as my voice echoes through the building. With the interview complete, his thanks are followed by cheering and clapping from the remaining die-hards, or those waiting for the traffic to clear out. Walking back to the dressing room, I enter, and take in the sweet feeling in the room that exists after a big win. The music is on, the stereo is loud; there's lots of chatter, smiles and laughter. I slowly take my gear off and hang it in my stall as I absorb the energy. What a hockey game, what a day, what an unforgettable memory!

Coach Murray asks to see me in his office. I enter, and he informs me that the injured boys are healthy again. I'm being reassigned to Baltimore, and will be expected at Skipjacks' practice tomorrow. I'm disappointed, but leave him with no such impression. In fact, I view this experience as a huge positive in my career. I gained an education watching the veterans deal with success and failure. Time spent with disciplined, dedicated, determined players who play with desire shapes the young, professional player in me. I will go down, work hard, and earn my way back up. I've tasted life in The Show, and I want more.

I walk out the side door of the Capital Centre. Eager fans of all ages stand behind the blue security gates on both sides of the wide concrete walkway creating an artificial passage to the parking lot. My suit and wet hair reveal that I'm a hockey player. Young fans eager for an autograph stick out their programs, and other pieces of paper. I sign with a smile, but inside I'm disheartened because I've just been sent back to the minors. However, as long as I'm walking along this pathway, I'm a Capital. I enjoy signing the autographs, and it's good for my bruised ego. I return the young kids' signed programs, and they enthusiastically accept them. I'm a role model for these youngsters. They look up to me, and a certain behaviour is expected. Athletes are heroes for some, and if I make it big, my signature could be a future autograph to sell for others. I become robotic as I make my way through the crowd, as the fans continue to push forward.

"What's your name?" Says a boy in front of me.

"Are you John Druce?" says another little guy.

"No, Steve Seftel," I reply.

"What number are you?" He asks enthusiastically.

"40," I reply back.

He takes his signed program, and looks down the line for the next Capital. This has been a great developmental experience, and more steps in my journey. I've spent a lifetime labouring to get to this moment. I just spent a week in the National Hockey League, and it was everything I dreamed about. The apprenticeship will continue in the AHL. I've been fixated on this hockey life for what seems like ages. It is my obsession, my passion, my journey.

I get into my car, turn it on, and listen as the V-8 engine rumbles. Tomorrow, I will drive north on I-95, and not the desired south. Driving home, my mind wanders. The Skipjacks play at home Tuesday, and I need to answer the bell. The last thing I want is for Coach Murray or Mr. Poile to think I'm sulking about being sent back down.

I think about the Gulf War, and the military troops fighting in Operation Desert Storm. The nightly news says to be vigilant, and watch for any suspicious characters or behaviour. I scan the sides of the Interstate. Nothing looks suspicious. I observe the overpasses on the highway as my car approaches. They look mostly empty. I'm hungry! I'll stop at Waterloo Pizza for their takeout lasagna. Their huge portions, inexpensive price, and great taste always hits the spot, and fills me up. It's time to eat. Sounds good!

Win, You Baltimore Skipjacks

Monday morning, I travel north on I-95 with Malts for practice. Arriving at the arena, I'm ready to go. Hockey etiquette says take your reassignment like a professional, and play determined to get back to The Show. I need to play so well that Mr. Poile has no choice but to give me another shot.

Two days after the game against the Islanders, I'm suiting up in Baltimore versus the Springfield Indians. The crowd tonight is quiet and thin; a typical sparse Tuesday night at the arena. Our big home night is Friday. It's challenging playing in front of 2,000 people again in the 11,000 seat Baltimore Arena. Playing in front of thousands of people in the NHL gave me an instant shot of energy.

Playing in front of a much smaller minor-league crowd requires more self-motivation.

We defeat the Indians 8-4 tonight. The *Skipjacks' Fight Song* plays eight times. We love it because we're sure the old, outdated tune drives the visiting team crazy. After each goal, the arena loud-speakers bellow to the delight of the crowd,

> *Win you Baltimore Skipjacks, win you Skipjacks from Baltimore.*
> *Fight you Baltimore Skipjacks, faceoff! Fight for a Baltimore score.*
> *Defencemen, forwards and goalie, we'll win without a doubt.*
> *For Baltimore, and Maryland, every Skipjack fan will shout,*
> *Fight! Fight! Fight!*
> *Win you Baltimore Skipjacks, win you Skipjacks from Baltimore.*
> *Fight you Baltimore Skipjacks, and score, score, score.*

The fans love it, and shout in unison and on cue: "Fight! Fight! Fight!" It certainly must annoy the visitors, especially if they have to hear it eight times, as Springfield does on this night. The first time I heard it was a few years ago when I played for the Binghamton Whalers, and I raised an eyebrow. Like all things unique to your home rink however, it becomes part of the home ice advantage and I have to admit, the unconventional fight song has grown on me.

After the Springfield win, the Jacks go on the road to play in Rochester and Newmarket picking up a tie and a loss. That makes three-games-in-three-nights for the Jacks; you know the drill, a typical minor-league schedule. For me, it's nine games in the last fourteen days, however, the way I'm feeling, the more the better. After scoring in three straight games, I'm digging deep for another shot in The Show. I'm determined to put the effort in for another taste of the good life, the dream life, the NHL life, and I want back in the Club.

A few calendar days pass. I'm eating supper with one of my teammates and his wife when news spreads that once again the Capitals have injury woes at forward, opening up an opportunity. There are a bunch of prospects in the pipeline deserving of this shot but I can only worry about myself. The NHL is the dream we're all chasing. In truth there is always a skilled, hungry player waiting for the moment when they can strut their stuff in the big leagues.

In my mind, I was recently recalled, and Coach Murray said I did everything he asked of me. I've come back to the minors, I'm scoring, working hard, and leading. This is my time. Instantly I become anxious as I try to guess Mr. Poile's next move. The same nervousness I feel before I play swallows up my chest cavity, and I believe the call is coming. It's going to be tough to sleep tonight.

At practice, Coach Laird walks in the room and informs the team that speedster Reggie Savage has been recalled by the Capitals. The scoring winger has already left for D.C. The news feels like a punch in the gut. I digest the announcement. I wanted this opportunity. Maybe the Caps are trying to make me hungrier for the job, or maybe they want to give Reggie a look-see. The reason doesn't matter. I want back in, back in the club, back to the dream. I just experienced the sweet taste of life in The Show, and it is right in front of me. I can taste it, smell it, and feel it.

After practice, I knock on Coach Laird's door. Don't shoot the messenger they say, but I'm looking for answers. Spewing my venom for a few minutes, which for me isn't very lethal, I make my point, and take satisfaction from that. My supportive and thoughtful coach says all of the right things I expect about hard work, patience, and staying the course. I appreciate it. I'm at the point where I can almost touch my dream, but it's just out of my reach. All I can do is keep stretching for it, hoping to one day grab hold, and never let it go.

It's been a busy schedule recently, as you know, and the boys have a couple of days before our next go-round. We decide it's time for a team-bonding activity. Events off the ice can bring teams closer together on the ice.

Recently we discovered a small pub outside Columbia. The parking lot is mostly empty, and inside the confines are tight. There's a long bar up front with three patrons; perhaps Norm, Cliff, and Fraser from *Cheers*. Not likely, but they do look like their seats are designated. Our presence agitates the older, out-of-shape-looking regulars who are conspicuously holding up the small bar.

We're a noisy group of young, athletic-looking males. Maybe we're too disruptive, too boisterous for this quiet, local watering hole. Tables are at a minimum, and we push the light pieces of furniture closer together in order to seat our group. Norm, Cliff, and Fraser stare at us defiantly as they sip on their mugs of beer, and discuss how we arbitrarily rearranged the setup in the bar without permission.

We introduce ourselves to the strangers, and discover the larger fellow's name is Ray. A round of beer is ordered by our table. The man and woman behind the bar are pleased with the additional business on this otherwise quiet weekday afternoon.

One of the guys pulls out a deck of cards, then another deck, and an impromptu euchre tournament commences. We need music! There's a jukebox on the far wall; a throwback novelty even for us. Quarters are needed for this sound machine, and the woman at the bar provides us with coins in exchange for our U.S. greenbacks. The jukebox comes alive with music; good songs, and bad; songs that inspire laughter; and others awkward participation. "Who sings that song?" a voice chirps. "Aerosmith," says another. "Why don't you let 'em," barks one of the fellas, and I laugh.

We order another round, and this time, add one for Ray, and his two buddies. From our tables, we raise a glass to our newfound acquaintances. There's no talk of hockey. We're just guys bonding on this quiet, sunny afternoon.

"Whose lead is it? Someone barks out.

"Pay attention," says another voice.

"Who has the Bauer?" Shouts one of the fellas at the other table.

"Winners move on!" I hear someone say.

"You didn't follow suit, you cheating sack of shit! Show me your cards."

The pub has come to life. "Another beer for Ray," a loud voice calls out, and the barkeeper gives our new friend another beer on the boys. In unison we break into raucous song:

Who's the greatest guy in town? Ray, Ray!
Who's the greatest guy in town? Ray all the way!
Ray all the way! Ray all the way!
Who's the greatest guy in town?
Ray all the way!

Ray is beaming with the widest grin I've ever seen, as his mates pat him on the back and give us a thumbs up. Laughing hysterically at our completed serenade, we continue to deal the cards. Time speeds by when we're sharing these moments. The euchre tournament champions are crowned, and it's time to exit. We shake hands with our new friends as we leave. Who knows if we'll ever see them again, and it doesn't matter. We came here to bond, and that was accomplished!

Afternoons like these are special! Future days will see attempts to duplicate moments like this, but the special ones come by unexpectedly, and then poof, they're gone, only to serve as memories, stories for the room, bus rides, and the off-season. Who's the greatest guy in town? Today, it's Ray!

Birds, Bones & Beer

Mid-March, the Skipjacks have another road trip with stops in Springfield, Hershey, New Haven, and Newmarket, finishing back in Springfield. Malts and I scramble around the apartment, trying to get our luggage together, so we can drive to the Columbia Arena and meet the bus that's leaving soon.

Malts is fond of country music and listens to Randy Travis when we're getting ready for games, and road trips. I'm not a country music fan, but have come to enjoy it, and even purchased my own CDs from my roomie's influence; artists like Alabama, and the Nitty Gritty Dirt Band. "Listen to the words," Malts says because country music tells stories.

Heroes and Friends by Randy Travis is playing on the CD player while I sit on the living room couch, and advise Malts to hurry so we're not late for the bus. Being late will be a 2-5, a team imposed penalty; a $25 fine for being tardy.

"C'mon we gotta go," I chirp. "Yep coming, give me a minute," he replies faintly from his bedroom. Sitting, waiting, holding my luggage, listening to the music, I sing quietly: "Your heroes will help you find good in yourself. Your friends won't forsake you for somebody else. They'll both stand beside you through thick and through thin, and that's how it goes with..." Thwap! I hear a peculiar sound. Thwap, thwap, thwap, thwap, thwap. "What the fuck?" I murmur. Standing up, I walk over, and turn down the music. Thwap, thwap. I follow the source of the odd noise into the foyer by the front door. Thwap. I turn left, and walk down the hall to my sunny bedroom. Thwap, I push open the door. Ahhh, no!

A frickin bird, a bird, a big, black starling is flying uncontrollably around my bedroom. Stupid bird! The starling is flying straight into the mirror in the middle off my dresser, bouncing off, sliding to the bottom, flying back to the wall, and trying again. Malts comes running into my room. "What's up?" He says. "There's a fuckin' bird in here!" I shout. "We gotta go, we're late. Get it out of here!" I holler. I distract the bird, and chase him out into the living room. "Open the patio door man!" I yell. "Okay," Malts shouts back while we pursue the scared bird until it escapes out the wide-open patio door. "C'mon we gotta go, we're late. Stupid bird!" Hustling over to the arena, we make the bus just in time. Whew, made it man. No fines today.

We board the waiting bus and are back on the road. Long road trips are a good time for team bonding, and it's impactful early on. Later in the season, when we're more fatigued, and banged up, road trips can get wearisome. Games on consecutive nights, arriving at hotels or shitty motels at 5 a.m., sleeping on buses, watching *Slap Shot*, *Caddyshack*, and *Fletch* again can lose their appeal. Having said that, there's a certain amount of excitement whenever the bus pulls out for a roadie.

Accompanied by the expected chirping, and laughing, our bus rolls onto the Interstate, a familiar piece of highway, and the coaching staff doles out the meal money for the entire trip.

The crew is rolling on the ice too. The trip starts with a 4-3 win vs the Springfield Indians, followed by a 6-3 romp over the rival Hershey Bears, and then a slim 1-0 victory over the New Haven Nighthawks. Post-game we're back on the bus and driving to Newmarket for a matchup with the Saints.

The tired, sleeping team is awakened as we arrive at the Canadian border. After clearing customs, I look out the window and see a road sign directing us to the familiar Queen Elizabeth Way. Only a couple more hours before we reach the city north of Toronto. Arriving at our Newmarket hotel we head straight to bed. There's no morning skate tomorrow. Night all!

Ring! Ring! Who? What? Fucking phone! I reach for the telephone that is causing my heart to pound. "Hello," I say gruffly. "Can I speak to Steve," says a voice. "Speaking," I growl. It's the Skipjacks' front office, informing me that my truck has been stolen. "Sorry to be the bearer of bad news," says the voice on the end. "Okay, see you," I murmur and hang up. C'mon man! My brand new Blazer. Shit!

Sleep is not possible now as my mind darts in dozens of directions. However, there's still hockey to play so the truck will have to wait. Family arrives to watch and we skate to a 2-1 win over the Newmarket Saints. Post-game, I meet up with the assembled crew of relatives, and share the lousy news of the day. "The Skipjacks' front office called, and said the Maryland State Police reported that my truck has been stolen," I say despondently. The police said my Blazer was taken for a joyride before being abandoned in a parking lot.

While exchanging hugs and good-byes with everyone, voices are calling out to the group. It's time to get on the bus; we're moving out. Grandma Betty has provided a care package for me complete with banana bread covered in maple icing, muffins, cookies and other quick eats. I'm looking for her to say thanks and good-bye but she's disappeared for the moment. I quickly scan the hall and

I see her huddled up with Jack. He starts to walk in my direction and as he gets closer, he looks at me and says, "I just ordered a cherry pie!" Really? Hey, those pies are for me. I walk over and give her a big hug and it is back on the iron lung.

On the bus, I carefully secure my package of sweet foods. These bags of goodies always make me feel closer to home. Driving to the border, we clear U.S. customs. There is one more game to play, back where we started in Springfield. After a week on the road, we're a tired team, but know we have one more game to focus on before going home. Truthfully, four-straight road wins finds us feeling not quite as tired as we might otherwise be.

The game with Springfield is a scrappy affair. Midway through the second frame, I'm standing in front of the opposition's net screening the goalie. A big, aggressive defenceman wants me out of there, and takes a mighty swing at me with his stick. The wild chop strikes the underside of my glove, and blasts the tip of my thumb. 'Ahhh!' I want to jump through the roof, and as the play moves up ice, I skate to the bench. Sitting down, I bend over, and rock back and forth.

Sliding down the bench, as the forwards change quickly, my line is up again. Hopping over the boards, my linemates are attacking the goal, and I drive the net. A shot comes from our defenceman stationed on the blue line and strikes my glove, another massive blow to my already throbbing thumb. Like a wounded wolf, I let out a huge howl! Slowly I glide to the bench, and our trainer comes over. "My thumb, my thumb," I snap. Can't grip my stick. I can't go!

I sit on the bench for the remainder of the night. Nothing can be done now. The game ends in a 5-5 tie, and we pull in nine out-of-ten possible points; a successful road trip. Post-game, the Springfield doctor looks at my swollen, black and blue thumb. "Could be broken, you'll need an X-ray," he says. Thanks Captain Obvious!

Outside the rink, random fans holding Sharpies ask for autographs. I sign and throw my hockey bag under the humming motor coach. The bus slowly fills, and we depart for home; a drive of just over five hours. In order to help out the trainers, we stop at the arena to unload and hang our cold, wet equipment.

Back on the bus, we travel south down I-95 to Columbia. We arrive about 5 a.m. and half asleep. Malts and I pick up a ride home from one of our teammates. On the drive we're laughing and joking with giddy fatigue. This week was anything but smooth sailing between my throbbing thumb, my stolen truck, and the stupid bird! "I know, I know, what else could go wrong eh?" I say to Malts.

Staggering out of the car when we arrive at the apartment, we slowly walk up the three flights of stairs. I unlock the door, and push it open. It's dark, and cold in our two-bedroom digs.

"Turn on the lights Malts," I say

"It's bedtime for Bonzo," he replies as he flips a switch on.

"Yah, me too," I announce, and turn on the kitchen light.

"What's this?" I say curiously while staring at the dirty countertop.

"What is that?" Says Malts.

"Look, here's more," I say, and walk over to the dark living room.

"Bird shit!" I shout.

"What?" Malts shouts.

"Yah, bird shit!" I repeat louder.

That stupid bird from a week ago found his way back into the apartment.

"Look at this!" Adding to our disgust, I find a half-eaten loaf of bread, and more bird shit everywhere and on everything.

"Where is he? He's gotta be in here," says Malts. We start hunting room to room for the avian intruder; stupid bird! Lifting up the lid on the kitchen garbage can, I find the lifeless, dead, black starling. Like I thought, stupid bird! In his attempts to escape, or forage for food, the bird opened the light plastic lid on the can, and became trapped inside. Sweet justice!

"I'm going to bed," says Malts,

"Well I'm certain my thumb is broken, so I'm staying up to clean this shit," I respond.

Scrubbing the counters and furniture for a couple hours, I curse the fucking bird with each push of the black, dirty sponge. With the sun coming up, and my cleaning complete, it's now 7 a.m., so I decide I'll stay up for the day. I'm injured anyway and I know I won't be playing for few weeks with a fracture. At best it's a severe bruise, and I'll be out a week.

At 9 a.m., I start the search for my truck. Earlier this season, I purchased the new Blazer in Virginia from Malt's buddy Larry, a Newfoundlander, now living in the U.S. The strange thing is, I still owned my Firebird. Why did I need two vehicles? I didn't. My plan has been to sell the Firebird in the summer.

Making phone calls to start the hunt, the police are able to give me the address of the pound where my truck is waiting. Malts is awake now, and drives me. We arrive, and it's a scene right out of the movie, *Mad Max*. There it is – my Chevy Blazer – a disaster. Feeling violated, and a little less safe all of a sudden, I discover the joyriders have shredded all of my personal belongings. The front driver's side window is destroyed, and hundreds of tiny fragments of glass litter the floor. The starter is gone, removed to allow the car thieves a quick hot-wire. Not being an experienced car thief, I wonder how I will start this vehicle.

I know, I'll ask the pound's wise attendant for advice. "How do I start this truck with the starter gone?" I say to the rough-looking stranger, and he says he can help. "Okay," I reply. "$20," he adds. The hopes for me to start my truck now hinge on the hot-wiring skills of this shady character. What a scammer, I think, but still, I pass him $20. He sits in the vehicle and the engine is running in seconds. He hops out, I hop in and, drive back to the apartment.

Pulling into my parking space, I stare at the location where the starter would be. Next problem, 'how do you turn off a car with no starter?' "What a joke!" I shout out. I wait for Malts to arrive, so I can share my new dilemma. He shrugs his shoulders, and says he's not a mechanic either. "The gas gauge reads below one-quarter, so I'm going up to the store to buy a case of beer. I'm going to sit here and drink until this truck runs out of gas," I say to Malts in an exasperated tone.

With that, I drive up to the corner, purchase a case, take it back to the apartment, park, and start drinking beside the still running Blazer. Several pints in, a couple of the boys who heard about my misfortune arrive, and one, a wise veteran named Chris Felix, helps his younger apprentice turn off the truck. "Thanks Feeler!" I say. Our work here is done.

I go to bed about 2 p.m. with one found dead bird, one recovered stolen truck, and one broken thumb. I've heard people say things happen in threes. Birds, bones, and beer. What a week! Stupid bird!

Obliterated

An X-ray is on the schedule for my aching, colourful, swollen thumb, and the result is, it's broken. I'm knocked out of commission for the remainder of the regular season. The team doctor says I won't be playing for several weeks. His timeline will have me back for the start of the Calder Cup tournament.

An unfamiliar player agent has been around the rink recently, and talking to his clients. I have free time due to my fractured thumb; maybe too much time. I find myself in a private conversation with the player representative who is aligned with an agency out of New York City. After our meeting, I believe perhaps a change is in order, and I agree to sign on with his organization.

It is an impulsive decision. Rick has been my agent since I was 16-years-old. He was with me at the OHL draft, NHL draft, and when I signed my first two contracts. I've seen him less in recent memory, and maybe that makes this rash decision easier. Regardless, I send a letter to his Toronto office, simply stating that I'm making a change, and no longer require his services. It's not the best way to end our working relationship, and I know that.

Some time later, I receive the expected phone call from him. Rick is furious! The call is short and awkward, and unfortunately will be the last time I speak with him. Looking back, it was a knee-jerk reaction that I regret and if I could do it over again, I would not have made the change. You know what they say about hindsight; it truly is twenty-twenty.

At the end of the 1990-91 regular season, the Skipjacks are sitting in third in the Southern Division with a record of 39-34-7 for 85 points. This sets up a first-round playoff matchup with the second-place Binghamton Rangers, the New York Rangers' affiliate. Coincidentally, our parent Capitals finish the regular season in third in the Patrick Division, setting up a playoff series with the New York Rangers. NHL clubs and their AHL affiliates are squaring off.

A long Calder Cup run will be beneficial for all of the Skipjacks; allowing Caps' management more opportunity to see us play in the post-season when games are more intense. Despite a fractured thumb, I feel ready, and like our chances.

To start the series, Binghamton wins Game One and Game Two at home by scores of 5-4 and 2-0, and are led by playmaker Rob Zamuner, defenceman Peter Laviolette, and a veteran lineup. The series shifts to Baltimore for the next two tilts.

Game Three gets underway, and we're desperate for a win. I don't feel sharp after missing the last few weeks. I'm struggling with timing, and try to ratchet up the intensity. Skating through the neutral zone, I chase a puck dumped into the Rangers' end. My legs churn faster, and I enter the offensive zone looking for a big hit on the freewheeling defenceman. As I make contact, he twists away, and I abruptly cut with my left skate to stay on his heels. Pop! I feel a strange twinge inside my knee, as if it has shifted, and settled back in place. There is a feeling of instability I haven't experienced for a long time. I glide to the bench for a needed line change. At the final buzzer, the Rangers double us up by a score of 6-3, and take a commanding 3-0 lead in the best-of-seven-series.

Over the last four years, I've adapted to playing with a large, cumbersome brace on my left leg. I've never stepped onto the ice without the custom-made appliance I'm required to wear to protect and support my torn ACL. For me, it's another piece of equipment. No different than shin pads, elbow pads, or any other protective gear. It hangs in my stall, is packed in my bag for road trips, and comes home in the summer.

Post-game with Binghamton, I mention my wonky knee to our trainer, Dan. He suggests I let the Skipjacks' team doctor look to be safe. The orthopedic doc arrives in the training room, and asks me to hop up on the evaluation table. "Your knee Steve?" He says. "Yah, I tweaked it. You know, it kind of made a popping sound but it doesn't hurt," I reply. I want him to know that. In my mind I believe I'm fine and this is a formality. He asks me to lay back on the table. I know what's coming next as I've been through this battery of ACL tests many times. He performs a couple of simple maneuvers to check stability of the wobbly joint.

I don't like the strained look on his face as he completes the exam. Maybe I'm just seeing things, or making mountains out of mole hills. "Steve, there's nothing we can do here today," he says. "But after the season, you may need this knee surgically repaired." Surgery? What? No need, I'm fine. Thanks for the opinion. Can't I just get a bunch of anti-inflammatory pills for the road? I've been playing like this since junior hockey. I'll be fine. I hustle out of the training room, replaying the doctor's ominous words over and over in my uneasy mind. 'Screw surgery, I have hockey to play, and this series isn't over.'

We buckle down with our backs against the proverbial wall, and dig deep to win Game Four and Game Five by scores of 6-5 and 5-3 only to be eliminated by the Rangers in Game Six at home by a 2-1 count. The disappointing playoff loss means there will not be a Calder Cup parade for us this spring.

Meanwhile, up in The Show, the Caps knock off the New York Rangers in six. In doing so, they advance to round two of the playoffs against the spectacular playmaking abilities of Super Mario, the always dangerous Jaromir Jagr, and the rest of the star-studded Pittsburgh Penguins.

Within five days of starting the series with the Pens, the Capitals are eliminated by the crew that will go on to win the 1991 Stanley Cup. Incidentally, in leading the Pens to the Cup, Mario Lemieux le Magnifique will finish his Cup run with 16 goals, 28 assists, 44 points in 23 games played, and win the Conn Smythe trophy as playoff MVP.

Just like that, Stanley Cup and Calder Cup dreams fizzle out for another hockey season. The players and management tend to the business of end-of-season meetings, locker clean out, packing up gear, and loose ends. Medical follow-ups are on the agenda if needed, and it appears that the news of my rickety knee has been reviewed by Mr. Poile, Jack, and the Skipjacks' medical staff. Therefore, I'm going to receive an examination before departing for home.

Arriving at the suburban D.C. office for the familiar ACL exam, I take a seat in the quiet and clean waiting room. The Caps' calm team doctor invites me in, completes the examination, and I watch his face closely, looking for any piece of information he telegraphs unintentionally. Leaving the office, I quickly drive back to the Capital Centre; I'm meeting Jack after my appointment.

When I arrive, he's waiting. I enter the room, and sit down calm and cool like. I'm comfortable with Jack, and I trust him. Let's get this meeting over with and I'll be on my way.

"Hi Jack," I say confidently.

"Have a seat Steve," he says matter-of-factly.

"Sure," I reply and take my position in the chair.

"I spoke to the doctor this morning," he says calmly.

"What did he say?" I reply anxiously.

"He thinks we should repair your ACL," Jack says as he leans forward folding his hands together.

"No, I don't want surgery," I state as I lean back in my chair, fidgeting with my hands, and feeling my heart beating a little faster.

"This is the best thing for your long-term career," he says convincingly, while he sets his folded hands on the table.

"No, I don't want surgery. I can't do it," I say, as my pulse continues to rise. A lump forms in my throat, and I slowly move back from the large table.

"Why can't you do it?" He asks inquisitively, like a wise father who knows best.

"I feel fine, and, ah, what if I don't wake up after? I heard that happens to people," I add, and search for valid reasons to delay this idea. My mouth is dry, and my distracted mind is wandering in and out of the conversation.

"This is the best decision for your long-term career," he repeats for the second time.

I trust Jack, and if that's what he and the doctor think, maybe I should do this. My knee is unstable at times, and I do hate wearing the brace, but I've played well this year. I'm so fucking close to the dream, and now you want to shut me down for months. I'm poised to make a move in the organization. This is the best I've ever felt on the ice, and The Show, it is right in front of me. I sit back and stare at Jack. I have to trust him and the doctor.

"Shit. When will it be?" I ask.

"Our doctor will have you in within the week," he replies quickly.

"Yah," and I relent. Surgery. It's on.

Jack reaches for the phone on the large desk, and within moments engages in a conversation confirming reconstructive knee surgery is to go ahead. My mind is darting from thought to thought. I'm no longer listening to any of the words coming out of Jack's mouth, not out of disrespect, but out of disbelief and confusion.

Within hours, I have a confirmed surgery date and time. The off-season procedure will be performed in a suburban D.C. hospital. Making the difficult calls home, I have to explain to my family that I'm having knee surgery, even though recently I played in a playoff game and appear healthy. The torn ACL from my sopho-more year of junior is the culprit. "Everyone says this will help my long-term career," I say to my family and friends. That's all I can say, and really, I don't want to talk about it.

Surgery day I arrive at the upscale D.C. hospital. It's quiet, clean, and quite posh for a medical building. It's not the type of large, busy medical centre I expected, and in fact, seems like "Club Med" for pro athletes.

The Caps' orthopedic surgeon will perform the procedure. Completing the normal admission procedures, I follow the nurse into my private room. I change out of my clothes, into the thin hospital gown provided, lay on the bed, and anxiously wait for the orderly to whisk me away. My nurse reappears, and says it will be a few more minutes. Inserting a needle into my hand, she says it will assist with the anesthetic required. I begin to think about what it's like to be cut wide-open. Visions of saws, blades, drills and sharp knives fill my mind. My complicated inner voice toys with me. The orderly appears and says, "Time to go." The sides of my hospital bed are raised, and I'm rolled down the hall to the OR.

The operating room door opens, and my bed is rolled in. The room is cool and bright. Dressed in the expected surgical gowns, the medical team is positioned and waiting for my arrival. The surgeon briefly speaks with me about the upcoming procedure. With that, the anesthetist begins the process to knock me out. I close my eyes, and then, an odd taste is present in my throat. Strange, what is? Zzzz.

"Steve, Steve, Steve." 'What, huh, where, what?' My eyes open slightly, but it is difficult to keep them like that. In a dark, quiet room, I see a young nurse who is calling my name. "How do you feel?" she says softly. "Nauseous, I think I'm going to throw up," I reply. "I have something for that," she says. My mouth is pasty and dry. I want to wet my tongue. "Can I have a drink?" I mutter. She passes me a cup of water. I have a sip, and drift back to sleep.

Awakening again, my knee does not feel good. It is wrapped tightly in a dressing and is throbbing. The soft-spoken nurse reappears, and provides me with a painkiller for my swollen leg and a miracle drug is inserted in my IV; morphine I hear her say. The morphine gives me a warm, fuzzy feeling all over, and feeling like I'm floating, I drift back to sleep with ease.

The next time I awaken, the nurse appears with a small apparatus for my surgically repaired knee. You want me to use this? "What about the morphine?" I ask, as that seems more appropriate to me. She calmly secures the machine on to the bed, and it houses my knee while gently flexing and extending the joint. This is to allow for immediate improvement to my range of motion, and to lessen recovery time. Sounds good to me, but will I get more morphine after? I have to wait how long? Alright, I'll wait.

The surgeon pays me a visit to review the procedure. He explains to me that inside the joint, he discovered the ligament was completely obliterated. In other words, it was no longer functioning or recognizable. Obliterated, he says. Reconstruction was necessary, and I can't say I'm surprised. The rehabilitation time from reconstructive knee surgery will be about nine months. I do the quick math, and realize my return to play will be in January or February of the upcoming season. That seems like a long way off while laying in my hospital bed in May of 1991.

I feel helpless being there in the quiet room alone. I'm in pain, and depressed. I have a tiny television in my room to help pass the time. Adding to my stress, I discover on the local news that a major riot has started. A shooting incident involving police has resulted in chaos in the capital city. Uptight and paranoid with the unrest, I see cars on fire, looting, arrests, and anger are in the D.C. streets. Two days of violence result in a state of emergency being declared, and a curfew implemented. Being heavily medicated, and isolated, my anxiety level increases, as I anticipate the hostilities spilling over to the hospital. Watching the nightly news on my bedside TV fuels my delusions while the capital is under siege.

Returning to Ontario after my release, I'm looking forward to being married in June, to my best friend, Lisa. In order to walk down the aisle in six-weeks-time, I start physiotherapy as soon as I return. I should have no problem walking by then according to the surgeon. I'm outfitted with a large brace to wear under my tuxedo, as I still need to support the new, healing ligament.

The wedding day is a perfect one in Kingston, and many of the boys, current and former, attend, along with family and friends. The ceremony is at St. Joseph's Roman Catholic Church, followed by a dinner, a Thousand Islands' boat cruise, and a reception that comes together for a terrific day.

This summer is different than any other that I've experienced before. There is no skating, running, squats, Brigitte Wolf, or summer hockey, only physiotherapy to prepare a surgically repaired knee for hockey next winter.

The Metro

My new ACL is a loaner. In other words, the surgeon used a ligament from a cadaver. He says that using this technique will speed up my recovery time. The road ahead, and my routine this summer and fall, will be dominated by intense physiotherapy sessions. Let's get this knee ready for hockey games, shall we?

However, first things first, I still need to sell my Firebird. I've run ads in the classified section of the Whig-Standard all summer, and nobody is banging down my door for this car. In fact, there are no phone calls at all, nothing. Remember, I paid $16,000 for this vehicle, and I started this summer asking for $9,000. The closer I get to training camp, the lower the asking price is going.

Mid-August and two short weeks before we leave, I'm getting increasingly frustrated with the lack of interest. I decide to dangle the carrot, a price that can't be refused; I want a response, just one! My new ad in the Whig-Standard reads as follows: "1987 Pontiac Firebird $4,500. Moving to U.S.A. Must sell." Hey, I wanted to sell it, and fast. Not surprisingly, the phone starts to ring, and I arrange a meeting with a potential buyer. Arriving at my apartment, he checks out the powerful, muscle car. "I'll give you $4,200." Says the older, wise gentleman. Oh boy! Well, I guess I asked for it. "Okay, fine," I say. He leaves and returns shortly thereafter with a certified cheque. With payment in hand, I pass him the keys, and watch as he drives away with the biggest smile I've ever seen.

Training camp is days away and it's time to go. Lisa and I load up a U-Haul trailer, and attach it to our silver, four-wheel drive Blazer which will carry us and our dog, Tyson. We cross into the United States at the Thousand Islands Bridge, leading to I-81 south for Maryland. I'll be present at training camp, but unable to participate in on-ice activities; physiotherapy is my main assignment.

The Capitals signed a lease over the summer to use the newly built Piney Orchard Ice Arena. The facility, located in Odenton, Maryland, will be the new practice rink for both the Capitals, and the Skipjacks. There's excitement around the organization as we prepare to move into our new training home. There's enough space for each team to have a large dressing room and we'll share a weight room, trainer's room, and players' lounge. There are tidy, modern offices for the coaching staffs, and Mr. Poile has an office upstairs overlooking the ice surface.

Training camp starts for the Capitals. It's a difficult time for me. Watching from the sidelines is not enjoyable, and it frankly sucks! I'm isolated from the team, missing scrimmages, practices, and meetings. There will be off-ice workouts for me but my focus, and task, is still physiotherapy, now in downtown D.C., three-times per week, Monday, Wednesday, and Friday. Tuesdays and Thursdays, I work out in the weight room with the squad.

The Caps provide me with the clinic address. My therapist's name is coincidentally Lisa. She will be in continuous contact with trainer Stan Wong, providing weekly updates on my progress. Appointments are scheduled in the morning. In order to avoid the snarling downtown D.C. traffic and lack of parking, I decide to ride the subway into the city. The D.C. subway system is called the Washington Metro, or as the locals say; the Metro. To catch the train, I drive thirty-minutes to the closest Maryland stop on the route.

I become a skilled operator of the underground subway system. In time, I memorize all the major stops – you take the green line for the University of Maryland; for the Smithsonian Institute, take the blue line; Landover, take the orange line.

My trips on the Metro from my suburban pick-up point to downtown D.C. are approximately thirty-five minutes, and then there is a short walk on the bustling city streets. Each day, I take along my Sony Walkman, and a couple of cassette tapes to pass the time.

Once I arrive, I go through rigorous therapy. Improving strength, and stability are the early goals. Motivation to get healthy and play hockey again drives me. Physiotherapy for an ACL repair is a slow and tedious process. It takes time, and there are no shortcuts. It requires personal drive, and I have to push myself daily. There's no training partner to work out with, no coach screaming in my ear. There is guidance, yes, from my therapist Lisa, but largely, self-motivation is required.

Physio has its share of pain too, namely the massaging of scar tissue that developed in the joint post-op. Scar tissue forms in joint spaces after surgery but through manual massage, it can be reduced. The pain from the scar tissue massage leaves me clutching the table, and cursing under my breath. Range of motion exercises, leg extensions, leg flexions, leg raises, flexibility, and more are each designed to get me ready for skating, and in time, contact hockey games.

The upcoming season is the NHL's 75th anniversary. The Capitals will start their 1991-92 schedule at home versus the Flyers, and the Skipjacks will start at home versus the rival Bears.

The Caps get off to a flying start with an 8-2 record through their first ten under returning Coach Terry Murray. The Skipjacks have the coaching duo of Rob Laird, and Barry Trotz back for their second go-round with the club. A number of player personnel changes have taken place in the off-season, and the makeup of the Skipjacks has changed considerably. In mid-June, Malts was traded, along with prospect Trent Klatt to the Minnesota North Stars for defenceman Shawn Chambers. I'm gonna miss my roomie! We lived together for two years and shared a lot of laughs and good times. The pure goal scorer will play 120 NHL games.

The new season is underway for both clubs and I feel disconnected. The days spent in physiotherapy are days away from the rink, the team, the comradery, and relationship building. Missing training camp, games, and practices leaves me on the perimeter. The coaches give me statistical tracking tasks to keep me involved. I review the stats with Trotzy before each game, and then take the elevator up to the press box and chat with Baltimore Sun sports columnist Nestor. I get a small sense of purpose helping out with stats, but it doesn't take long before tracking data loses its luster.

In order to stay more involved with the crew, I offer to represent our club as the player representative for the Professional Hockey Players' Association. The PHPA represents the interests of AHL hockey players, negotiating benefits like medical, dental, travel expenses, meal money, playoff shares and other programs. It gives me a chance to be involved in another aspect of hockey and to work with the PHPA's management group and representatives.

I want to be on the ice, I want to play, but I need to be patient. Having said that, I don't feel like being patient anymore, I want to play hockey! Despite being sidelined, a contract offer has been extended to me by Mr. Poile. This will be my third with the organization. I'm certainly not in a position of strength, as a former second rounder who has spent the bulk of the last three seasons in the minors, and is coming back from major reconstructive knee surgery. Having said that, I don't immediately sign the proposed deal. I, like other players, want more money!

After workouts in the weight room, I watch practice from the stands at Piney Orchard to stay connected. Jack is walking through the rink, and I suspect he wants to observe practice too. He starts moving up the stairs in my direction, and takes a seat beside me. I like to shoot the breeze and talk hockey with Jack. I expect this will be one of our hockey talks. "How is physio going?" he asks. "Right on schedule," I reply confidently. "Good to hear," he says. Bring on the hockey talk Jack.

To my surprise, his next question is about my new contract. "Why haven't you signed your contract?" Says the experienced hockey man. I immediately stare down at the floor and pause as I think about the appropriate answer. As I said, I want more money, and I nervously try to explain this to him. I've never been involved in this kind of contract roulette before; agents look after contracts. I can tell from his eyes, and the look on his face, what his position is on the issue, and at that point I get close-mouthed. This isn't the hockey talk I had in mind Jack. This is agent and GM stuff. The dialogue about my contract is short. I sort of explain my position, and he listens. After this face-to-face meeting, I feel pressure to put pen to paper, and get this deal signed.

In short order, I do in fact sign my new contract, and in the end, I receive an extra $5,000 in guaranteed money. My new salary will be $160,000 U.S. and my new guaranteed salary will be $35,000 U.S. I sign my third contract with the Capitals, and it feels fantastic!

Back in the Saddle

Big Al Iafrate makes a generous offer to a few of the boys in Baltimore. He simply says, if we can get to the Capital Centre tonight, he has tickets for us to see Van Halen. Agreeing without hesitation, we drive down to meet the easy-going Michigan native. It's a great show and equally great time with Al!

Mid-December rolls around, and I finally have the opportunity to put my dusty blades on for the first time this season. No equipment, just skates. After practice, I'm permitted to skate easy laps as part of my rehabilitation. I'm on the ice alone to prevent any accidental contact. It's awesome for my hockey spirits to have my steel blades cutting through the ice again, as I cautiously skate lap after lap. With each passing minute, I push my blades a little harder, and listen to them carve out the ice beneath. My heart rate begins to elevate. I back off, because it's light skating only at this point. The team is in the dressing room getting ready to go out on the road again. I miss being on the road. Returning to the room, I find they're slowly loading the bus and preparing to depart. Today is another step for me. I'm getting closer to playing hockey again.

In the wintery month of January, my physiotherapist Lisa gives me her blessing. "You're ready," she says. We've spent three-days-a-week for the past five months together. We've become closer over that time, having gone through my intensive rehabilitation process together, working towards a common goal, and my lengthy recovery is now complete.

I feel rebuilt, and my leg is strong. Thanking her, I suggest we attend a Capitals' game together as a final farewell. She agrees, and I pick up two tickets to the next home game. A hockey fan she is not, therefore, I answer her questions as we watch from our lower bowl end-zone seats. The final siren sounds, we both stand, she gives me a hug, and wishes me luck with my career. We exit the rink and walk through the jammed parking lot. It's time to start practicing with contact to prepare for game play. I haven't played hockey in months, but now, it's go time!

After an extended layoff and practicing hard through the remaining days of the month, I have my sights set on playing soon. It's so close now – it will be my first action since last April. Almost one-year has passed, and needless to say, I'm eager to get back playing. Missing more than half of the season I need to level up my conditioning, and participate in full-contact drills. Coach Laird and I are targeting the first week of February for my return. Aerosmith released a song in the 1970's named *Back in the Saddle*, and after an intense drawn-out absence, I can say I'm back in the saddle again and it's a relief!

Coach suggests I start off with an assignment in the East Coast Hockey League, with the Capitals' affiliate, the Hampton Roads Admirals. Truthfully, I want to play in Baltimore. It isn't necessary, I'm ready to play, and I assure him I will not disappoint. It's my fourth-year in the American Hockey League, and I know I can contribute and compete right out of the gate without a conditioning assignment. After a closed-door discussion, Coach Laird agrees, and pencils me into the Skipjacks' lineup for our next game.

Practicing in advance of my reappearance, I'm on a regular line and skating well. My return will be at home vs the New Haven Nighthawks, months after my surgery. Tonight will be a crucial test for my knee. Sitting in my stall, I do my pre-game visualization routine. Eyes closed, I picture myself taking pucks off the boards in my own end, making a tape-to-tape first pass, shooting the puck quickly, seeing the puck enter the net, finishing checks, and back-checking. I say a quick prayer, and open my eyes wide.

It's almost time, and the chatter in the room ramps up. "Here we go boys! Big game, big game!" I miss this energetic chatter, and realize how much as I rock back and forth in my skates beside the full stick rack. It feels awesome making the long walk out to the ice surface, hearing the home fans cheer, to be skating for warm-up, to hear the arena music-man play, 'The boys are back in town,' to stand on the bench for the national anthem, and to be back playing hockey!

The puck drops, and this game and my career are back on! With my lungs on fire, I realize my conditioning still needs work, but that will come. This is a good debut against the Northern Division's Nighthawks. My knee passes the first test, and I believe it will only get better from here. I'm ecstatic to be back on the ice; that goes without saying. However, the team is falling in the league standings and the pressure on the coaches and players to win is increasing daily.

To end the month of February, we leave town for a six-game road trip with stops in Rochester, Utica, Binghamton, Hershey, and New Haven. I'm stoked to be travelling with the fellas again.

The fourth game of the trip is in the State of Connecticut against the New Haven Nighthawks. At breakfast, I walk into the hotel restaurant, and notice Jack is in the lobby. That's odd. The boys' Spidey senses are instantly elevated. Jack showing up on the road is not normal course, and especially when the team is struggling. The rumours swirl, and the players buzz on the bus ride to the arena for the morning skate.

The trip ends in Binghamton. Our suspicions become a reality after returning home when we are given the news that Coach Laird has been fired by Mr. Poile, and replaced by assistant coach Barry Trotz.

Mr. Poile explained the firing to James H. Jackson of the Baltimore Evening Sun: "The determining factor in our decision was the recent won-lost record of the Skipjacks. It is my feeling that, to give the Skipjacks any chance of turning their season around in the remaining 20 games, a change was necessary at this time."

Coach Laird and I had a good working relationship, and he trusted me on the ice. The news is disappointing, and I feel for him on a personal and professional level. He has a family and a passion for hockey. He's a hardworking coach who put everything into his job, and the team. However, this is business decision.

I speak with Trotzy. It is a difficult position he finds himself in as well. Coach Laird mentored him the last couple years so he is replacing the man who helped him cut his coaching teeth at the pro ranks. Coaches have goals too. Mr. Poile offered this stepping stone to Coach Trotz, and he is seizing the opportunity.

The team plays five of the next six at home with our new bench boss. I'm feeling better on the ice, and fitting back in. My goal is to continue to improve, and finish the season playing well. If the Skipjacks can put a streak together, perhaps there will be future Calder Cup playoff games down the road to extend this season, and my development.

On the mid-March schedule is the annual road trip to the Canadian Maritime provinces for games versus clubs in the new Atlantic Division of the AHL: Cape Breton Oilers, Halifax Citadels, Fredericton Canadiens, St. John's Maple Leafs, and Moncton Hawks.

The first game of the trip takes place in icy cold Sydney versus the Oilers, where the crowd is lively and boisterous. The game in the bright arena starts like any other. The Canadian rinks have good ice; fast and hard.

The Oilers come out flying to start. Early on, I'm skating towards their goal, I cross the blue line, and a fast-skating defenceman closes in on me. I fire the puck, an-inch off the ice, and it pounds the goalie's pad. A rebound drops in front of the net, and a d-man clears the puck for the home Oilers. Out of gas, I hustle to the bench for a line change. "C'mon boys," shouts a voice from down the bench. "We have to match their speed," says another.

Back and forth the two sides go, and my line is back up. I hop the boards, and skate towards our defensive zone. The frozen puck is flipped out to centre, and I scoop it up. An Oilers' defender engages quickly, and forces me to make a play. I bend over, using my body to protect the puck, and the opposition checker leans hard on my lower back. I feel like I'm supporting his entire body weight. I lift my left leg off the ice, and expose my stronger right leg. Pressure bears down on my knee as I dig my sharp blade harder into the ice for needed torque to hold off the strong opponent. POP! Suddenly my leg goes limp, and I put it down to stop from falling. Instantly I forget about the puck, and glide, bent in half to the bench. Stepping through the door, I sit down. Dan comes over to check on me. "It's my knee," I spit out. Limping down the runway to the dressing room, I sit down, perplexed, confused; perhaps in denial. I hear nothing, only muffled sounds. I remove my equipment slowly knowing my night is over. I sit and stare at the dressing room walls while waiting for the final buzzer, and the team to return. I replay my last shift over and over in my anxious mind. 'That popping sound was familiar, but no, there's no way. It must be something else, it has to be.'

Post-game, and after an assessment, I'm given a new itinerary. This is the first game of the road trip, and it's clear that I will be out of the lineup indefinitely. Therefore, the best course of action will be to have me fly home instead of travelling around the Maritimes for a week with an injured knee. Before departing for the airport in Sydney, I'm informed that an MRI has been ordered by the team doctor.

Lisa is waiting for me at BWI when my flight arrives. It's nice to see her smiling face when I gingerly walk into the silent terminal. It will be a quiet week waiting for the gang to return from the roadie. Lisa and I talk about my knee, and what the injury might be.

I'm crushed to be down and out again after playing just 18 hockey games. Hopefully it's a short-term setback. As instructed,

I drive to the suburban Baltimore clinic for the MRI which will definitely display the extent of my injury. The big machine shows images of soft structures like ligaments. The friendly technician asks me to lay on my back, and then proceeds to push my body into the large apparatus. My heart begins to beat faster as my feet enter the slender tube. Panicky, I try to control my breathing as I'm pushed in until the table comes to a sudden stop. The technician asks me to remain still during the thirty-minute procedure, and within moments the piercing, loud noises from the giant machine begin. The firing of the electric currents make peculiar sounds. Focusing on my breathing, I close my eyes, and try to regain my composure in the tiny confines of the tube.

Post-procedure, it's now a waiting game; waiting for results. The group returns from the Maritimes, and I drive to the rink to watch practice. Dan asks me to meet him in his office. Waiting nervously, I sit down. He appears and I stare at him, as he sits in the chair across from me, only a few feet away. "I have the MRI results," he says quietly. The look on his face is not encouraging; he looks like someone shot his dog. "You have a torn ACL," he says. Kaboom!

The stone-cold silence that follows his blunt message leaves me feeling devoid of any feeling whatsoever. The grim, painful words feel like a punch in the face, but I cannot respond and I suddenly feel completely alone. Looking down at the floor his words continue to penetrate my crumbling mind. This season-ending injury feels catastrophic. I'm speechless; not angry, but numbed by the devastating results as I walk zombie-like out the players' entrance at Piney Orchard. Needless to say, this is an unforeseen fork in the road. There are no words that will help.

The season ends abruptly for the Skipjacks, as we fail to qualify for the playoffs. The Capitals finish the season in second-place in the Patrick Division with a healthy 45-27-8 record for 98 points. This sets up a first-round playoff series with the defending Stanley Cup champion Pittsburgh Penguins.

The Capitals storm out to a 3-1 lead in the best-of-seven, only to see superstar-centre Mario Lemieux lead his team back with three-straight wins including a Game Seven victory at the Capital Centre.

This marks the second consecutive year the Caps are eliminated by the Pens. The reigning champion Penguins go on to win their second consecutive Stanley Cup, sweeping the Chicago Blackhawks in four games.

Mr. & Mrs. Bud Poile

The hockey season is over; only weeks after the fateful game in Sydney that left me with a torn right ACL. It's grossly unfair, but nothing in life or pro hockey is fair. Injuries are part of hockey.

What now? A decision must be made. I know the risks of surgery, and the risks of not having surgery. In my spinning mind, the anticipation of missing another season due to surgery is a hockey death sentence. Or am I just afraid again? My head is scatter-brained, and worrisome. The anxiety is swallowing me whole.

The decision must be made however, and it is, swiftly. Rehabilitation will be the course of action. I will no longer wear a brace on my left leg, but will now wear a custom-made brace on my right. The Caps send me to the suburban Maryland community for the fitting.

Still struggling mentally with the injury news, I keep that tucked away inside. Most of the boys leave town, as they do every spring at the end of the season. Sitting down with Jack to discuss summer plans, I tell him that I prefer to stay in my apartment. I can rehabilitate here. After a short discussion, he agrees, and says the Caps will pay for two of my four months' summer rent costs.

Post-meeting, and arriving home, I start to think about an upcoming trip. The PHPA's annual meeting is fast approaching. I, along with player representatives from the other clubs, will assemble in Tucson, Arizona. Lisa and I fly out of BWI for the once-a-year encounter. Arriving in the Grand Canyon State and picking up a rental car, we quickly acclimate to our surroundings at the picturesque Tucson National Resort.

Wandering into the comfortable hideaway's restaurant, we find it's quiet and mostly empty. A polite couple who arrived only moments before us are taking their seats. Following their path towards a table for two, we pass the friendly pair. I say hello and engage them in familiar chatter. In this serene environment, the laid-back chitchat turns into a hockey conversation and to my surprise, we find we're speaking with Mr. and Mrs. Bud Poile. "I know your son, Mr. Poile, I mean my boss, the GM, the GM of the Capitals, David," I loudly stammer. The calm, senior Mr. Poile easily responds to my sputtering. Mrs. Poile happily interjects about her son, David. There is common ground with these genuine folks; for one, their son David, I mean Mr. Poile and two, love for hockey. The welcoming folks invite us to join them at their table and we happily accept.

I always knew Bud Poile was David Poile's father but I knew little about his storied hockey career. I begin to quiz the senior Mr. Poile about our game, and his knowledge is endless.

Born in the Northern Ontario town of Fort William, he began his playing career in 1942, suiting up for the Toronto Maple Leafs. Remarkably, he put his hockey dreams on hold to serve his country in World War II. Returning from the war, resuming his hockey career, he was a key member of the Maple Leafs, helping them win the 1947 Stanley Cup.

Later, in his impressive hockey life, he became GM of the expansion Philadelphia Flyers and later yet, the expansion Vancouver Canucks. This is only a sample of the contributions he made over his six-decades in hockey before being inducted into the Hockey Hall of Fame in 1990.

After dinner, and at the end of our engaging conversation, I pronounce, "It has been a pleasure meeting you Mr. and Mrs. Poile! I'll make sure I tell David, I mean Mr. Poile, about our visit."

With the week's meetings complete, we depart Arizona, and return to Maryland. The NHL is expanding by two teams for the upcoming 1992-93 hockey season with the addition of the Tampa Bay Lightning and Ottawa Senators. Two new clubs for the league's growing family. Hockey in Florida? Sounds interesting but will it work in South Florida? Time will tell I guess.

To kick it off, the expansion draft takes place on June 18th. Players left unprotected by their clubs are available for selection by the two new franchises. Names fly off the board, and in the end the Capitals lose defenceman Shawn Chambers and plucky-grinder Tim Bergland. Bergy is a character guy, and another great teammate moving on to a new opportunity. The former Minnesota Golden Gopher is a patient, diligent hockey player who helped the younger me in the minors.

Expansion draft complete, it's time to get back to business. Summers here are hot and humid, so I get workouts done in the morning before the heat. I add a Rod Langway training tool – rollerblades. Using skates on wheels in the streets of Columbia, I receive strange looks from the curious residents.

Mid-August arrives, and training camp is on the horizon. Capitals' prospect Keith Jones arrives in town early. The Western Michigan grad played for the Skipjacks at the end of last season. After a solid, college hockey career, he's turning pro. Jonesy and I were minor-hockey rivals. I remembered him as a smallish player back in the day, but he's a big guy now at six-foot, 200-pounds; a classic late bloomer.

We hit it off immediately when he arrives. He's brash, confident, with a good sense of humour, and a hearty laugh that I hear often. Lisa and I enjoy his company, wit, and outgoing personality. Spending a lot of time together leading up to the 1992 training camp, we talk about the old days back home, junior hockey, college hockey, pro hockey and more. He's a breath of fresh air for me. Jonesy will go on to play 491 NHL games. Today he is a respected, network hockey analyst.

Summer is coming to a close and Helen and Tim invite us over for their Blue Crab Party; a Maryland tradition. They can always be counted on for friendship and hospitality. As always it feels good to be welcomed over to join in with their close family and friends for this end-of-summer bash. Picnic tables are covered with newspaper and bushel baskets full of steamed Maryland Blue Crab. First things first: learning how to shuck the crab if we want to eat it. I ask Helen for advice and a voice shouts, "Eat what tastes good and spit out what doesn't." The assembled group of experienced locals laugh and we promptly take our seats.

Tools are scattered on the picnic tables – a crab mallet, a knife, and a claw cracker. It looks easy enough. Lisa and I start with a short, thin crab leg, turn it over, and attempt to retrieve the larger pieces of meat on the underside. Now it's time to crack the claws for the larger pieces. The spicy seasoning is the addictive flavour that keeps me grabbing more: a mixture of cayenne pepper, paprika, black pepper, garlic pepper, salt, oregano and thyme. Oh, it's good! Drinks are a must as the mixture is hot; too hot for some, but I love it! This event is an experience meant to be done slowly, sitting in the sunshine, soaking in the warmth, chatting, sharing, and laughing with friends and family. Cheers Helen and Tim!

Dire Straits

Training camp is here and the boys are back. The site of camp will be the Piney Orchard Ice Arena for the second consecutive season. Physicals and paperwork are complete, the practices start, and I feel slow.

At our first intra-squad game, after picking up a loose puck, I'm dumped on my ass, unable to provide the torque required to fend off my strong opponent. I'm rusty. Later, the disc enters my team's defensive zone, and I'm puck watching, not paying attention to my defensive assignment, and in a split second, Kevin Hatcher quickly skates in off the blue line. He's big and strong, I feel him fly by me, receive a pass, and I watch as he scores with a quick snap shot.

I'm not sharp, and I'm not decisive. I'm two steps behind the play. Perhaps playing tentatively is to be expected since I haven't been involved in a lot of meaningful hockey in recent months. At the conclusion of a less than stellar camp, I'm assigned to Baltimore. This is not a bad place for me because I need to play and play a lot.

The Capitals start the regular season October 7th at Maple Leaf Gardens versus the Buds. Fresh off of playing for Team Canada at the Olympics, my old teammate, Brad Schlegel, earns a spot on the Caps' opening-night roster, and suits up for a 6-5 Washington win. The Skipjacks start their season on October 9th at home versus the Binghamton Rangers. Barry Trotz is back as head coach with former NHLer Paul Gardner serving as his assistant.

I need a plan to get back on track and be leader in the minors: back to basics, keep it simple. I want to get my career moving in the right direction; however, my strategy is put on hold when I'm a healthy scratch for the first game of the season. It's a difficult pill to swallow.

My prickly, opportunistic voice begins to question the decisions made since my injury in March. 'Maybe you should have pressed for surgery to get this knee fixed properly, you're too slow now, and you're damaged goods.' Perhaps I'll be back in the lineup tomorrow night. My head spins from all the internal, invasive scrutiny.

Our next game is at home versus the Hershey Bears and I'm a healthy scratch again. I see a trend here. Post-game we depart for a busy road trip and games versus the Bears, Rochester Americans, Capital District Islanders, and Hamilton Canucks.

The roadie begins in Hershey. After taking warmup, I get the tap from Coach Trotz on the leg, and in the next three to follow. Tap, tap, and tap. The tap means I will be a healthy scratch and not in the lineup. There's no communication or reason given from the coach, just the tap. Frustration and anxiety are rising. I hate the fucking tap! I know Trotzy well; he's been around since my first training camp. He was a confidant; now he's the boss and the relationship is different.

The bus departs for the Canadian border headed on to the Steel City. Visiting with my parents on the final stop of the trip in

Hamilton, I take a seat with them in the sparse Copp's Coliseum crowd. They've made the trip to the Hammer to see me play. They do see me, but they do not see me play hockey; not on this day! I'm sitting and not playing again tonight. Speaking at length about hockey and the future, we talk. Of course, no decisions are made, but it is a chance to vent. I pour all my feelings out about the situation and time flies by. I can see they're concerned about my present state of mind. Walking to the bus, we say our good-byes and it is back on the highway for the ten-hour drive to Maryland.

Returning to Baltimore, my frustration and anxiety has reached a fever pitch. There's no communication between Coach Trotz and myself, and we're both to blame. Hockey at the pro level is a, what have you done for me lately proposition, and I haven't done much lately.

The next day, the team has a golf tournament with local sponsors. Uptight on a good day, I endure even more uncontrollable anxiety. I have a new level of unrecognizable stress, and I can't sleep in the midst of these emotionally taxing days.

Rising early before hitting the links, I decide I'm not going to the golf event today. Fuck it! I consider it a sort of personal protest against being a healthy scratch for six-straight games. It's likely not the best tactic, but today, in this mental state, it feels right. Having never done anything like this before, it seems to me like a bold move. I'm staying home.

I pick up a pen and begin writing down the skills that make me a good hockey player. I fold the paper, push it into my pocket and pace in my quiet apartment. Back and forth. Back and forth.

Later in the afternoon, a couple of my teammates knock on the front door to check on me. "Where were you today?" They ask. "I didn't go," I assert, and justify my decision. They tell me it took a while, but Coach Trotz eventually realized I was missing. "Good," I quip. The typically non-confrontational version of me just sent notice to the coach that I'm ready to talk.

Arriving at the practice facility, I enter the dressing room. Trotzy walks in with purpose, looks in my direction, and motions for me to follow him with his index finger. Following him into his office,

I know full well that this is not going to be a discussion about the power-play breakout. The door closes, and he unloads on me with an upset verbal barrage. It's been a long time since I had a meaning-ful conversation with anyone in the organization. After his rant, I snap back, defending my actions. From my pocket, I pull out the paper I wrote on the previous day and say, "You know me. I don't do things like this." I need someone to acknowledge my presence. I'm here, a person, a hockey player. I read a couple of the bullet points I'd written. Coach Trotz nods in agreement, as I articulate my personal accounts. Fear and nervousness bubble up from deep inside, and at that point my anxiety, dissatisfaction, angst, and frus-tration come crashing to the surface of my thin skin. Tears form in my strained eyes. Slumping back into an empty chair, I'm buckling under the perceived internal pressure. The tension in the room is broken and we engage in a calm conversation for the next several minutes. Coach Trotz takes his coaching hat off, and speaks to me as a friend, a hockey guy. My anxiety level decreases as the discus-sion continues, and there is a moment of relief. Opening the door, I exit his office. I have to pay a $25 fine for missing the golf tourna-ment. The situation hasn't changed, but both Trotzy and I have cleared the air.

Returning to my apartment, I think about my options. My for-mer coach, Rob Laird, is now coaching the Moncton Hawks. Maybe there is interest in me elsewhere. However, the phone isn't ringing off the hook. In fact, it isn't ringing at all. 'Maybe I should have that right knee repaired.' Look what happened the first time – torn liga-ment at 18, surgery at 23 – that can't repeat itself with my right leg. Anxious and confused about my future, I decide to ask for another opinion regarding my wonky right knee.

The Skipjacks' team doctor is a logical place to go. After all, he's easily accessible, and available. Making an appointment to be seen at his clinic, I nervously wait. An assessment is done, and we talk about my choices, including knee reconstruction.

Dire Straits is a popular rock band, and their hit song *Money for Nothing* was played over and over on MTV to my music-video gen-eration. The opening riff is certainly air band material. I'm not sure why they called themselves Dire Straits, but I know I'm now facing by own dire situation.

Daily, I'm spiralling out of control mentally. I no longer have my eye on the prize but have become distracted by the continuous noise in my head. From a young age, I was told to suck it up, and press on. Play like a warrior! From the time I was a little boy, the hockey manual for aspiring ice soldiers was clear; be tough and pay the price! Never show weakness or vulnerability to your team or opponents.

What I'm going through in my reeling mind feels like weakness, and I can't be seen as weak to my peers or family. My thoughts abuse and betray me. I'm afraid of the uncertainty that lays ahead. My inner voices torment and crush my hockey spirit. There is a tug-of-war going on in my mind that feels endless. The internal tiger is once again chasing me. I need an escape. Help me! Searching desperately for solutions in these dark moments in time and place increases my stress levels, and I fear for the future. I'm making the biggest decisions of my career in the grips of fear, anxiety and panic. This is dire straits!

Loss of the Pack

Our eight-month-old boxer puppy Lacy quietly sleeps in her medium-sized crate. At times, she snores and wakes us up. Two-year-old boxer Tyson occupies half of our bed at night and forces Lisa and me to the other side of the queen-size mattress. Pushing his eighty-pound solid body with my legs isn't easy or fun, and I force him to move. Tyson sees me as the leader of our family pack but the stubborn dog isn't willing to give up his precious sleeping space without resistance. The bedroom window is open and a cool breeze filters in through the screen. Rolling slowly out of bed, I can't sleep again. I have a meeting today with Mr. Poile to discuss my hockey future. I wonder if the discussion will be a heart-to-heart or a pep talk from the GM.

Meeting Mr. Poile at the practice facility, he is frank and to the point. My subconscious mind does not want to hear his penetrating words. The discussion is a blur and the meeting leaves me with so many questions. Returning home to my apartment, I feel desperate.

I've been groomed as hockey player from an early age not to be soft, to soldier on even during the hardest of times, taught to deal with problems by setting them aside, and focusing on the next shift, period, or game. The culture we promote takes pride in toughness and sacrifice. This is an attitude that is necessary when times get tough on the competitive ice but does it translate as well to my life off the ice?

I'm confused and distressed. The ominous, crippling, mind-numbing anxiety is taking a toll. I'm scared! I frantically lecture myself. Hockey is my life. I feel my stress thermometer rising; like water filling a tub and flowing uncontrollably over the edges. Something is not right. A radiating burn develops in my chest, con-suming my body – like smoke slowly filling a tiny room. Pacing, my heart beats faster, as I continue to debate with myself. I'll sit down for a minute. I sit on the couch, but as soon as my ass hits the cush-ion, I pop back up to my feet. I can't sit still. I can't! In my mind, I'm sprinting away from the tiger chasing me. This is now panic!

My life has been spent as a hockey player and there has been little preparation for life without it. My identity and self-worth emerged from hockey, and I feel like I'm losing a grip on the game I love. This isn't riding off into the sunset, it's walking the plank.

Days pass. I'm floundering, and with a spinning mind, and heavy heart, I inform Mr. Poile that I have decided to retire from hockey. Lisa returns to Canada with the Blazer and dogs ahead of me. I am now alone in my apartment. Without a vehicle, I call Tim and Helen to discuss my precarious situation. They have been a constant source of support as I was trying to sort through my bot-tled-up feelings.

Helen joins me to watch a movie, and her presence calms my weary, anxious mind. We say little, both knowing I'll soon be returning home. It's bittersweet knowing I turned Helen and Tim into hockey fans, and I will no longer be around to play and share the sport they've grown to love. They will be okay – I've introduced them to a number of the boys, like Jonesy, Martin Jiranek, Taylors, and others. Soon they will be following the Capitals more than the Skipjacks, and making road trips to Philadelphia and Pittsburgh.

The phone rings. I'm summoned to the Capital Centre to sign my release papers. Driving south on I-95 to the saddle-shaped arena located on 1 Harry S. Truman Drive in Landover for the last time is painful. Arriving at the rink, I feel like a dead man walking.

There's a short meeting, and exchange of floundering pleasantries with the staff on hand. Pat Young has the paperwork ready for me to sign. She's known me since I was drafted as an 18-year-old kid back in '86. Always helpful and smiling, our smiles are difficult to find today. Picking up a pen, I sign the document, and with the paperwork complete, Pat wishes me well. We exchange good-byes, I leave the room, and slowly exit the Capital Centre. Walking out the doors of the rink for last time is tough. I feel like I'm leaving a chunk of my hockey soul at the gates. Outside, I look up and see that the sun is setting. Returning to the truck, I exit the parking lot and drive north on I-95.

Tim Taylor and I have played together for the last four years. He and his wife Jodi-Lynn are good friends of ours. The Taylors have opened up their home to us many times, and in my mind, there are plenty of good memories of those times to scan through. Tim and I both came into this hockey season with a certain level of uncertainty, and that has served to bring us closer together. He will be traded shortly to the Vancouver Canucks for Eric Murano. In fact, he will go on to play 746 NHL games and win two Stanley Cups.

I pack up a large Ryder truck with assistance from T-Bone and the boys. Truck packed, there are handshakes – no tears – and it's time to leave. I return to Canada with Christmas just three-weeks away. The holiday season provides a needed distraction. Helen calls me, concerned and wondering if I'm okay. She arranges for Jonesy to phone me at home. He is his talkative, comedic self, but I'm struggling with the change of life. I've lost my pack. What do I mean?

Well, hockey teams imitate life in a wolf pack.

Wolves belong to family groups. My hockey team is like family, and I miss that relationship the most.

Wolf packs comprise 8 to 15 members. My hockey teams have comprised 17 to 25 members, and I feel alone without them.

Wolf pack range is 6 to 600 miles. My hockey team's range had been 1 to 1000s of miles, and I miss the road trips with the boys.

The alpha-male is the leader of the wolf pack. The captain is the leader of the hockey team. I was a captain many times, and I miss being a leader in the dressing room, and learning from and watching respected leaders I played with.

The wolf pack hunts together to ensure success. My hockey teams competed together to achieve team goals, and I miss the thrill of the hunt, of playing, of winning, and the feelings in the dressing room after.

The wolf pack provides support for the individual members of the pack to ensure pack survival. My hockey teams supported each other on and off the ice, and I miss the comradery, laughs, friendship, team meals, travel, being with the boys, and so much more.

The wolf pack communicates with sounds: growls, yips, and howls. My hockey teams communicated in a similar fashion, and I miss the chirping, barbs, jokes, and laughter.

The wolf pack must survive. If a wolf breaks its leg in the wild, it will lay down and die alone. The pack must keep moving! I have now become a lone wolf, and as a lone wolf I spend my time alone; the team must move on without me.

I feel isolated and alone without the comfort of my pack. I'm frightened by the future. 'Who am I?' I've only done one thing, play hockey, and that is now gone… I begin to withdraw. I do not want to be seen or talk to anyone, and I don't want to face questions about my hockey career.

The ice beneath my feet is shattering, and I need to find the strength to stay upright or I will permanently sink. There is mental strife without my pack, my team, and hockey. Help me! Detaching, I don't want contact with the outside world. I'm miserable without hockey and the lack of direction in my life.

On daily outings, I try not to be seen, and I don't want to be. As I see it, if I'm spotted, it will lead to the inevitable questions about my failed hockey career. Yes, I see my career as a failure. I grapple with that notion daily in these days after hockey. My prickly, anxious voice measures my individual success by games played in the NHL, and money earned playing.

Lisa and I receive great news early in 1993, and my focus instantly changes. Our first child is due in December. We are excited parents-to-be. Perhaps this remarkable new role of father is a blessing from a higher power to give me a new purpose. Being a parent is a responsibility I'm excited about, and may be the most important role any adult takes on.

During my time in Baltimore, I had the pleasure of meeting Cal Ripken Jr. at a charity event. The respected Orioles' shortstop is a class individual. He reminds me of my hero Wayne Gretzky in the way he conducts himself on and off the field. I reveal to Lisa that if we have a boy, I want to name him Calvin after the soon-to-be Hall of Fame shortstop who played 2,632 consecutive games for the O's. A true ironman! Our first son Calvin is born December 8th 1993 in Kingston, Ontario.

I Played Hockey

Attempting to get on with a new life, I decide to give post-second-ary school a try. Pleased with my new sense of purpose, I'm educat-ing myself and parenting a new baby. We're moving forward with this new chapter.

Not having put on skates in a number of months, and receiving an invitation from a group of Kingston prison guards to play pick-up hockey, I lace 'em up. Familiarly, it is game on and the fellas are chirping each other. I'm skating, and it feels good for the hockey soul. Picking up a loose puck at the opposing blue line, I skate towards the net. I make a play, lean on my right leg, tightening my quadriceps to support my weight. In that moment, my knee slips forward, and I hear a clunk. There's minimal pain but I can't straighten my leg. A warm rush originating in my chest fills my body as I begin to repeatedly try and straighten my gimpy limb. The game is less than fifteen-minutes old, and I have to ask for the dressing room key. I know it's over for me as I limp off the ice. Dropped off at home, I hobble into our living room and realize I need to seek medical attention sooner, rather than later.

After an appointment with my doctor, I'm sent to see an ortho-pedic surgeon. He puts me through the all too familiar tests, and says he suspects I have a meniscus tear to go along with a torn ACL. Surgery will be required. It's scheduled at Hotel Dieu Hospital tomorrow.

Post-op, the surgeon visits me, and says that he discovered a bucket-handle meniscus tear which caused the locked-knee condi-tion. He repaired the ligament using a portion of my patellar ten-don. I'm in no mood for rehab; my only goal is to get walking, and that will take about six weeks.

Attending school on crutches, I rehabilitate at home. Surgery sinks me into a deep state of depression. Lisa pleads with my Grandma Betty to stay with us for a week to help out. I mean I can't walk, Calvin is colicky, we have two boxers, and a litter of puppies. Grandma agrees, and boards a bus in Kitchener bound for the Limestone City. Her presence in our home is needed loving support for all of us.

Back on my feet, we decide to move our young family to Kitchener-Waterloo. Lisa is expecting our second child, with a due date of March 1996. Adjusting to life back in K-W is exciting for me with a new job, a new house, a son, and a new baby arriving shortly. I have renewed energy being back in my hometown. Most of my friends are gone, but much of the family still lives in the area including my parents, brother, grandmothers, aunts, uncles, and cousins.

Lisa says if our new baby is a boy, she will name him Nicholas, a name associated with one of the world's most generous souls: Saint Nicholas. This is the perfect name for our son, born on March 26, 1996.

Time passes quickly and suddenly, it's September, and that means training camp. The calendar year has four seasons: spring, summer, fall, and winter. The hockey calendar has four seasons: training camp, regular season, playoffs, and off-season. I've been out of hockey for a while, but as soon as September hits, my insides begin to stir and feel agitated, as my internal hockey clock begins to prepare my mind and body for a training camp that's not coming. Shutting off these feelings is difficult, and I find it painful to pay attention to the goings-on as pro training camps get under way.

The Toronto Maple Leafs are holding camp in Kitchener this year, including an exhibition game at the Aud. It's a chance for Leaf fans to see Mats Sundin, Doug Gilmour, Wendel Clark and Scotty Pearson, who signed as a free agent. This is his second stint with the Buds.

I call him in advance of camp, and we make arrangements to have him over for dinner. Eating out for a month gets tiresome. Therefore, a home-cooked meal, and a chance to catch up with friends away from the rink is a welcome break.

Calvin and Nick are too young to entirely grasp the idea of having a Maple Leaf player over to the house. Still, we invite the neighbourhood kids over for a meet and greet with my good friend. He shares thoughtful memories, handshakes, and stories on the deck with the youngsters before I drive him back to the downtown hotel.

Attending the exhibition game today at the Aud, Calvin, Nick, and I cheer on the Leafs. Mats Sundin is in the lineup today, and that draws extra excitement from the noisy Auditorium crowd.

I'm still trying to sort out my own feelings about hockey. Being this close to the Maple Leafs' camp only fuels my ignited senses. It's hard to turn hockey off. Maybe over time these strong feelings I'm experiencing will vanish. However, I'm not going to share these thoughts. This transition isn't easy, or the same for everyone. I still have a fire burning in my belly, and at times I wonder if these sensations will ever go away. Perhaps not.

Keeping that in my thoughts, I remind myself that it is a privilege to play this great game. I want to share my love of hockey with my two sons, like many Canadian dads and moms before me. Like my dad! Perhaps this explains why we're a hockey nation.

Over time, Calvin develops into an athletic goalie, a fan of Patrick Roy and the famed Montréal Canadiens. In big games he has ice in his veins, always appearing calm, cool and collected. Nick, from day one of Learn-To-Skate, could fly. He is a gifted, effortless skater with speed and skill who can turn on a dime and bury a snap shot faster than you can say Erik Karlsson. Yes, he's a fan of the Ottawa Senators and the dynamic defenceman.

I find my way back into the rink – to my safe zone – to the place I like to be. There are times when I wonder if I'm doing this for myself, or Calvin and Nick, and the answer is both. I want to share my passion for hockey with them.

They play in tournaments I played in when I was their age: the K-W Oktoberfest, Burlington Golden Horseshoe, Peterborough Lift Lock, Kitchener Blue Line, and others. We drive hours to watch them play. Yes, it's what we do; it's what parents do for their kids playing hockey. The new hockey families become our friends, and our new wolf pack.

There are wins, losses, happy car rides, quiet car rides, good games, not so good games, parent parties, year-end parties, comradery, and friendships. In a matter of a couple of winters, I've managed to manufacture my four hockey seasons again with my two boys: training camp (or tryouts), regular season, playoffs, and off-season. One difference though is that the off-season is lacrosse season, so there is no off-season for our family.

I return to the arenas I played in as a kid, and I'm now watching as a parent. Some have changed, some look exactly the same. We enter Queensmount, Don McLaren, Waterloo Memorial (the Bubble), Centennial in Guelph, Brampton Memorial, Iroquois Park in Whitby, and more. Even where the arenas are not the same, the feeling is.

The arena feels like home as it always has; the hockey community that provided me comfort as a kid is still there. The rink attendant flooding the ice is there, however, the old-school tractor has been replaced by a Zamboni or an Olympia.

The canteen is open, and kids are asking parents for loonies and toonies, instead of the quarters that I requested. The trophy case, with its glistening hardware, is now filled with faces and names that are familiar to me. The busy lobby is the place where parents still chat, and excited players still stack hockey bags and sticks while they wait for the dressing rooms to be vacated.

Now I'm talking with parents about coffee and skate sharpening. Without even being aware, or maybe I am subconsciously, I'm spending time in my childhood safe place – the arena. Here, I found confidence, accolades, challenges, a career, and a lifetime of memories.

I want to give something back to the game I love. Maybe I need a new role; perhaps as a coach. Coaching is a natural way to fulfill three needs: to teach young players about the sport, give back to the game that has given me so much, and feel the comradery of the team.

I coach minor hockey and in doing so I manage to pay-it-forward to the new generation of young, aspiring players. I share thoughtful quotes from my mentors, Larry Lyman, Murray Fried, Bill Seaman, Jim Scott, Jim Jenks, George Knisley, Fred O'Donnell, Bryan Murray, Terry Murray, Doug MacLean, Rob Laird, and Barry Trotz.

Coaching is addictive for me; I love practices and games. I want the players to enjoy the sport, and all it has to offer. I pass on my knowledge and passion. This year, I'm coaching a ten-year-old atom hockey team, the Waterloo Wolves Black. Today, we have a game in Kitchener against the Jr. Rangers. It's Saturday, and I drive to Grand River Arena for the 10 a.m. game. I arrive early as I always do; I can't be late. There's a minor-atom game being played when I arrive between longtime rivals Kitchener and Waterloo.

I'm feeling anxious and short of breath today. Anxiety still haunts me. I walk into the arena with my Tim Hortons' coffee, and proceed to the playing surface. The game is well underway. The air is cold, and smells crisp like arenas do in winter in Canada. I suck in the arena air, and it flows deep into my chest, and the cells in my lungs devour it. I exhale, the water vapours in my breath condense, and form a cloud on the glass. I inhale again, and listen to the sounds of the game: pucks hitting sticks, skates carving the ice, sticks tapping, a referee blowing his whistle. The soothing sounds on the ice are replaced by cheering voices in the crowd: clapping, chanting, and shouting. I don't know any of these players or parents, but I feel grounded by their energy. I'm calm, and in the moment, present with this hockey community. This is my safe zone. I see it clearly now! Perhaps this is what Canadians mean when they say, "Hockey is in your blood."

The bright-eyed, innocent boys I'm coaching arrive, and I enter the small dressing room to listen to their idle banter. I line up the sticks; my routine. I have to see the sticks aligned. Perhaps this is my own superstitious pre-game ritual or an obsessive-compulsive behaviour but it doesn't matter.

"Coach Steve, can you tape my stick?" A youthful voice asks. "Yes, I can Alex," I reply easily. "White or black tape?" I ask. "Black," he says. He tosses me a roll of black and I begin to tape the blade heel to toe, and carefully round the blade with each pass. The motion is therapeutic, calming, and it feels right. This is the sacred hockey player's task of taping the stick. The youngsters are observing my meticulous method. I get another request from Heppy (nickname), followed by another, another, and yet another. I can't get enough. Unknowingly, these little hockey players have helped to bring back the joy of the game for me. This hockey culture is in my heart and soul!

It took a long time, but I can finally see my hockey career as a success! My best friend stuck with me through the most difficult of times and helped me crush the prickly, anxious, panic-filled, depressed voice in my head. I still struggle with my mental health, and it is becoming easier to say. However, my wife Lisa patiently helped me to realize my success in hockey came from the journey; the journey you have taken with me. The teams I played on, the players I competed with and against, the coaches I played for, the friends I made along the way, the arenas I played in, and the cities, all combined to form my passion for this great game. I played hockey in the NHL, just as my heroes did – the Kraut Line, Danny Gare, Darryl Sittler, and Wayne Gretzky.

I love hockey! The game and the people in it taught me how to work hard, be a part of a team, to never quit, lose with dignity and win with class. It has brought me joy and pain. I played hockey!

Overtime

Players and parents ask me, what it is like to play in the NHL. I reply, "I loved it! It was a dream come true. Choose a job you love and you'll never have to work a day in your life."

People I've met are always intrigued when they inevitably hear I played in the NHL. Having said that, here are the 10 most common questions I've been asked over the years by family, friends and acquaintances.

Why did you stop playing in the NHL?

Did you ever play against Wayne Gretzky?

How much money did you make playing?

Do you have a hockey card?

How many NHL games did you play?

Did you score any goals?

Did you ever play against Mario Lemieux?

What NHL team did you play for?

What round were you drafted?

What the hell's a Skipjack?

Today, if I could have a conversation with my five-year-old self who is shooting plastic pucks at his mom's seventies-style yellow stove, I would tap his shoulder and say, "Steven Jerome Seftel, love your family, talk to your friends, and always remember that you deserve to be happy." And I would pass him the note below, inspired by song lyrics from One Republic's *I Lived*.

I Played Hockey

Hope when you hit that ice, you don't feel the fall,

Hope when that puck hits your stick, your hands feel sweet!

Hope when the crowd screams out, they're screaming your name,

Hope when all the kids leave the rink, you choose to stay,

Hope you fall in love with this game,

The only way you can know is if you can say, "I gave it all I had!"

I hope you don't suffer but erase the pain,

Hope when you're all done you'll say, "I loved this great game!"

Hope you say "I played my best…gave my all!"

I owned every second that this game can give,

I saw so many places and the things I did,

With every broken bone, I swear to you, "I played hockey!"

I hope after playing this game, you have no regrets

At the end of your career, I hope you raised a cup….maybe even Lord Stanley's!

I want you to know, I witnessed all your joy, defeats, and pain,

Hope when you're all done you'll say, "I loved this great game!"

Hope you say, "I battled for my teammates and coaches…gave it my all!"

I owned every minute that this game can give, I met so many people, and the things I did!

With every broken bone, I swear to you, I played hockey!

Barons, Kavaliers, Krackers, Krauts, Keewees, Kruisers, Knights, Kings, Greenshirts, Canadians, Whalers, Skipjacks, Capitals!

With every save I watched Calvin make!

With every goal I watched Nick score!

With every smile on the face of a kid I coached!

With every outdoor game I played, road hockey game, Stanley Cup winning goal I scored outside, stick I taped, skate I tightened, hat-trick, one-timer, saucer-pass, hard-around, dump-in, finished-check, big-hit, apple, scrum, scrap, backhand, forehand, power play, penalty-kill, snipe, celly, crossover, start, stop, screen, tip-in, redirect, blocked shot, snap-shot, wrist-shot, slapshot, with every broken bone,

I swear I bled, I played hockey!

I swear I lived, I played hockey!

I played hockey! I did!

Acknowledgements

A lifelong fan of hockey statistics, trivia, stats, and streaks, I'd like to take this opportunity to thank the following newspapers and websites for their contributions to the game of hockey and filling my hunger for hockey information: Kitchener-Waterloo Record, Windsor Star, Kingston Whig-Standard, Washington Post, Rochester Democrat and Chronicle, Hockey News, Baltimore Sun, www.hockeydb.com, www.hockey-reference.com, www.legendsofhockey.com, www.flyershistory.com, www.hockeydraftcentral.com.

A special thank-you to three talented professionals: Doug Smith for your guidance and inspirational story; Laura Duchesne and the staff at Westmont Signs and Printing for your patience and remarkable graphic design skills; and Genevieve Prevost and the staff at Interscript for your excellence and professional assistance. Thank-you-Merci!

Every effort has been made to search for and acquire the permission necessary to reproduce the photographs in this book. The publisher welcomes notice of any omissions, corrections, or errors.